Drupal 7 Social Netwo

Build a social or community website with friends lists, groups, custom user profiles, and much more

Michael Peacock

[PACKT] open source *
PUBLISHING
community experience distilled

BIRMINGHAM - MUMBAI

Drupal 7 Social Networking

Copyright © 2011 Packt Publishing

All rights reserved. No part of this book may be reproduced, stored in a retrieval system, or transmitted in any form or by any means, without the prior written permission of the publisher, except in the case of brief quotations embedded in critical articles or reviews.

Every effort has been made in the preparation of this book to ensure the accuracy of the information presented. However, the information contained in this book is sold without warranty, either express or implied. Neither the author, nor Packt Publishing, and its dealers and distributors will be held liable for any damages caused or alleged to be caused directly or indirectly by this book.

Packt Publishing has endeavored to provide trademark information about all of the companies and products mentioned in this book by the appropriate use of capitals. However, Packt Publishing cannot guarantee the accuracy of this information.

First published: October 2011

Production Reference:1150911

Published by Packt Publishing Ltd.
Livery Place
35 Livery Street
Birmingham B32PB, UK.

ISBN 978-1-84951-600-6

www.packtpub.com

Cover Image by Asher Wishkerman (a.wishkerman@mpic.de)

Credits

Author
Michael Peacock

Reviewers
Kazi Ataul Bari
Nedo Laanen
Ronald J. Simon

Acquisition Editor
Sarah Cullington

Development Editors
Kartikey Pandey
Hithesh Uchil

Technical Editors
Pramila Balan
Joyslita D'souza

Project Coordinator
Joel Goveya

Proofreader
Aaron Nash

Indexer
Hemangini Bari

Graphics
Valentina D'silva

Production Coordinator
Aparna Bhagat

Cover Work
Aparna Bhagat

About the Author

Michael Peacock (www.michaelpeacock.co.uk) is a web developer and Zend Certified Engineer from Newcastle, UK with a degree in Software Engineering from the University of Durham.

After working as Managing Director and Lead Developer overseeing the development team at the web agency he co-founded almost five years ago, Michael stepped back from the business and now acts as Senior/Lead Web Developer on the telemetry project for Smith Electric Vehicles.

In October 2010, Michael presented his thoughts on specific web application architectures at the popular PHP North West conference, and has presented to the PHP North East user group on automated deployment systems and to North East technical community group Super Mondays on Jenkins Continuous Integration.

Michael loves working on web related projects, and is currently incubating a number of ideas for launch through his latest venture, Central Apps Limited (www.centralapps.co.uk).

He is the author of *Drupal 7 Social Networking*, *PHP 5 Social Networking*, *PHP 5 E-Commerce Development*, *Drupal 6 Social Networking*, *Selling online with Drupal e-Commerce* and *Building Websites with TYPO3*. Michael acted as technical reviewer for other publications like *Mobile Web Development* and *Drupal for Education and E-Learning*.

You can follow Michael on Twitter: www.twitter.com/michaelpeacock or find out more about him through his blog: www.michaelpeacock.co.uk.

Acknowledgement

I'd like to thank all the staff at Packt Publishing, in particular: Douglas Paterson, for working with me to develop my first book ideas; Sarah Cullington for working with me on developing this book; Joel Goveya, the Project Co-ordinator for helping keep the project on track and Karthikey Pandey, the Development Editor. Thanks are also due to the Technical Reviewers: Kazi Ataul Bari, Nedo Laanen, and Ronald J. Simon, who helped ensure the technical quality of the book was up to scratch.

I'd also like to thank everyone who left feedback about Drupal 6 Social Networking; their feedback really helped shape this book, so that as well as being updated to cover Drupal 7, it is more relevant, more interesting, and builds a more powerful Social Networking site.

My thanks also go to my friends and family, in particular my fiancée Emma for her support while working on the book.

Finally, I'd like to thank you, the reader; I hope you enjoy this book and produce a fantastic social network of your own. I look forward to seeing what you come up with, and hope you will provide me with your feedback so that Drupal 8 Social Networking can be even better still!

About the Reviewers

Kazi Ataul Bari was born in Comilla, Bangladesh. He has been working on PHP and MySQL, JavaScript, jQuery,CMS (Joomla, Drupal), Adobe Photoshop, Adobe Flash, and Action Script 3.0 for three years. Currently, he is working for GraphicPeople | Enfatico | WPP as Web Developer. He also worked at BRACNet Limited, and GoldenHash Technology as a Software Engineer and Quality Assurance Officer.

> I would like to thank Hithesh Uchil, Joel Goveya, my grand father for giving me the encouragement to explore new opportunities, and my friend Fatema Akter Puspo for supporting me to work hard. Also, I would like to thank my Mom and Dad.

Nedo Laanen graduated in 2003, where he studied Applied Mathematics and Computer Science. He then started working for a large company in the computer industry. There he worked for several clients as a Novell System Administrator. Soon he developed a keen interest in Linux and Open Source software and started to pursue a career as a Linux professional at a Utrecht based company. Nedo has worked for companies like the Dutch department of the World Wide Fund in Zeist and the Dutch Council for Refugees in Amsterdam, as well as for several different Dutch Hospitals. He was also involved in the 'Antonius Open' project at the Antonius Hospital in Utrecht/Nieuwegein, a prestigious project of the Antonius hospital to cut back costs by implementing Linux and Open Source software in their computer network, replacing expensive proprietary software and eliminating vendor lock-in.

In 2011, Nedo started his own business as an all-round Linux engineer, providing Open Source solutions for other businesses: http://www.laanen-ict.nl.

Next to Linux and Open Source he is also an enthusiastic photographer (http://www.nedolaanen.nl). In 2009, he therefore started the website http://www.opensourcephotography.org to promote Open Source photography.

Nedo has also been a reviewer for Packt Publishing on the book *GIMP 2.6 Cookbook*.

Ronald J. Simon has been working with the development of shared information and database design dating back to the days before the Internet and has worked in many different areas of information management and writing documentation to support users.

Ron is also an Adjunct Instructor for Grand Valley State University and has worked in the legal field in Document management and security.

He is also an owner of RJS Designs, which is a small business consulting company.

I would like to thank my Coffee Machine for always being by my side.

www.PacktPub.com

Support files, eBooks, discount offers and more

You might want to visit www.PacktPub.com for support files and downloads related to your book.

Did you know that Packt offers eBook versions of every book published, with PDF and ePub files available? You can upgrade to the eBook version at www.PacktPub.com and as a print book customer, you are entitled to a discount on the eBook copy. Get in touch with us at service@packtpub.com for more details.

At www.PacktPub.com, you can also read a collection of free technical articles, sign up for a range of free newsletters and receive exclusive discounts and offers on Packt books and eBooks.

PACKTLiB®

http://PacktLib.PacktPub.com

Do you need instant solutions to your IT questions? PacktLib is Packt's online digital book library. Here, you can access, read and search across Packt's entire library of books.

Why Subscribe?
- Fully searchable across every book published by Packt
- Copy and paste, print and bookmark content
- On demand and accessible via web browser

Free Access for Packt account holders

If you have an account with Packt at www.PacktPub.com, you can use this to access PacktLib today and view nine entirely free books. Simply use your login credentials for immediate access.

Table of Contents

Preface

This book uses Drupal, a powerful and extendable Content Management System (CMS), to set up and manage a social networking website. This is achieved using a range of powerful and feature-rich social networking modules that are available, as well as creating a few of our own along the way. By using Drupal, the site can be built and extended rapidly and changed as the needs of our users and site change and evolve.

This book is packed with practical tips, not only for setting up a social networking site, but also for promoting and marketing the site, working with the site's users to help the social network grow, and preparing for growth so that our users get a reliable, enjoyable experience on the site.

What this book covers

Chapter 1, Drupal and Social Networking, looks into the basics, dealing with various social networking concepts, and also why you may wish to create a social network. You will start by looking at the concepts of social networking, Content Management Systems, and Drupal. Then you will be guided to install Drupal, look at its features, and see how it works.

Chapter 2, Preparing Drupal for a Social Networking Site, looks at Drupal in more detail, particularly at how to use its administration options, which should help you in building your site. This should prove to be a useful reference point in future. You'll be able to plan some of the static content for your site, and start to create content for it.

Chapter 3, User Content: Contributions, Forums, and Blogs, focuses very much on content; with these features in place you can now look at users, their profiles, and allow them to connect with one another to create a powerful social network.

Chapter 4, Users and Profiles, teaches how to manage users, roles, and their permissions. It talks about Gravatars and how to enable them. You'll learn how users can track the activity of each other and how to extend user profiles. Settings and rules for users will be talked about and you'll also learn how to give authenticated users a more relevant home page.

Chapter 5, Enabling User Interaction, explains how users can build relationships and friendships within the site, and how they can communicate with each other. With this, you will learn how to create a social site which is truly a network using Drupal.

Chapter 6, Social Seasoning, sprinkles in third-party social features to the site, including sharing content on other social networks, and using more advanced comment features from services such as Disqus.

Chapter 7, Module Development, rapidly teaches the basics of the Drupal 7 module system, through the creation of a suite of modules including a new bespoke content type and a map. This covers module development, extending the default content types, and allowing modules to interact with one another.

Chapter 8, Designing Our Site, discusses the default themes available to us, how we can customize it, where we can get new themes from, and the basics of the Drupal theming system. This provides the ground work for making your social network look the part.

Chapter 9, Communicating with Our Users, helps administrators communicate directly with users through e-mail, contact forms, and using the theme and reminders.

Chapter 10, Deploying and Maintaining Our Social Network, details the processes involved in taking a site from your local computer to the web. This discusses concepts including hosting, domain names, and the methods used to get the site running online. Once the site is online, it discusses how to maintain the social network.

Chapter 11, Easing Growing Pains, provides help and advice for scaling the social network and how to prepare with a large number of users. These tips speed up the site and show how to make the site more reliable when under load.

Chapter 12, Promotion, SEO, User Retention, and Monetization Strategies, looks into effectively marketing and promoting websites and social networking websites with online marketing techniques, search engine optimization, and user retention strategies. You'll also be looking briefly into how you may wish to monetize your site.

What you need for this book

For this book you will need:

- A local development environment (see *Appendix A*)
- A text editor, such as Crimson Editor (http://www.crimsoneditor.com/)
- An FTP client to deploy your site online, such as FileZilla (http://filezilla-project.org/)
- An SSH client if you wish to maintain your site using the command line (http://www.chiark.greenend.org.uk/~sgtatham/putty/)

Who this book is for

This book is aimed at anyone looking to create their own social networking website, including:

- Businesses: Building a social network around a product or service can improve your company profile and increase customer loyalty, while an internal social network gives you employees a place to keep resources, discuss ideas, raise concerns, and keep up-to-date on company policies.
- Hobbyists: Create a community around your hobbies and interests; create a local or distributed user group.
- Organizations and charities: Raise your profile, promote your events, services, and fundraisers, and get help from the community in organizing them.
- Families: For large families based across the country or across the globe, keep up-to-date with everyone, and let everyone know what you are up to.

You don't need any experience of Drupal or PHP to use this book. If you are a Drupal user you will find this book a great way to rapidly tailor an existing installation into a socially orientated website.

Conventions

In this book, you will find a number of styles of text that distinguish between different kinds of information. Here are some examples of these styles, and an explanation of their meaning.

Code words in text are shown as follows: "To make use of friendly or clean URLs, the mod_rewrite module for Apache, and the ability to use .htaccess files is required."

A block of code is set as follows:

```
<a href="http://twitter.com/share" class="twitter-share-button" data-
count="vertical" data-via="dino_space">Tweet</a><script type="text/
javascript" src="http://platform.twitter.com/widgets.js"></script>
```

When we wish to draw your attention to a particular part of a code block, the relevant lines or items are set in bold:

```
<iframe src="http://www.facebook.com/plugins/like.php?href=
  <?php

    $path = isset($_GET['q']) ? $_GET['q'] : '<front>';
    $link = url($path, array('absolute' => TRUE));

    echo urlencode( $link );
  ?>
  &amp;layout=standard&amp;show_faces=true&amp;width=450&amp;

    action=like&amp;font&amp;colorscheme=light&amp;height=80"
```

Any command-line input or output is written as follows:

```
sudo apt-get install apache2
```

New terms and **important words** are shown in bold. Words that you see on the screen, in menus or dialog boxes for example, appear in the text like this: "This page contains download links for **Drupal Core**, **Installation Profiles**, **Themes**, **Translations**, and **Modules** ".

[Warnings or important notes appear in a box like this.]

[Tips and tricks appear like this.]

Reader feedback

Feedback from our readers is always welcome. Let us know what you think about this book—what you liked or may have disliked. Reader feedback is important for us to develop titles that you really get the most out of.

To send us general feedback, simply send an e-mail to feedback@packtpub.com, and mention the book title via the subject of your message.

If there is a book that you need and would like to see us publish, please send us a note in the **SUGGEST A TITLE** form on www.packtpub.com or e-mail suggest@packtpub.com.

If there is a topic that you have expertise in and you are interested in either writing or contributing to a book, see our author guide on www.packtpub.com/authors.

Customer support

Now that you are the proud owner of a Packt book, we have a number of things to help you to get the most from your purchase.

Downloading the example code

You can download the example code files for all Packt books you have purchased from your account at http://www.PacktPub.com. If you purchased this book elsewhere, you can visit http://www.PacktPub.com/support and register to have the files e-mailed directly to you.

Errata

Although we have taken every care to ensure the accuracy of our content, mistakes do happen. If you find a mistake in one of our books—maybe a mistake in the text or the code—we would be grateful if you would report this to us. By doing so, you can save other readers from frustration and help us improve subsequent versions of this book. If you find any errata, please report them by visiting http://www.packtpub.com/support, selecting your book, clicking on the **errata submission form** link, and entering the details of your errata. Once your errata are verified, your submission will be accepted and the errata will be uploaded on our website, or added to any list of existing errata, under the Errata section of that title. Any existing errata can be viewed by selecting your title from http://www.packtpub.com/support.

Piracy

Piracy of copyright material on the Internet is an ongoing problem across all media. At Packt, we take the protection of our copyright and licenses very seriously. If you come across any illegal copies of our works, in any form, on the Internet, please provide us with the location address or website name immediately so that we can pursue a remedy.

Please contact us at copyright@packtpub.com with a link to the suspected pirated material.

We appreciate your help in protecting our authors, and our ability to bring you valuable content.

Questions

You can contact us at questions@packtpub.com if you are having a problem with any aspect of the book, and we will do our best to address it.

1
Drupal and Social Networking

Welcome to Drupal 7 Social Networking! During the course of this book we are going to learn how to develop a flexible, powerful, and interesting social networking site using the **Content Management System**, **Drupal 7**. We will start by looking at the concepts of social networking, Content Management Systems, and Drupal. Once we are more familiar with the concepts we will install Drupal, look at its features, and see how it works. By using a combination of existing features, modules, themes, and some simple custom development, we will enable user interaction, user contributions, and the ability for our users to communicate with each other.

In this chapter you will learn:

- What social networking is
- About social networking concepts
- What a Content Management System is
- What Drupal is
- Why Drupal is an excellent platform for Social Networking sites
- How to install and configure Drupal

Throughout the book we will use Drupal, and our increasing knowledge of it to develop a site for a fictional project, DinoSpace!—a Social Networking site for keepers of pet dinosaurs.

Social Networking: An introduction

Social Networks are a relatively new aspect to the Web that are really taking off. Many businesses, organizations, communities, and families are using social networking to promote themselves, communicate better with others, and to engage with their audience.

Social networking relies upon users building up their own network of contacts on the site, which in turn introduces them to new contacts. On many social networking websites, it allows them to be found more easily, and for new contacts to be recommended or introduced, helping to grow the user network.

Let's look at an example of how a user's network of contacts can be built up:

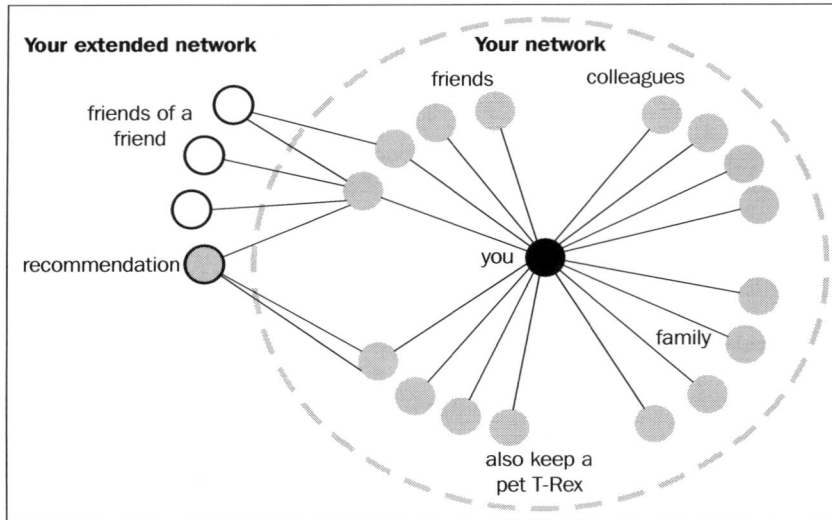

This social network representation shows the connections between contacts. It also illustrates how a user may be able to discover friends of a friend, and friend recommendations (based on friends in common), making it easy for the user to build up their social network, to communicate with new people, or reconnect with lost contacts.

Social networks generally serve two primary functions; firstly they allow users to connect with each other and build a contact network as we have just discussed. However, they also provide a community with collaboration and contribution features, allowing the content and information within the social network to be grown by the users themselves. Later in this chapter we will discuss some of the features available in existing social networks and social networking software, to build up a list of key features we will need to include, as well as things we might like to include.

Business logic to social networks

There is some very compelling business logic to using both existing and custom social networks. Creating your own social network or social network tools gives a dedicated customer area where feedback on products and services can be obtained, for instance, use of support forums to discuss and resolve problems. Areas which allow customers to share tips, resources, and product care tips help promote those products and services.

Examples: Businesses making use of existing social networks and their own social networks

There are some examples of businesses making great use of existing social networks and their own social networking type websites to improve their businesses. Let's have a look at a few specific examples:

Dell: Twitter

Dell, a popular computer manufacturer, was recently able to attribute $2 million of sales to their Twitter account www.twitter.com/DellOutlet. By regularly posting discounts and discount codes to followers, Dell was able to entice more customers to their online shop to make a purchase. More information is available on the Mashable website: http://mashable.com/2009/06/11/delloutlet-two-million/.

NameCheap: Twitter

NameCheap is a domain name registrar, and they use Twitter for two purposes. Firstly, they collect and respond to feedback from customers mentioning their company, and more prominently, they run various competitions giving away free domain names. These viral competitions encourage more users to follow them, and promote the competition, therefore increasing their own brand awareness. The NameCheap Twitter account is http://twitter.com/namecheap.

BT: Twitter

British Telecom uses Twitter to help improve customer service and manage their reputation. You may have seen this used in response to customer complaints to try and assist them with their problems, and escalate matters such as fault testing and engineer call out. This makes them seem more caring (also emphasized by their choice of Twitter username www.twitter.com/BTCare), and increases customer satisfaction by resolving problems more quickly.

Netgear: Custom

While not strictly a social network, Netgear have various social aspects to their website, both through a dedicated community area and the support section of their website. The support section integrates community generated content from their discussion forums, and brings this into product pages, making it easier for customers to find answers to the questions that the staff have not answered directly. Discussion forum software is also quickly becoming social networking software to an extent, in its own right.

Why not join or use an existing social network?

There are already a number of popular and powerful social networks available, which we will discuss in a moment, so why would we want to create our own social network? We will want to create a social network for the following reasons:

- **Provide a service**: With the site we are going to create throughout this book we will be providing a service through the exchange of knowledge and information relating to owning pet dinosaurs. Having our own social network provides a fantastic platform for sharing and expanding this knowledge.

- **Improve business**: A social network can allow businesses to interact informally with customers, gathering feedback and in some cases giving value to the customer. One particular instance of this that I have noticed is that radio stations often advertise their websites as social network type websites, where listeners can get in touch, connect with other listeners, request songs, share photographs, and so on.

- **Improve communications**: Communicate with users informally, easily, and cheaply — Drupal can be used for Intranets too and can easily handle group communication functions.

- **They are fun!**: Social networks help break down the barriers of time and distance, and are a good way to meet new people in a relatively safe way. Recent years have also seen an increase in the number of niche social websites focusing on dating and real-world socializing.

Some of the reasons I've just listed still don't answer why we should create our own social network, as opposed to using an existing one. Let's look at some of them in more detail.

Provide a service

There are many ways in which websites and social networks provide additional services which are relevant to the social network or the target audience, though these are often through third-party applications. For example, there are features for both Facebook and LinkedIn which can provide a list of books which a user has read; these link off to book retailers so that more information can be discovered and the books can be purchased. Additionally, some social networks contain knowledge bases of information which can be improved by the user.

With existing social networks, any additional service provided either directly through the social network or through third-party applications and plug-ins would, or could, be restricted in a number of ways. The terms and conditions of the social network would be the main restriction, followed by how the features themselves can be added.

For example, if we wanted to add a map of dinosaur-friendly restaurants to an existing social network, it would rely upon:

- Data collection / use provisions with the social networks terms of service
- Promotion within that social network, which can be a challenge
- Provisions for third party applications, which would most likely limit and restrict the functionality and design
- Design and user interface guidelines enforced by the social network

Improve business

By tapping into the existing user base of established social networks, we can communicate with a new group of users, increasing awareness, and hopefully improving business. One slight flaw with existing social networks is providing extra enhancements.

Taking Facebook as an example, third-party developers create additional features, and embedded them as applications, and some of these applications add business functionality. One example allowed users to book a table at a restaurant. The limitation with using Facebook is that before information is sent to the application, the user is subjected to several dialogs asking for their confirmation. These dialogues are important to prevent abuse, and to ensure user data is used properly, however it is an obstacle for developers. As more and more applications become available, there is more competition for a user's attention, which recently has led to applications requesting users to invite their friends to use it. These mass invitations have the opposite effect, and discourage users from using the applications in question.

With our own social network, the data and functionality would be hosted by ourselves, giving us the freedom to extend the functionality of the social network to help us improve business as we see fit, leading to a more relevant and user friendly social network!

Improve communications

Social networks remove most barriers to communication, such as geographical location (the only barrier which remains is Internet access), and this is the case for both existing and custom Social Networks. The primary advantage over using our own system is that we are less restricted in how we can communicate with users. With existing social networks you must be connected to the user, and restrictions may be imposed over which communication methods you use within the social network, or which external communication details are shown to you.

Existing social networks

There are many existing social networks available, some of which are already very popular, and have some excellent features. I'd imagine you have heard of all these before, and more likely use them on a regular basis, but let's take a look at the most prominent features of some of these more popular sites.

Facebook

Facebook is very much a global social networking website for everyone over the age of 13, starting out for students at Harvard University, branching out to all universities, and now available for everyone. Features available include:

- A customizable profile
- Users can update their statuses
- Users can connect with other users by adding them as "friends"
- Statuses of friends can be commented upon and users can indicate that they "like" a particular status
- Friends can post messages to each other's profiles
- Photos can be posted and shared
- Events can be posted and shared, with attendees sending their RSVPs online
- Groups can be created and joined, promoting specific activities or interests
- Topics can be discussed
- Third-party developers can create their own applications for Facebook, to add more to the platform

LinkedIn

LinkedIn is a business social networking site which encourages business contacts to connect. Features available on LinkedIn include allowing users to:

- Customize their profile
- Connect with colleagues
- See how users are connected to others
- Recommend other users with respect to a job
- Integrate Twitter with their account profiles
- Create and view business profiles

MySpace

MySpace is a social networking website used primarily by a younger audience, very popular with bands, particularly because of how many profiles can be customized with HTML, and how music can be embedded within profiles. Features available include:

- Customizable profiles, complete with:
  - ° HTML customization, allowing users to customize the colors, look, and feel of MySpace
  - ° Music integration
  - ° The user's current mood
  - ° Comments
- Groups: small subsets of users
- MySpace TV: video sharing
- Applications through an API
- Forums: for discussions
- Polls: to get user opinion

Twitter

Twitter is a microblogging social networking website, which primarily deals with very short messages of 140 characters or less. Despite this, it has a large number of prominent features, including:

- Profiles can be customized, both in terms of colors and background image
- Users can update their status

- Users can reply to each other's status updates
- Users can repost another user's status update, using the ReTweet function

The ease of use and small set of core features have made Twitter very popular.

Drupal

We are going to create our own social networking website, and to do that, we are going to use Drupal, an **Open Source Content Management System (CMS)**. So, let's look at exactly what a CMS is, and what Drupal is.

What is a CMS?

Before we look into exactly what a CMS is, let us look at the problem with websites which lead to the need for content management solutions.

Most websites available on the Internet involve a degree of complexity, be it that they are large websites with a lot of content; they may deal with dynamic user interactions, or they may involve a number of different people updating different sections. Even small websites can be complicated to manage, particularly if the design needs changing, or a particular piece of information needs changing on every page.

One of the key features of a content management system is that it separates the design of a website, the content of a website, and the logic or features of the website, making it easy to change any aspect of the website independently without affecting the rest of the website.

The following diagram shows the separation of these key layers, and how, when a visitor to the website requests a page, the content management system takes the design template and takes the content from the database. It combines the two, along with any logic (such as checking to see if the visitor is logged in, in which case it may display a username too) and then sends the result to the visitor's web browser.

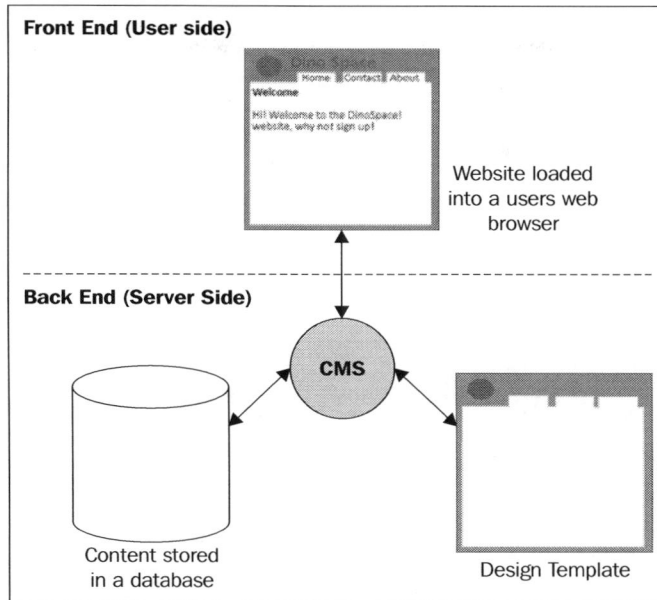

Generally, Content Management Systems have the ability for users to:

- Create content
- Edit, delete, and manage content
- Provide and restrict access to content, and the ability to edit the content
- Allow multiple users to easily edit and control different areas of a website simultaneously
- Separate the design, content, and logic layers of the website
- Collaborate effectively
- Manage different versions or drafts of content (referred to as revisions in Drupal)

What is Drupal?

Drupal is a free open source content management system that allows individuals or a community of users to easily publish, manage, and organize a wide variety of content on a website.

The project was started by Dries Buytaert and is now assisted in development with a large community. One particular advantage with Drupal is its modular framework, which allows additional features to be plugged into it, in the form of modules. The Drupal website maintains an extensive list of modules and themes (custom designs) which can be used.

The Drupal website address is `drupal.org`, and it contains the core Drupal downloads, news and updates related to Drupal, discussion forums and information, and downloads for many of the user contributed modules and themes, which can be downloaded to enhance Drupal.

Drupal as a social networking platform

Because of the way Drupal is structured, it is very flexible to adapt to the needs of a wide range of different websites. Permission to perform various actions such as creating content, writing a comment, writing a blog post, and so on can all be assigned to different roles within Drupal, be it the role of an administrative user or the role of a standard user who is logged in. This means that we can grant the permission to contribute and help manage the content of the website to the users of the website.

Many social-oriented features are included with Drupal "out of the box" (without the need to download extra files or modules) including:

- Blogs
- Forums
- Contact forms
- Content Construction Kit
- Collaborative content through the Book module and also through permissions allowing users to edit different types of content, such as pages

Drupal's modular framework, as mentioned earlier, allows new features to be installed at a later time. There are many modules available designed to enhance Drupal's ability to work and act like a social network. It also means that once our site is up and running, we can easily expand it at a later date with new modules to add extra functionality. Such modules include:

- Views
- Organic groups
- Extended profiles
- Blog themes

- Gravitar
- OpenID
- Janrain Engage (formerly RPX)

With Drupal being a Content Management System, we also have the advantage that a part of our site could be controlled and managed by us, as is typical with most websites, and other areas can be contributed to by the community.

Alternatives to Drupal

Drupal isn't the only option available, though since you are reading this book I'd imagine you are planning to use it! It is worth being aware of the alternatives, to ensure that before we start creating our site, we know we are using the right platform to do what we want.

Roll your own

Off-the-shelf products provide quick access to most common features, but their main lacking is in specific customization. One alternative is to create your own social networking website; by rolling your own, you can ensure it functions exactly how you want it to. The downside is the additional development time, technical skills required, and the difficulty in implementing some of the social features which off–the-shelf products have out of the box.

If you want to know more about how you could roll your own social networking site, Packt has a book published on the subject, *PHP 5 Social Networking* at `https://www.packtpub.com/php-create-powerful-dynamic-social-networking-website/book`.

Elgg

Elgg is an open source social networking platform, complete with functionality for setting up profiles, sharing files, adding friends, blogging, aggregating RSS, content tagging, and social graphs. Elgg also has an API allowing developers to extend Elgg by adding additional functionality, as well as a RESTful API to allow other applications to interact with the platform. More information on Elgg is available on their website: `http://www.elgg.org/`.

Hybrid approaches

There are of course options available which combine using an off-the-shelf system and a custom system, however, these mainly facilitate extending the functionality of the existing social networking platform, or by integrating some of those social aspects with our own website. Such approaches include:

- **Facebook Applications**: Creating applications which are accessed through Facebook's main site, providing additional features to users, for example, a Map of Dinosaur friendly restaurants these are hosted externally, by the developer.

- **Facebook Connect**: Allows websites to interact with Facebook, using it as an authentication protocol, pulling friend data from it, as well as pushing and pulling status updates to and from Facebook.

- **Google OpenSocial**: A set of common APIs which make applications for social networks interoperable with supporting social networking sites. It also enables site developers to integrate the API so that other developers can build applications for that site too.

There are many other social networking engines available for this type of approach, although they are not as common as the ones listed earlier. A simple web search will provide a list of additional engines which we can investigate if we wish.

DinoSpace!

Throughout this book we are going to be creating our very own social networking website using Drupal; this website is called DinoSpace! and it is aimed at owners of pet dinosaurs (yes, I know, nobody really owns a pet dinosaur…it would be too expensive and impractical) to interact with one another. In particular the website aims to:

- Connect owners of pet dinosaurs and allow them to build and maintain friendships with other users

- Allow owners to share stories about their pets

- Help promote dinosaur-friendly places to visit

- Provide interactive help and support to fellow dinosaur owners

- Allow owners to chart their activities with their dinosaur

Of course the website needs to enable more than just user to user interactions; it also needs to provide other content, and allow communication between us, the managers of the website, and our users to keep them up to date.

Installing Drupal

We know what Drupal is, we know what social networking is, and we know what we are going to create with Drupal throughout the course of this book; let's get started! The first thing we need to do is install Drupal. This section contains some detailed technical information regarding the requirements and installation of Drupal.

> For most of the book, we will be working with Drupal installed locally on our own computers (see *Appendix A*, for setting up a development environment if you don't have web server software installed on your own computer). As we build up the site we will then deploy Drupal onto a web server in *Chapter 10, Deploying and Maintaining our Social Network*.

Requirements

Provided we used the instructions in *Appendix A* to set up our development environment, we will already have a suitable development environment which meets the minimum requirements to run Drupal. For reference, or if you are using a custom development environment and want to check if it meets the requirements for Drupal, the minimum requirements are:

- A web server:
    - Apache 2.0 or greater is recommended
- PHP 5.2.4 or greater.
- Database engine: Either MySQL 5.0.15 (or greater), MariaDB 5.1.44 (or greater), PostgreSQL 8.3 (or greater) or SQLite 3.4.2 (or greater). MySQL is assumed during the course of this book.
- To make use of friendly or clean URLs, the mod_rewrite module for Apache, and the ability to use .htaccess files is required. However, this is optional.
- PHP's XML extension may be required to utilize certain XML-based services using Drupal. This is also optional.

The Drupal Handbook also has a page on installation and usage requirements; however this page is currently for several versions of Drupal, with accompanying notes, and is marked as requiring an update: http://drupal.org/requirements.

Download

We can download Drupal from the download page, http://drupal.org/download. This page contains download links for **Drupal Core**, **Installation Profiles**, **Themes**, **Translations**, and **Modules**. We want to download Drupal core:

Download & Extend

Download & Extend Home	Drupal Core	Modules	Themes	Translations	Installation Profiles

Download Drupal core files, and extend your site with modules, themes, translations and installation profiles.

Core	Installation Profiles	Themes	Translations
Download Drupal 7.2	Community Site	About Themes & Subthemes	Catalan
	E-commerce	Most Installed Themes	French
	News Site	New Themes	Hungarian
Download Drupal 6	Wiki	Most Active Themes	Dutch
Other Releases	**More Profiles**	**Search for More Themes**	**All Translations**
More Information			

Installation

Now that we have downloaded a copy of Drupal 7, we need to install it on our local web server, to do that we need to:

- Extract the Drupal files
- Create a database
- Run the Drupal installer

Extracting the Drupal files

The file we have downloaded is a compressed file containing all of the individual files which make up Drupal. We need to extract this into the web folder in our development environment (see *Appendix A*) using an unzipping program (such as WinZip, PowerArchiver, or Windows, built in "Compressed folders" system, or the default program for handling compressed files on your computer).

> **Technical installation details**
> Further details on these requirements are available in the INSTALL.txt file in the Drupal download zip.

Creating the database

We need a database for Drupal to use to store information such as the website's content, details of our users, settings, and so on. PHPMyAdmin is a web-based tool for administering MySQL databases; most web hosts provide access to it, and we have a copy on our local machine too.

Let's log in to phpMyAdmin and create our database, our local installation is located at `http://localhost/phpmyadmin/`. We will need to have our database username and password available (see *Appendix A*, if you are using that development environment). Most of the development environment software, such as WAMP, XAMPP, and so on have a default username of `root` without a password.

Once logged in, we have the option to create a new database, let's call it `drupal`, by entering it into the **Create new database** box:

localhost

- Server version: 5.0.45-community-nt
- ► Protocol version: 10
- Server: localhost via TCP/IP
- ► User: root@localhost
- MySQL charset: **UTF-8 Unicode (utf8)**
- MySQL connection collation: utf8_unicode_ci ▼ ⊚

Create new database ⊚

| drupal | Collation ▼ | Create |

> Keep a note of the database name, as well as the database username and password, as we will need them in a minute when we run the Drupal installer.

Running the Drupal installer

Now we have our database, we can run the installer; to do that we just need to visit the folder where we extracted Drupal, using our web browser. This should be `http://localhost/drupal/`.

Since we haven't installed Drupal yet, visiting this page will take us straight to the installer, which initially asks us if we wish to install the **Standard** (with the most commonly used features pre-configured) or **Minimal** (with only a few modules enabled) installations.

1. **Select an installation profile**: Let's select **Standard**, and then click the **Save and continue** button:

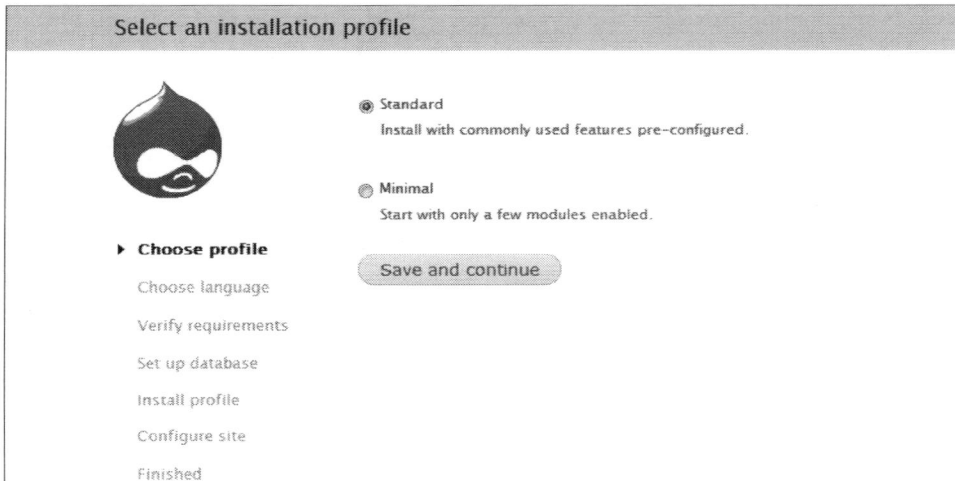

2. **Choose a language**: Next, we need to select the language we want to install Drupal in. The default download only includes English, though additional languages can be downloaded from Drupal.org, so we can click the **Save and continue** button again:

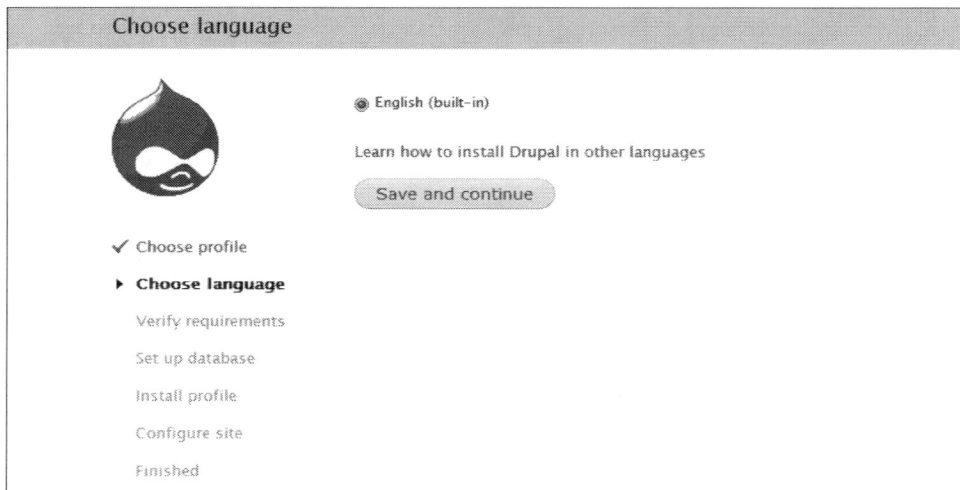

Drupal will then automatically verify the development server against the installation requirements; as we are using a suitable development environment, this won't raise any issues for us.

3. **Database configuration**: We are then presented with the **Set up database** screen where we can enter the name of the database we created earlier, drupal, and the username and password (working locally, the default WAMP installation gives us a username of root with no password) required to access that database:

Database configuration

Database type *
◉ MySQL, MariaDB, or equivalent
◉ SQLite
The type of database your Drupal data will be stored in.

✓ Choose profile

✓ Choose language

✓ Verify requirements

▸ **Set up database**

Install profile

Configure site

Finished

Database name *

| drupal |

The name of the database your Drupal data will be stored in. It must exist on your server before Drupal can be installed.

Database username *

| root |

Database password

| |

▸ ADVANCED OPTIONS

(Save and continue)

Once we have entered that, we again click **Save and continue.**

4. **Drupal installer**: Now the installer gets to work:

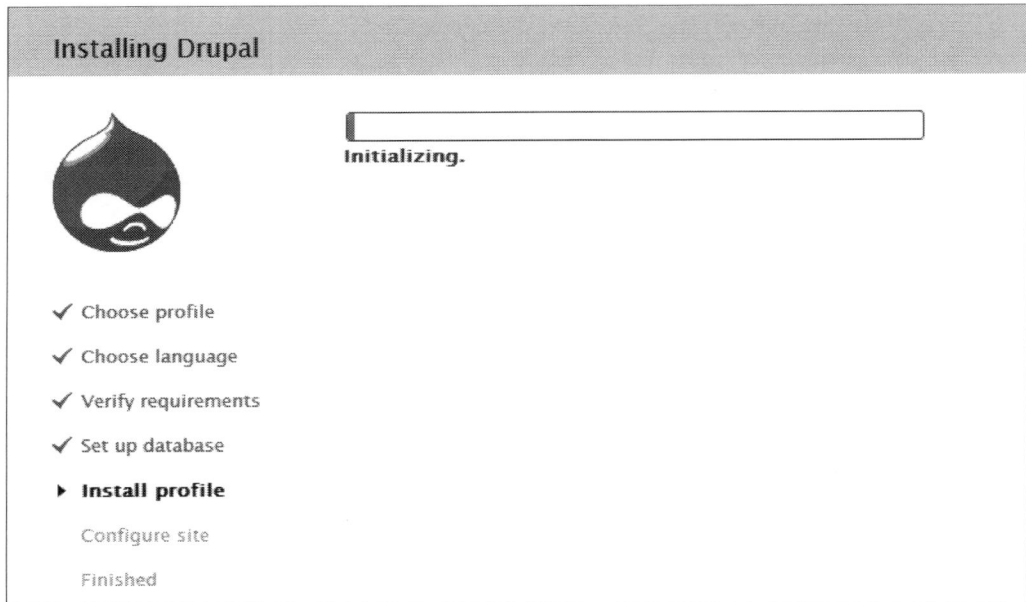

5. **Configure the site**: The final step in the installation process is for us to provide some basic configuration information, including the **Site name**, **Site e-mail address**, details for a maintenance account, server country and time zone, and update notifications.

We need to supply the site name, DinoSpace!, and e-mail address, so that our site has a name, and all site e-mails come from a site related e-mail address. The site maintenance account will be our initial administrative user account; it is important that we use a secure username and password:

Configure site

- ✓ Choose profile
- ✓ Choose language
- ✓ Verify requirements
- ✓ Set up database
- ✓ Install profile
- ▶ **Configure site**
- Finished

SITE INFORMATION

Site name *

DinoSpace!

Site e-mail address *

mkpeacock@gmail.com

Automated e-mails, such as registration information, will be sent from this address. Use an address ending in your site's domain to help prevent these e-mails from being flagged as spam.

SITE MAINTENANCE ACCOUNT

Username *

Michael

Spaces are allowed; punctuation is not allowed except for periods, hyphens, and underscores.

E-mail address *

mkpeacock@gmail.com

Password *

••••••••   Password strength: **Fair**

Confirm password *

••••••••   Passwords match: yes

To make your password stronger:
- Add uppercase letters
- Add numbers
- Add punctuation

The **SERVER SETTINGS** indicate the country to be used for the site, and the default time zone for dates and times displayed on the site. Finally, we can select to have our Drupal installation automatically check for updates and send notifications to us:

Once we have completed this page, we click **Save and continue**.

6. **Installation complete**: Our installation is now complete; the final screen confirms this for us, and provides us a link to view the newly installed Drupal site:

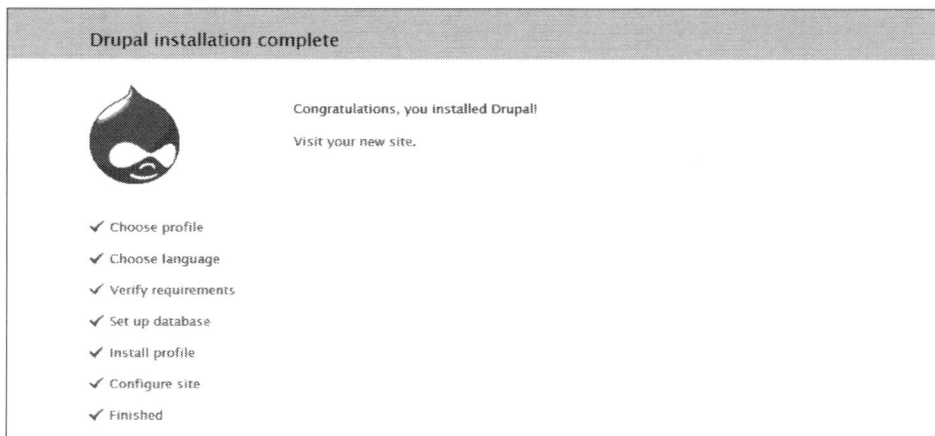

If we click that link, we see our new site, and we are automatically logged in:

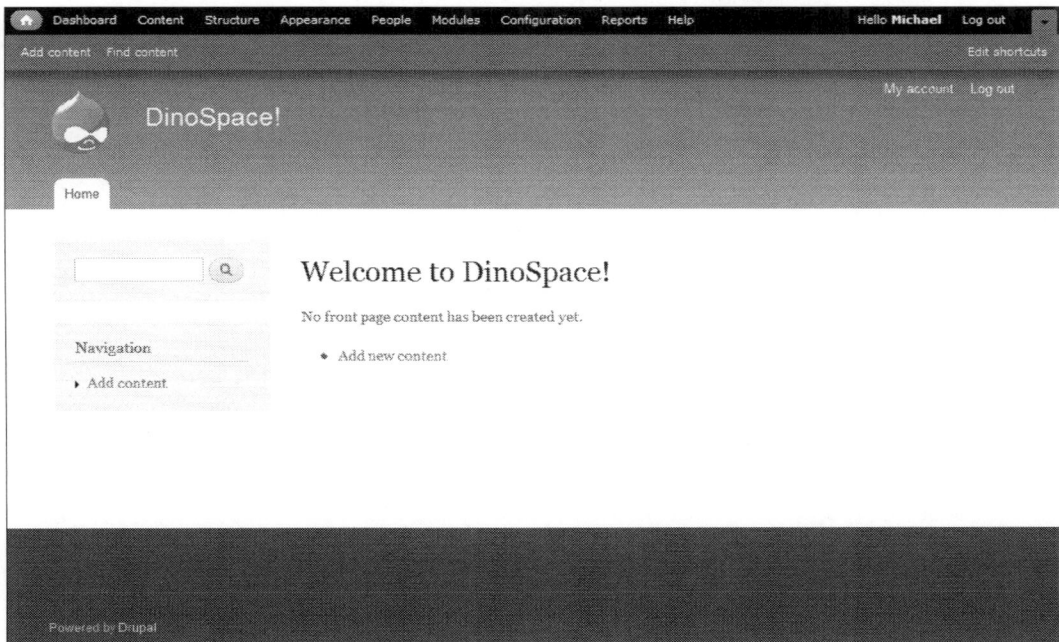

Configuring Drupal

We will discuss Drupal's administrative options more in *Chapter 2, Preparing Drupal for a Social Networking Site*; however, now that we have installed Drupal let's look at configuring our installation.

Provided we are logged in as an administrator, the administration bar is at the top of the page, listing the main administrative sections available. Click the **Configuration** option:

This then presents us with a pop up window overlay within our browser, containing the administration options available:

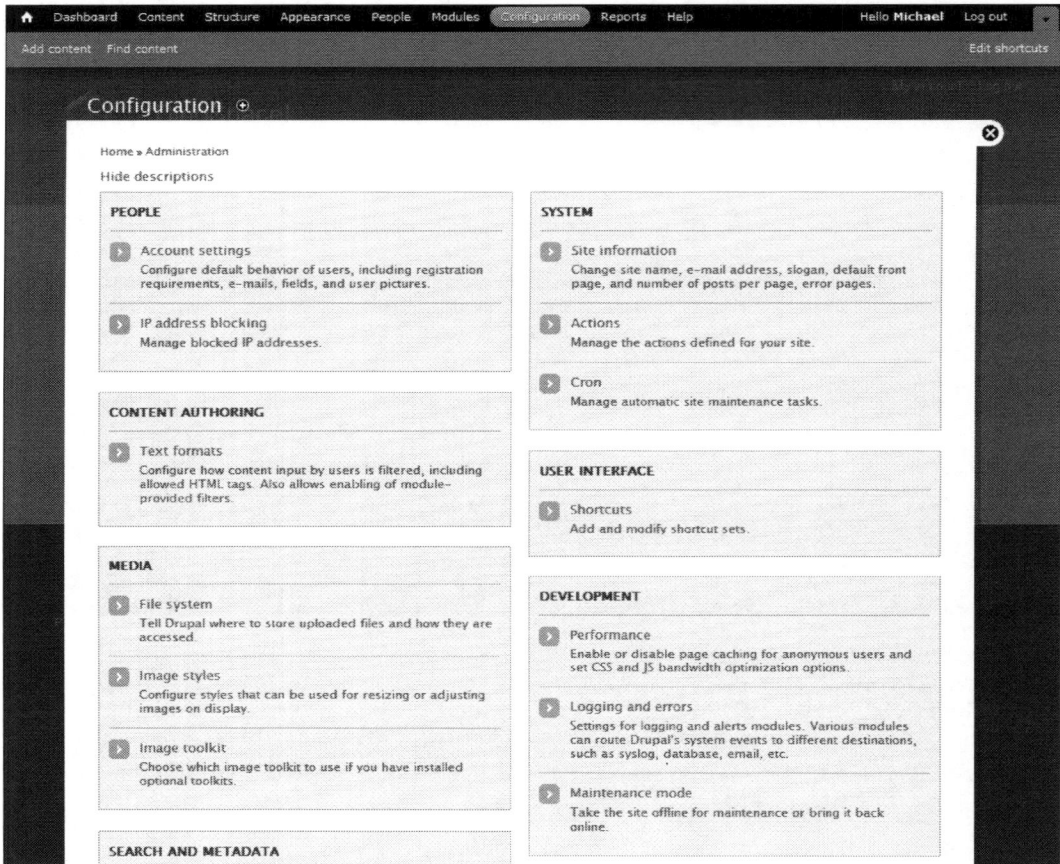

Let's go through these, focusing on the ones important to us for initially configuring our site.

People: Account settings

Here the first group of settings is for **ANONYMOUS USERS**; this has a setting **Name**, which is the name given to users who have not logged into the site, but who are interacting with the site. Any content that they create will be created under this name. Let's leave this as Anonymous:

Home » Administration » Configuration » People

ANONYMOUS USERS

Name *

Anonymous

The name used to indicate anonymous users.

The next group of settings is **ADMINISTRATOR ROLE**, the role for administrative users. Within Drupal, users have a number of roles within the site (such as administrator, editor, reviewer, and so on) and these roles have various permissions assigned to them. When new modules are installed, the administrator would automatically have full permissions for these modules; by selecting or changing the **Administrator role** here, we can change which role will automatically receive these permissions when new modules are installed. Let's leave this setting as **administrator**.

ADMINISTRATOR ROLE

Administrator role

administrator ▾

This role will be automatically assigned new permissions whenever a module is enabled. Changing this setting will not affect existing permissions.

Next we have **REGISTRATION AND CANCELLATION**, which defines who can register for a user account, if these accounts require e-mail validation, and what happens in the event of an account cancellation. Since we will want lots of visitors to sign up to DinoSpace! we should configure it so that **Visitors** are selected under **Who can register accounts?**. To prevent automated SPAM accounts registering and posting SPAM content, we should require all visitors to verify their e-mail account before they are able to log in.

Finally, we should leave it so that when accounts are disabled, the content created by that user is retained on the site. If we changed this, various pages, comments, and discussion posts would be removed when a user cancels their account.

REGISTRATION AND CANCELLATION

Who can register accounts?

○ Administrators only

◉ Visitors

○ Visitors, but administrator approval is required

☑ Require e-mail verification when a visitor creates an account.

New users will be required to validate their e-mail address prior to logging into the site, and will be assigned a system-generated password. With this setting disabled, users will be logged in immediately upon registering, and may select their own passwords during registration.

When cancelling a user account

◉ Disable the account and keep its content.

○ Disable the account and unpublish its content.

○ Delete the account and make its content belong to the *Anonymous* user.

○ Delete the account and its content.

Users with the *Select method for cancelling account* or *Administer users* permissions can override this default method.

The next section, **PERSONALIZATION**, allows us to provide some brief personalization options for our users, such as allowing them to upload pictures and use e-mail signatures. Let's enable signatures so that our users can have a custom piece of text added after their posts on the website, and add picture guidelines requesting that our users only upload photos that they are permitted to upload, and that are within the guidelines of our site:

PERSONALIZATION

☑ Enable signatures.

☑ Enable user pictures.

Picture directory

```
pictures
```

Subdirectory in the file upload directory where pictures will be stored.

Default picture

URL of picture to display for users with no custom picture selected. Leave blank for none.

Picture display style

thumbnail ▼

The style selected will be used on display, while the original image is retained. Styles may be configured in the Image styles administration area.

Picture upload dimensions

1024x1024   pixels

Pictures larger than this will be scaled down to this size.

Picture upload file size

800   KB

Maximum allowed file size for uploaded pictures. Upload size is normally limited only by the PHP maximum post and file upload settings, and images are automatically scaled down to the dimensions specified above.

Picture guidelines

Only upload photographs you have permission to post, and which are suitable for the age-range of the audience of this website.

This text is displayed at the picture upload form in addition to the default guidelines. It's useful for helping or instructing your users.

The final group of options here allows us to customize the text of any of the user account related e-mails which Drupal sends out:

```
E-mails

┌────────────────────────────────┐  Edit the welcome e-mail messages sent to new member accounts created
│ Show Welcome (new user         │  by an administrator. Available variables are: [site:name], [site:url],
│ created by administrator)      │  [user:name], [user:mail], [site:login-url], [site:url-brief], [user:edit-url],
├────────────────────────────────┤  [user:one-time-login-url], [user:cancel-url].
│ Hide Welcome (awaiting         │
│ approval)                      │  Subject
├────────────────────────────────┤  ┌──────────────────────────────────────────────────────────┐
│ Show Welcome (no approval      │  │ An administrator created an account for you at [site:name] │
│ required)                      │  └──────────────────────────────────────────────────────────┘
├────────────────────────────────┤
│ Show Account activation        │  Body
├────────────────────────────────┤  ┌──────────────────────────────────────────────────────────┐
│ Show Account blocked           │  │ You may now log in by clicking this link or copying and pasting it to │
├────────────────────────────────┤  │ your browser:                                              │
│ Show Account cancellation      │  │                                                            │
│ confirmation                   │  │ [user:one-time-login-url]                                  │
├────────────────────────────────┤  │                                                            │
│ Show Account canceled          │  │ This link can only be used once to log in and will lead you to a page │
├────────────────────────────────┤  │ where you can set your password.                           │
│ Show Password recovery         │  │                                                            │
└────────────────────────────────┘  │ After setting your password, you will be able to log in at [site:login-url] │
                                     │ in the future using:                                       │
                                     │                                                            │
                                     │ username: [user:name]                                      │
                                     │ password: Your password                                    │
                                     │                                                            │
                                     │ -- [site:name] team                                        │
                                     └──────────────────────────────────────────────────────────┘

( Save configuration )
```

We should leave the e-mail options as they are and click **Save configuration**.

System: Site information

After clicking **Save configuration** from the e-mail settings, the site information can be found under the **Configuration** menu. The first group of settings under **site information** is SITE DETAILS, this includes the **Site name** and **E-mail address**, which we set when we installed Drupal, and also the site's **slogan**, so we need to add that in here:

Home » Administration » Configuration » System

SITE DETAILS

Site name *

DinoSpace!

Slogan

The social network for keepers of pet dinosaurs

How this is used depends on your site's theme.

E-mail address *

mkpeacock@gmail.com

The *From* address in automated e-mails sent during registration and new password requests, and other notifications. (Use an address ending in your site's domain to help prevent this e-mail being flagged as spam.)

The next group of settings, **FRONT PAGE**, define which page should act as the front page, and how many posts should be displayed on that page. This isn't something we are ready to change yet, as we don't have any content, so we can leave that as it is:

FRONT PAGE

Number of posts on front page

10

The maximum number of posts displayed on overview pages such as the front page.

Default front page

http://localhost/drupal7/ node

Optionally, specify a relative URL to display as the front page. Leave blank to display the default content feed.

The final group of settings relate to **ERROR PAGES**, and which pages should be used for the default 403 and 404 error pages. Again, we don't have content in place for these pages, so for now, we should leave them as they are. Once we have created pages to act as the error pages, we simply add the pages' URLs into the appropriate boxes:

ERROR PAGES

Default 403 (access denied) page

http://localhost/drupal7/

This page is displayed when the requested document is denied to the current user. Leave blank to display a generic "access denied" page.

Default 404 (not found) page

http://localhost/drupal7/

This page is displayed when no other content matches the requested document. Leave blank to display a generic "page not found" page.

Save configuration

Other configuration options

The other configuration options are not immediately important to us, however now is a good time for us to take a look at what these settings do.

People: IP address blocking

This setting allows us to list a number of IP addresses, the Internet addresses assigned to computers, which we want to block from using our site. If we find that we are receiving troublesome posts from one particular user or SPAM account, we can block their access to the site. This isn't foolproof, as IP addresses can be **spoofed** to appear to be different, or the user could request a renewed IP address from their Internet Service Provider.

System: Actions

This allows us to define and manage actions within our site.

System: Cron

Certain tasks, such as bulk mailings or search indexing, need to be processed on a regular basis automatically. The cron settings allow us to manually run these tasks, and configure how frequently they should be run.

Content authoring: Text formats

From here we can configure types of formatting that we wish to enable in our site, and the types of users who are permitted to use that content. For example, allowing users to post full HTML could pose a security risk, and only administrators should be permitted to post that. Other users would be allowed to post a restricted sub-set of HTML tags with their posts.

User interface: Shortcuts

Allows us to manage shortcuts to commonly accessed areas of the administration section.

Media: File system

This section indicates where files are uploaded to, and the servers temporary folder; these are automatically set from the installation process.

Media: Image styles

This section allows us to group various image effects (resizing, cropping, and so on) together, for use by other features and modules.

Media: Image toolkit

By default, since we are using the GD image library, this allows us to set the default image quality for uploaded images; this is a compromise between image quality and file size.

Development: Performance

Various options to help with the speed and performance of our site are managed within this section. By default, Drupal caches (keeps its own copy, preventing the need for it to continually lookup or load it) certain information, which keeps things running fast. Sometimes, we may need to turn off caching or clear the cache so that new options and changes we apply (for example, adding a new template) can take effect.

Development: Logging and errors

This allows us to define which types of errors should be logged, and how many of these logs should be kept.

Development: Maintenance mode

This allows us to turn our website off, placing it into maintenance mode, and displaying a message to our users.

Search and metadata: Search settings

This contains various settings related to the search feature.

Search and metadata: URL aliases

This allows us to "map" one web address onto another, for instance, creating a shortcut link to a long URL to promote on marketing materials.

Search and metadata: Clean URLs

This allows us to enable or disable the use of Clean URLs in our site. Clean URLs convert URLs which make use of the query string (`?path=node/`) to ones which don't, making them cleaner and more user friendly.

Web Services: RSS publishing

This allows us to customize our default RSS feed, which is a list of publicly visible content that visitors can read through their favorite feed reader.

Regional and language: Regional settings

Time zone and locale settings related to our site and server; this is the default time zone and location information which is used when generating times or regional specific language or symbols.

Regional and language: Date and time

The format which dates and times should be displayed on the site, when they are used in long, medium, and short forms.

Summary

We have looked into what social networking is, looked at various social networking concepts, and also why we may wish to create a social network. We then looked at Drupal and are now aware of what it is and how it can be used as a social networking platform. Finally, we installed Drupal onto our local development environment, examined the configuration options available, and made some basic configuration changes to the default Drupal installation.

The next stage is to start preparing our site to be a social network!

2
Preparing Drupal for a Social Networking Site

Now that we have looked into social networking, how we can use Drupal as a social networking platform, and we have installed Drupal, we need to start preparing our Drupal installation for use as a social networking site!

In this chapter you will learn:

- How Drupal works
- How to use Drupal
- How to use the administration tools within Drupal
- About taxonomy and RSS within Drupal
- More about planning your site and its content

How Drupal works

Before we start building our social networking site, it is important to take a step back and look at Drupal in a little more detail, to see how it works and the thought process behind it. Having a better understanding of this will help when planning, expanding, and managing our site!

An abstract framework

Although in the previous chapter Drupal was described as a content management system, it can more accurately be described as a content management framework. Whilst being a content management system—in that it is a system which is used for managing content within a website—Drupal places more emphasis upon the ability to easily customize and configure it.

Drupal is an abstract framework, because instead of focusing on specific types of site, and solutions to those, it focuses on more generic problems and approaches to them, which makes Drupal useful for more situations. With a little customization Drupal can be tailored more to a specific type of site.

Nodes

Nodes are what make Drupal an **abstract** framework. Most content types within Drupal are variants of a central concept within Drupal, the node. While different types of node (that is, different **Content Types**) are managed and handled differently, they are all stored together in the database. The Drupal website explains this best on their general concepts page:

> *A node in Drupal is the generic term for a piece of content on your website. (Note that the choice of the word "node" is not meant in the mathematical sense as part of a network.) Some examples of nodes:*
>
> *Pages in books*
>
> *Discussion topics in forums*
>
> *Entries in blogs*
>
> *News article stories*
>
> *Each node on your site has a Content Type. It also has a Node ID, a Title, a creation date, an author (a user on the site), a Body (which may be ignored/omitted for some content types), and some other properties. By using modules such as the contributed Content Construction Kit (CCK) module, the core Taxonomy module, and the contributed Location module, you can add fields and other properties to your nodes.*

For more information on nodes, visit `http://drupal.org/node/19828`.

> Much of the functionality related to the Content Construction Kit mentioned earlier, is now part of the Drupal 7 core, and not a separate module.

Although our default Drupal 7 installation only has provisions for Basic Page and Article content types (or types of node), the optional core modules which come included have provision for the following types of node:

- Blog entries
- Pages of a collaborative book (similar to a Wiki)

- Forum topics
- Polls

> **Drupal terminology**
>
> Drupal makes use of a technical vocabulary that has been documented in detail. While new phrases, words, and concepts are explained there may be some which are not covered in as much detail as they deserve. A detailed list of Drupal terminology is available online at http://drupal.org/node/937.

Modules and themes

Drupal's functionality is enhanced through **modules**. A number of modules are included as part of the Drupal core providing out-of-the-box, or optional out-of-the-box functionality, and the Drupal.org website features thousands of third party "contributed" modules which can be downloaded and installed to add new features to our Drupal installations.

The look and feel of our Drupal installation is determined by the **theme**. A few basic themes are included out-of-the-box with Drupal, with thousands available to download to change the design of the site. Drupal's theme system makes it relatively easy to completely customize the site's design.

Administering Drupal—An overview

Now that we have a basic understanding of how Drupal works, let's look through the administration area in more detail, making appropriate changes to settings where necessary to improve the suitability of our Drupal installation for a social networking site.

> It is important to note that the focus of this book is about using Drupal as a platform to create a social networking site. As a result, we won't be able to discuss each of the various features of Drupal in as much detail as deserved. We will of course cover everything that we need to, in sufficient detail, to use the features successfully for our social networking site.

Logging in

Before we can access Drupal's administrative tools, we need to log in as an administrator. The login box is on the left-hand side of our Drupal installation (`http://localhost/drupal7/`). Let's log in with the user account we created during the installation process:

Once logged in, we have access to the administrative toolbar at the top, along with a bar of shortcuts which we can customize to provide links to the areas we frequently access:

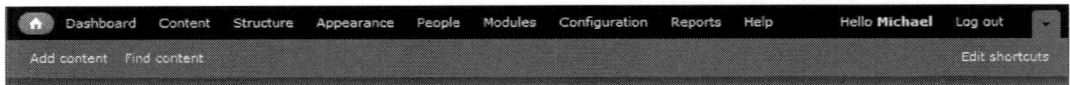

Dashboard

The first option on the administrative toolbar is the **Dashboard**. This is a simple screen which lists any recent content in the site, any new users to the site, and provides a search form for administrators.

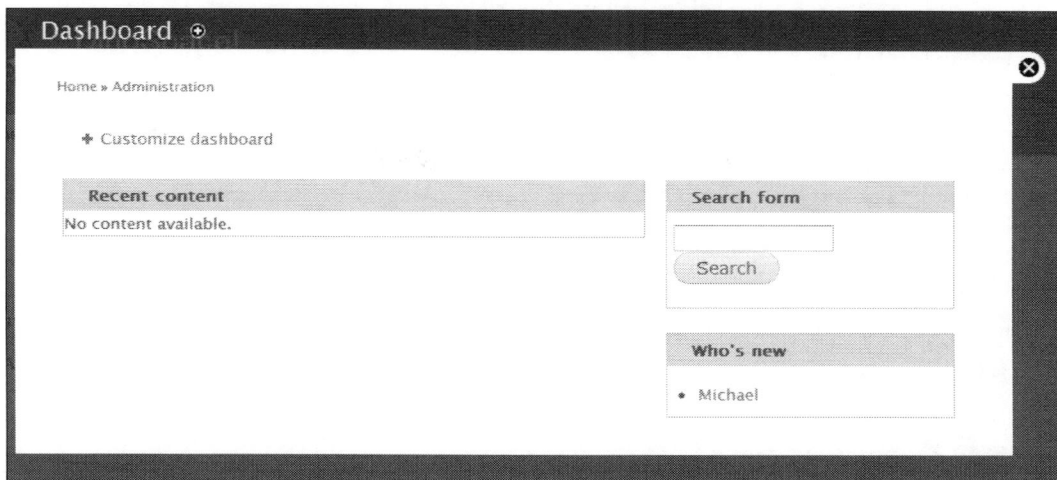

By default, the administration options in Drupal 7 appear in an overlay on the top of the main website, so that we can easily jump in and out of the administration area from the site itself.

We can customize the dashboard by clicking the **Customize dashboard** link, which allows us to configure the various blocks on the dashboard, move and reorder them, or select other blocks to add to our dashboard.

Let's add some more blocks to our dashboard:

1. First click the **Customize dashboard** link. This presents us with a list of blocks currently on our dashboard, and the ability to add more blocks:

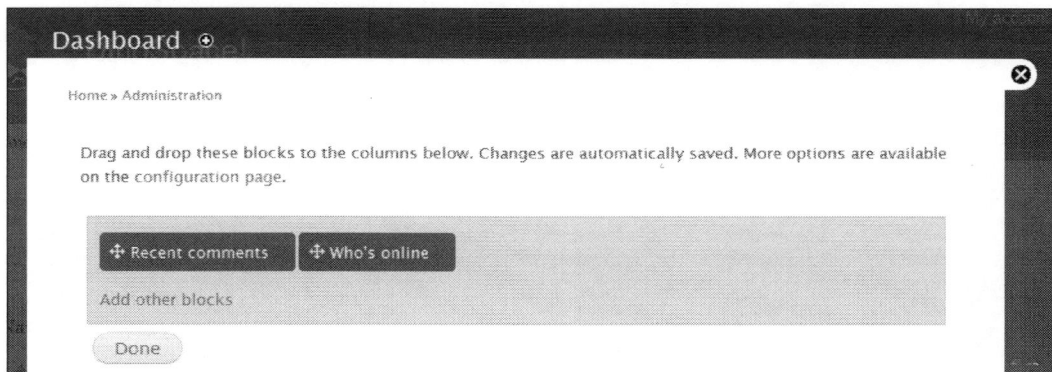

2. From here, we can click **Add other blocks** to add more blocks to our dashboard.

   As we are developing a social networking website, it would make sense for us to have the **Recent comments** block, showing recent comments which have been posted, and the **Who's online** block showing which users are online at the moment. This will give us, as administrators, a little more useful information from our dashboard:

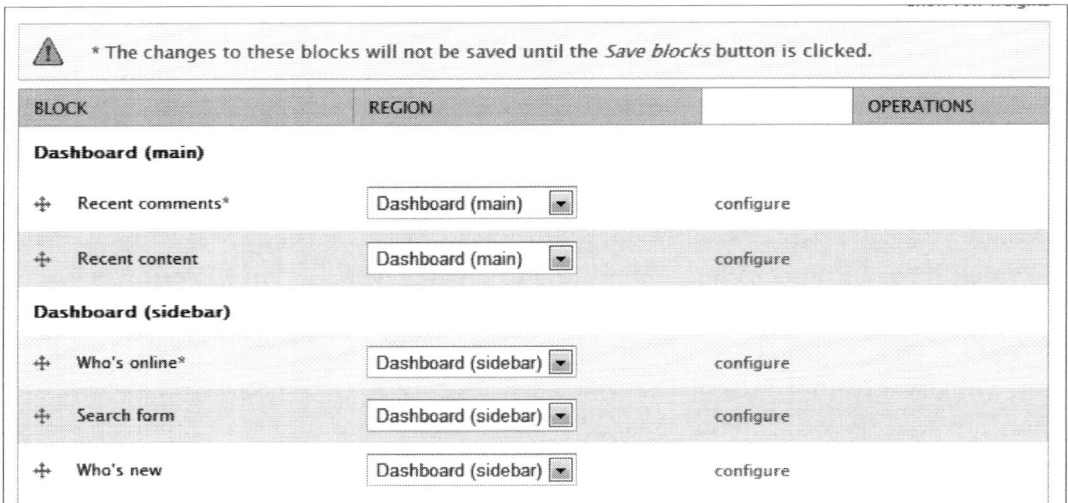

⚠ * The changes to these blocks will not be saved until the *Save blocks* button is clicked.

BLOCK	REGION		OPERATIONS
Dashboard (main)			
⊹ Recent comments*	Dashboard (main) ▼		configure
⊹ Recent content	Dashboard (main) ▼		configure
Dashboard (sidebar)			
⊹ Who's online*	Dashboard (sidebar) ▼		configure
⊹ Search form	Dashboard (sidebar) ▼		configure
⊹ Who's new	Dashboard (sidebar) ▼		configure

3. After making these changes, we need to click the **Save blocks** button at the bottom of the page:

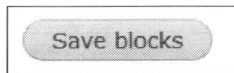

   Save blocks

Now, we have a slightly more useful and informative dashboard; or at least we will, once we have some users and comments on our site!

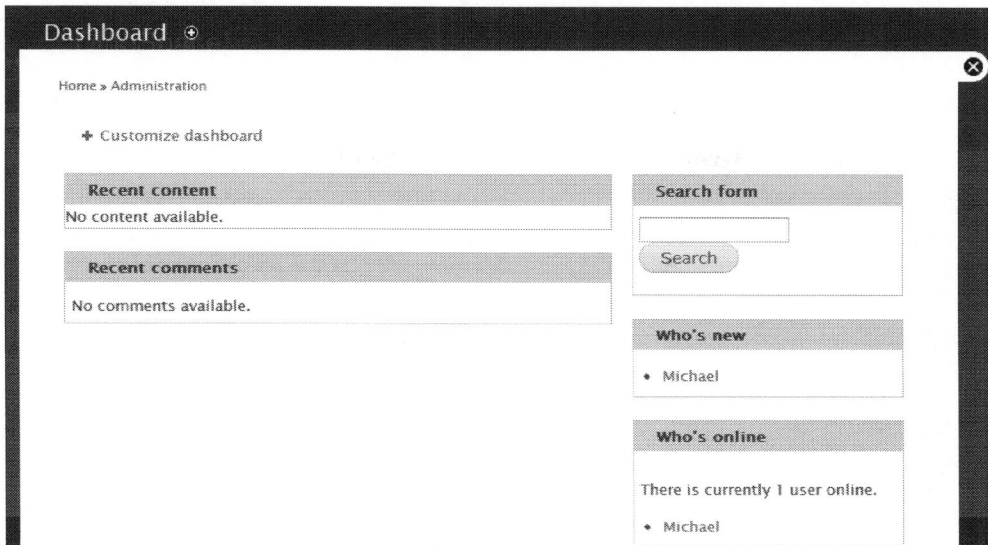

Dashboard ⊕

Home » Administration

✦ Customize dashboard

Recent content

No content available.

Recent comments

No comments available.

Search form

Search

Who's new

• Michael

Who's online

There is currently 1 user online.

• Michael

Content

The next section of the administration toolbar is **Content**, from here we can manage and create content for our site, and manage user contributed comments.

The main **Content** screen lists content in our site, and can be reordered by clicking the headings in the table listing the content. We can also select content and update its status, using the **UPDATE OPTIONS** drop down, or we can filter the list to only show content of a particular status or a particular type, using the options in the **SHOW ONLY ITEMS WHERE** section.

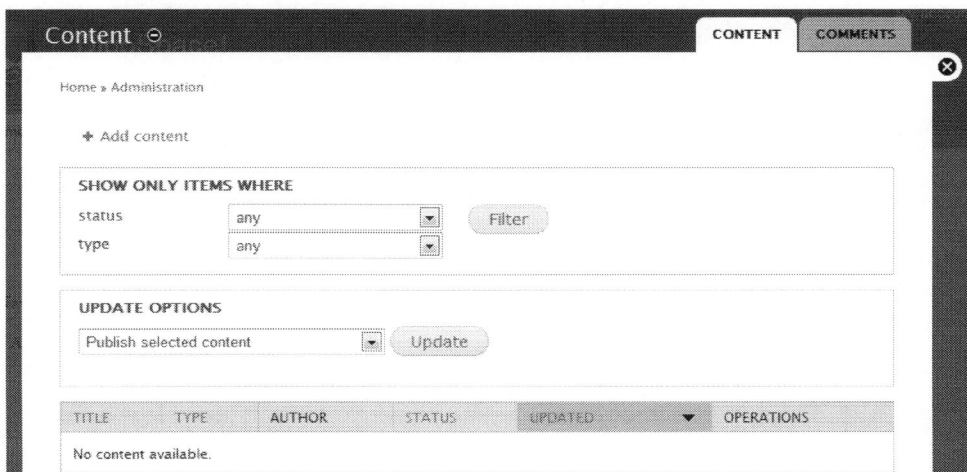

Content ⊖

CONTENT COMMENTS

Home » Administration

✦ Add content

SHOW ONLY ITEMS WHERE

status any Filter
type any

UPDATE OPTIONS

Publish selected content Update

TITLE	TYPE	AUTHOR	STATUS	UPDATED ▼	OPERATIONS

No content available.

Content statuses

Content in Drupal can be given different statuses to determine how (or if) it should be displayed in the site itself. The statuses available are:

- **Published**: This indicates that the content is published, and where appropriate is visible through the site itself.
- **Not published**: This indicates that the content has either been disabled, or is currently in a draft stage, and isn't visible through the site itself.
- **Promoted**: Where appropriate, promoted content appears on the site's front page.
- **Not promoted**: This type of content isn't displayed on the site's front page; the visibility of not promoted content on the site depends on the "published" settings.
- **Sticky**: In pages which list or display a number of nodes, sticky content appears first. If for instance, we had a page listing health care tips for T-Rex dinosaurs, and the page listed content newest first, we could create sticky content which would always display at the top, to describe the listing in more detail.
- **Not sticky**: This type of content hasn't been marked as sticky; the visibility of non promoted content on the site depends on the "published" settings.

Promoted content

The following screenshot shows the front page of our Drupal site, after a new page has been created and marked as "promoted". The content (if the page had more content on it, only a section would be displayed) is displayed with a link **Read more** for the visitor:

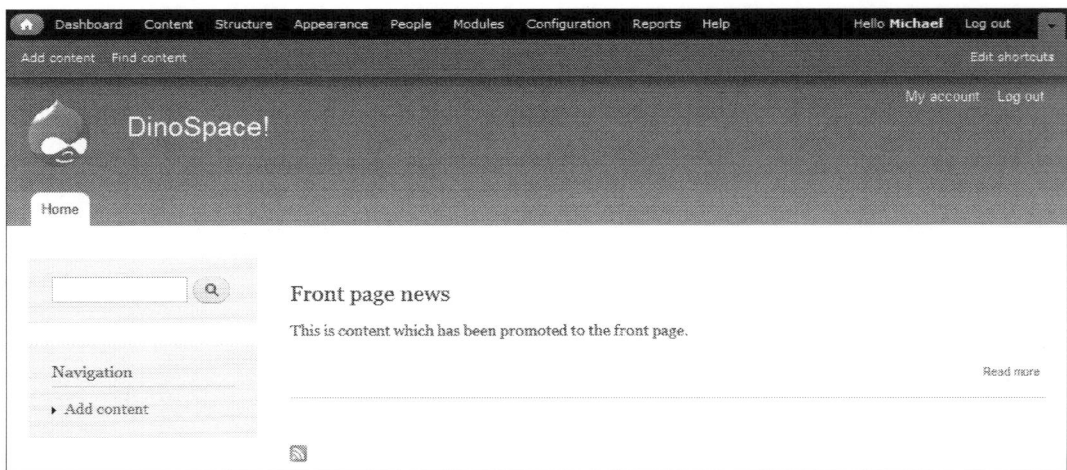

Sticky content

The following screenshot shows the front page of our Drupal installation, now with a new page promoted, this time marked as "sticky". The sticky content appears at the top, and is wrapped in a box making it stand out and appear more important than other content on the page:

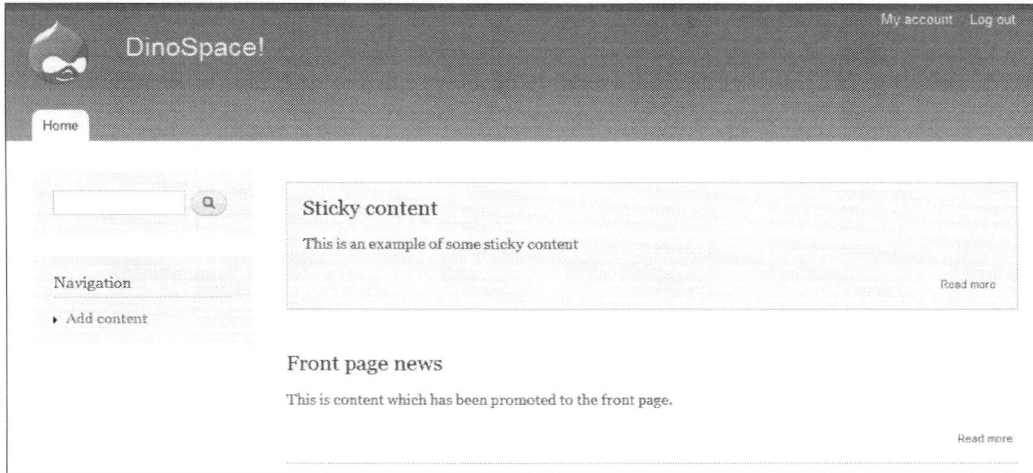

Creating content

To create new content for our site, we start by clicking the **Add content** link from the content section of the administration area. We are then presented with a list of types of content which we can create. By default, only **Article** and **Basic page** is available to us:

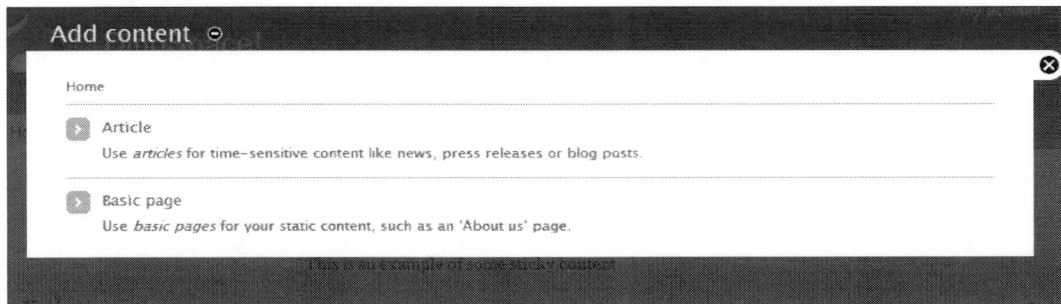

If we then select **Basic page**, we are presented with the appropriate screen to create a new page. There are two main aspects to the screen, the **Title** of the page, and the **Body** (or content) of the page. The **Title** is used as the name and the heading of the page, and the **Body** is the main content of the page:

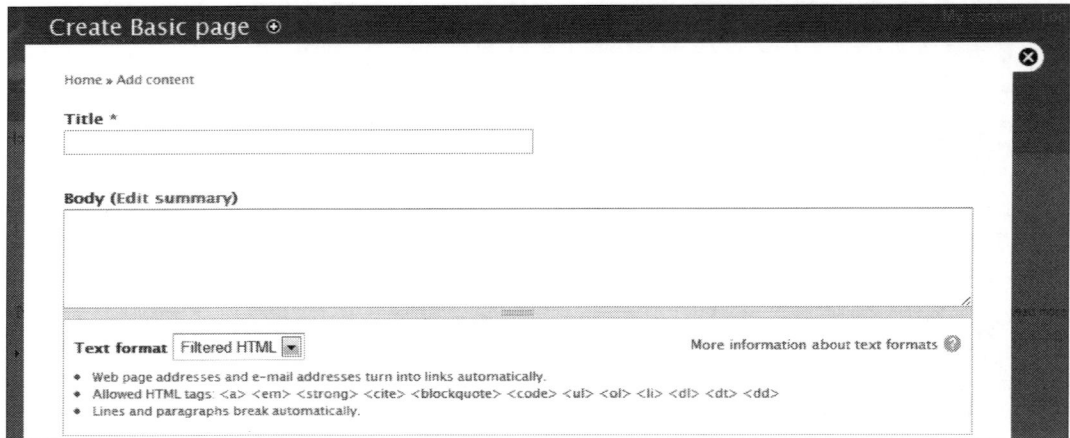

When a content type forms part of a list (for example, if we create a page which lists all T-Rex pages) only a section of the content is displayed; the reader then has to click a read more link to read the rest of the page. The section of the page which is displayed is, by default, automatically trimmed from the page's content. However, we can click the **Edit summary** link to display a separate textbox which allows us to specify the summary of a page:

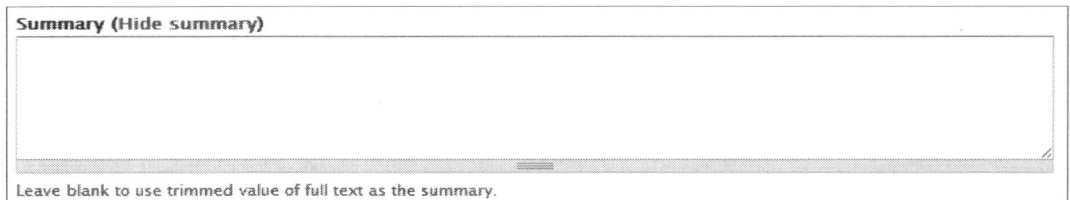

Finally, we have a number of different options and settings related to the new content, which we can configure, if we wish.

Each of the options down the left-hand side of the following screenshot are options which can be customized:

Show Menu settings Not in menu	☐ Provide a menu link
Show Revision information No revision	
Show URL path settings No alias	
Show Comment settings Closed	
Show Authoring information By Michael	
Show Publishing options Published	

These options include:

- **Menu settings**: This allows us to select if the page should appear in a menu, and if so, which menu and how it should be displayed.

- **Revision information**: This allows us to record a note when we create or change content, and select if the change should be saved as a new version of the content (which would allow us to undo changes at a later stage).

- **URL Path settings**: By default Drupal uses the ID (a number) of the node as the link to that page; we can create a more useful, readable URL to access the page by setting one in the URL alias box. In *Chapter 3, User Content: Contributions, Forums, and Blogs*, we will look at automating this process.

- **Comment settings**: Indicates if users can or cannot comment on a particular page (subject to the user's permissions).

- **Authoring information**: This allows us to change the author of the content (for example, if we are creating content on behalf of another user), and also the date that it was created.

- **Publishing options**: Here we can set if the content should be marked as Published, Promoted, or Sticky.

Comments

The **COMMENTS** tab allows us to view and manage comments which our users have posted on content within the site. Clicking the tab lists published comments, which shows the subject of the comment, the creator of the comment, where it was posted, when it was last updated, and allows us to view and edit the comment. The **UPDATE OPTIONS** drop down allows us to delete or unpublish comments. We can also click the **Unapproved comments** sub-tab to list any comments which are unapproved, so that we can moderate them and either approve or delete them:

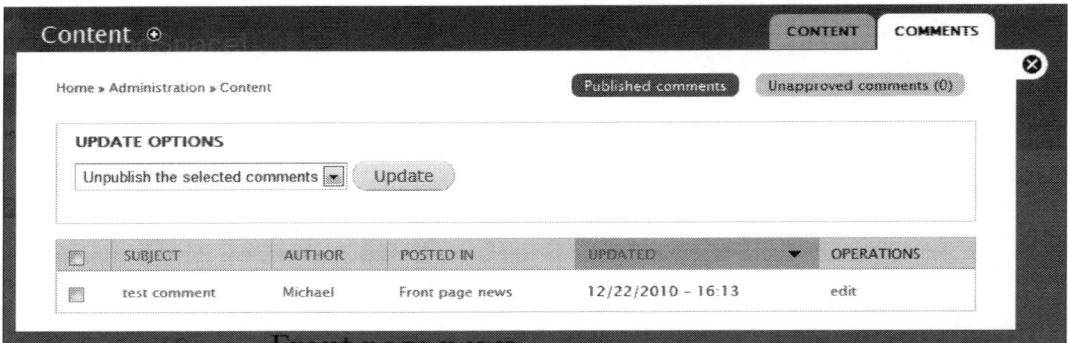

Structure

The **Structure** section of the administration area deals with various components which make up our site's structure. This includes blocks of functionality and content displayed on the site, the types of content which make up the site, menus which allow users to navigate through the site, and taxonomy which allows us to categorize content within the site:

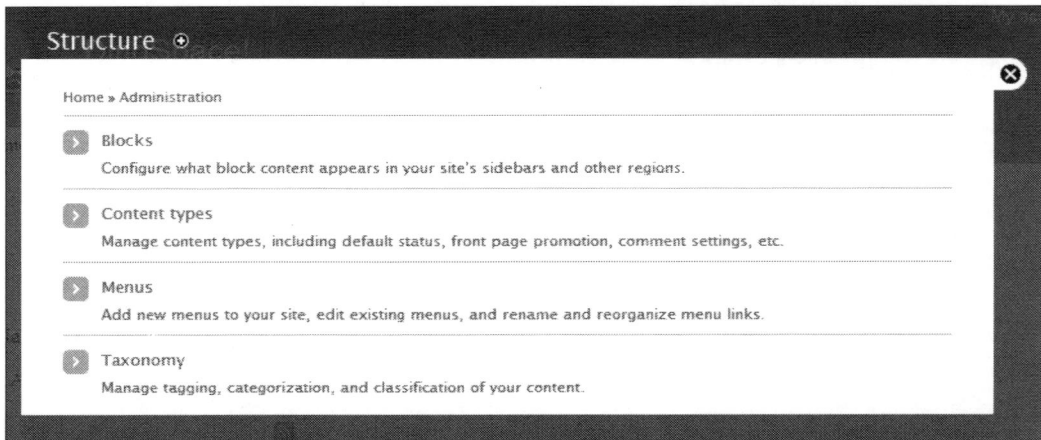

Blocks

Blocks allow us to place small sections of content or functionality in place across most of our site. For example, the location of a site-wide search box, or the user login box. The **Blocks** section allows us to reorder existing blocks, reposition them to different areas of the site, enable blocks which have been disabled, and create new blocks:

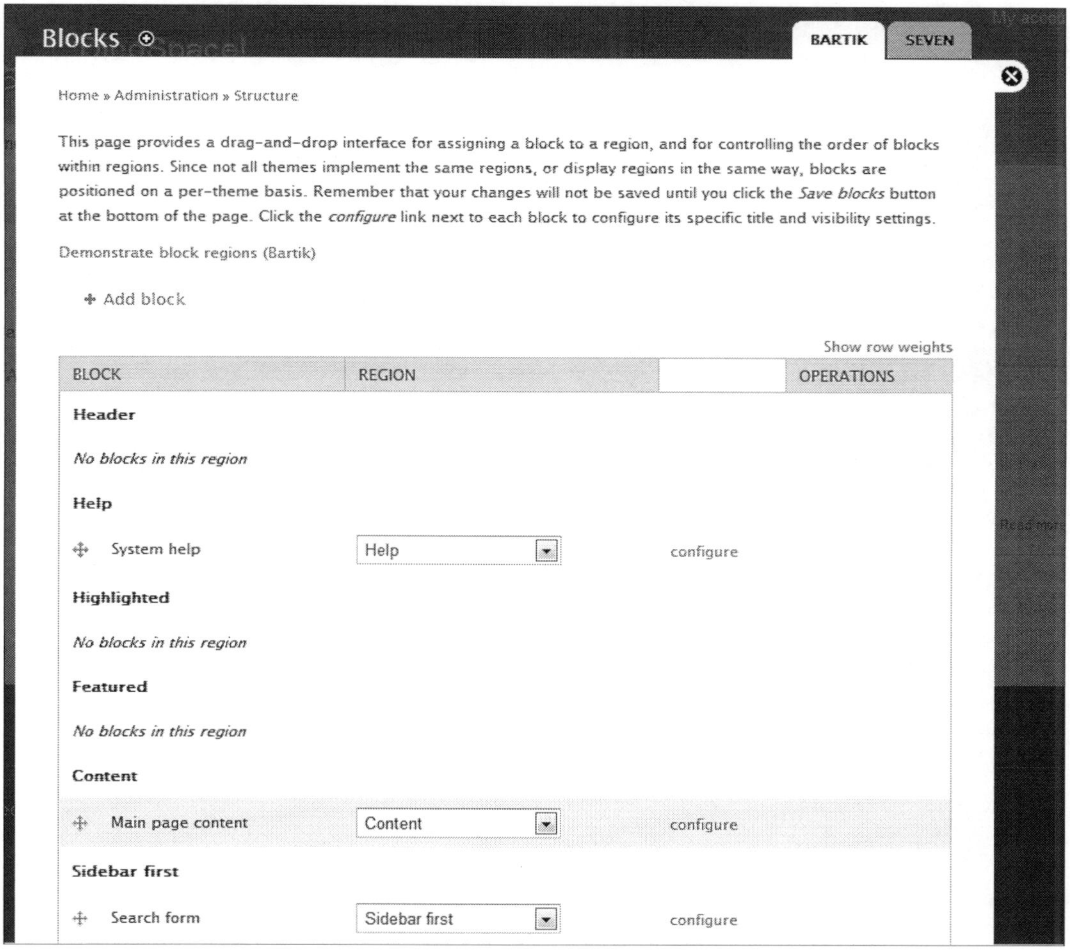

Blocks can be configured to specify which pages do or do not have the block displayed on them, which content types have the block displayed on them, which roles see the block, and if users can customize whether they see a particular block or not, all from the **configure** link next to each block. Blocks can be reordered by dragging the icon displayed next to the block's name, or be moved to a different section by changing the **REGION** drop-down list.

Struggling to reorder?

If you are struggling to reorder blocks using the drag-and-drop interface, you can click the **Show row weights** link, which will display a new column in the table listing the blocks. The column allows you to change the weight of a block, to make it appear higher or lower in the list. Block ordering won't be saved until you click the **Save** button, so remember to save any reordering before going into configuring or editing a block.

As there are quite a number of different locations that blocks can be placed, there is a helpful region demonstration which highlights on the screen which areas of the page match up to the region names.

A demo of these regions can be accessed by clicking the **Demonstrate block regions** link; such a demo is shown in the following screenshot:

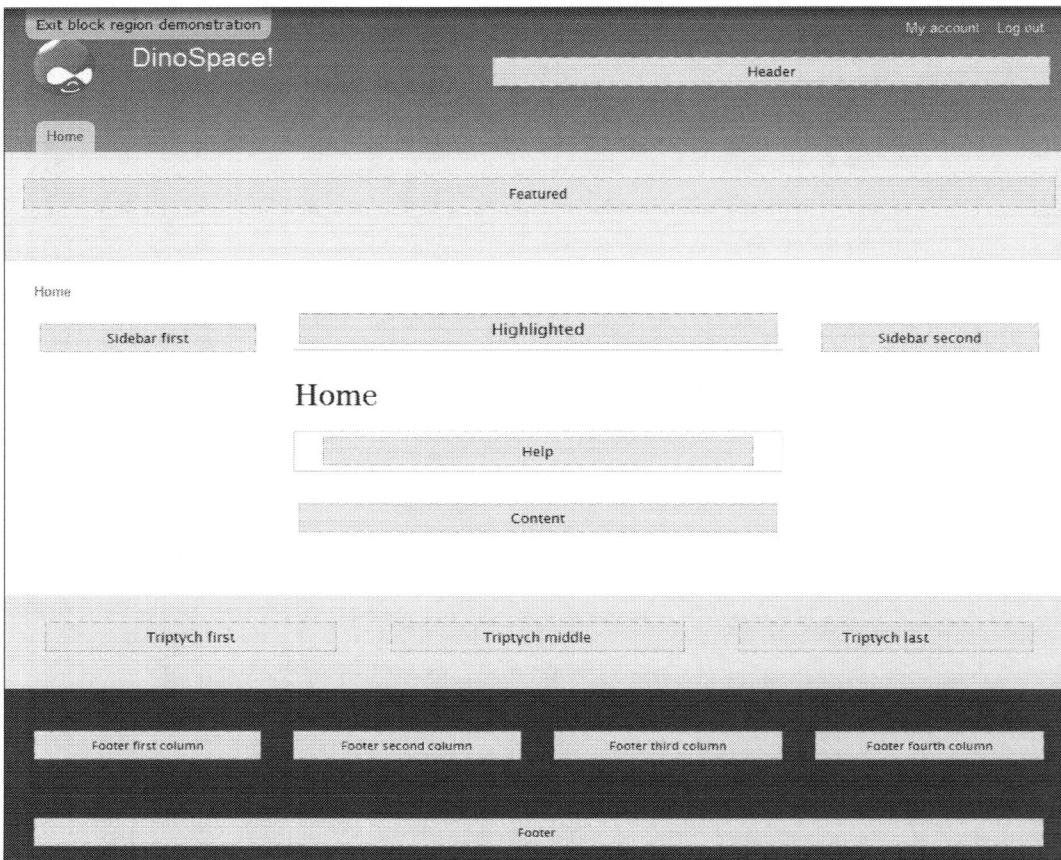

While configuring the blocks, the first installed theme is selected, and not the default theme. This is an issue with Drupal itself, and should be resolved shortly.

Content types

The content types section lists all of the available types of content which can be created in our Drupal installation. As we have previously discussed, currently we can only create Articles and Basic page content elements:

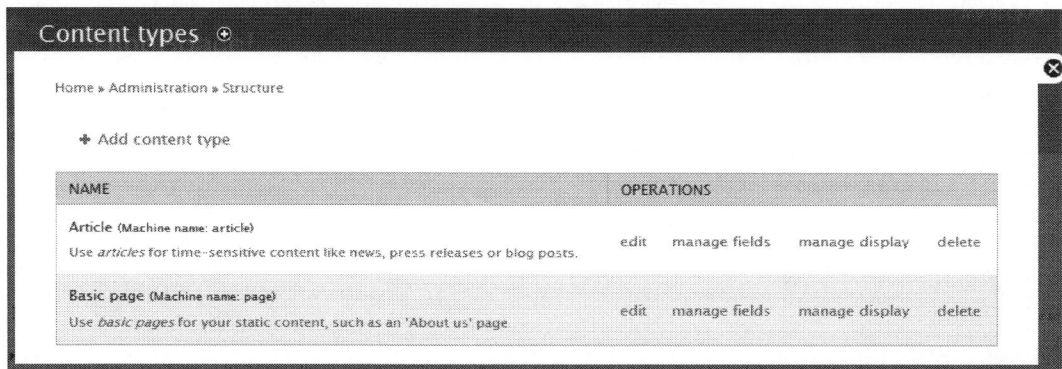

For each content type we can edit them, manage the fields which can be entered when creating content of that type, manage how the content is displayed, and delete the content type. We can also create new content types from here. We will discuss creating and editing content types in more detail, later in this chapter, as it is a very important section in its own right.

Menus

Menus are used by visitors to our site to navigate through the content, pages, and features available to them. By default, there are four menus available (more can be created):

- **Main menu**: This is often used to show the primary sections of a site
- **Management**: This contains links for administrative tasks, and is used to generate the administration toolbar at the top of the page when logged in as an administrator
- **Navigation**: This is the main menu used to allow visitors to navigate through the site
- **User menu**: This menu contains user related links, including the my account link, and the logout link

From the **Menus** screen we can list the links associated with it, edit the menu, or add a link to the menu. We can also create new menus, and from the **SETTINGS** tab, we can reallocate menus to act as either the "Main links" or "Secondary links" menus within the site.

Menus ⊙

| LIST MENUS | SETTINGS |

Home » Administration » Structure

Each menu has a corresponding block that is managed on the Blocks administration page.

✚ Add menu

TITLE	OPERATIONS		
Main menu The *Main* menu is used on many sites to show the major sections of the site, often in a top navigation bar.	list links	edit menu	add link
Management The *Management* menu contains links for administrative tasks.	list links	edit menu	add link
Navigation The *Navigation* menu contains links intended for site visitors. Links are added to the *Navigation* menu automatically by some modules.	list links	edit menu	add link
User menu The *User* menu contains links related to the user's account, as well as the 'Log out' link.	list links	edit menu	add link

When listing the links for a menu, we can reorder the menu links using the icon next to the link name (or, by clicking **Show row weights** and manually changing the order for the links), enable or disable a menu link, edit menu links, delete menu links, and add new links to the menu:

Main menu ⊙

| LIST LINKS | EDIT MENU |

Home » Administration » Structure » Menus

✚ Add link

Show row weights

MENU LINK	ENABLED	OPERATIONS	
✛ Home	☑	edit	delete

(Save configuration)

Taxonomy

Taxonomy is a powerful feature within Drupal, it allows content to be categorized, which in turn makes it easier to group, list, and sort content within the site. Words, phrases, and terms are grouped into vocabularies. From the taxonomy screen you can create new vocabularies, and within each vocabulary you can create and manage terms associated with them:

Taxonomy ⊕

Home » Administration » Structure

Taxonomy is for categorizing content. Terms are grouped into vocabularies. For example, a vocabulary called "Fruit" would contain the terms "Apple" and "Banana".

✦ Add vocabulary

VOCABULARY NAME	OPERATIONS		
Tags	edit vocabulary	list terms	add terms

A note to Drupal 6 users

Taxonomies have been completely reworked in Drupal 7. You no longer define which content types can be categorized by each vocabulary in the vocabulary settings; the only settings here are for name and description. Vocabulary is associated with content types through the content types themselves, thanks to the introduction of CCK to Drupal 7 core. We will discuss this in more detail later in the chapter.

Appearance

Themes which have been installed are accessible through the **Appearance** tab. By default, this tab lists all of the enabled themes we have installed:

Towards the bottom of the screen there is a section for specifying the **ADMINISTRATION THEME.** This allows us to have one theme for the public facing side of our Drupal installation, and another for the administration area. We can also opt to use the administration theme when we (administrators) create or edit content within our site:

There are a number of settings available for the themes installed, which can be accessed through the **SETTINGS** tab. These include the ability to enable or disable specific sections of the display, such as removing the **Logo**, or the **Site name** from the site's design:

People

The access details for users (visitors with a valid username and password) are managed through the **People** section of the administration area. This lists users within the site, and through the **UPDATE OPTIONS**, allows us to **block** or **unblock** particular user accounts, cancel a user's account, and assign or remove **roles** to a user account:

By editing a user account, we can change a user's username, reset their password, change their e-mail address, and modify their settings for using the site.

Permissions

Users, and administrators, are given permission to perform certain actions, such as creating content, commenting, performing searches, and so on, through the permission system. Each user is given a number of roles and these roles have permissions assigned to them.

The **Permissions** screen lists all of these permissions, with checkboxes showing which roles have permission to perform those actions. The permission allocations can be edited from this screen:

People ⊕   LIST | PERMISSIONS

Home » Administration » People   Permissions   Roles

Permissions let you control what users can do and see on your site. You can define a specific set of permissions for each role. (See the Roles page to create a role). Two important roles to consider are Authenticated Users and Administrators. Any permissions granted to the Authenticated Users role will be given to any user who can log into your site. You can make any role the Administrator role for the site, meaning this will be granted all new permissions automatically. You can do this on the User Settings page. You should be careful to ensure that only trusted users are given this access and level of control of your site.

Hide descriptions

PERMISSION	ANONYMOUS USER	AUTHENTICATED USER	ADMINISTRATOR
Block			
Administer blocks	☐	☐	☑
Comment			
Administer comments and comment settings	☐	☐	☑
View comments	☑	☑	☑
Post comments	☐	☑	☑
Skip comment approval	☐	☑	☑
Edit own comments	☐	☐	☑
Contextual links			
Use contextual links Use contextual links to perform actions related to elements on a page.	☐	☐	☑
Dashboard			
View the administrative dashboard Customizing the dashboard requires the Administer blocks permission.	☐	☐	☑

Roles

If we click the **Roles** sub-tab, we can see a list of the roles available in our site:

People ⊙   LIST   **PERMISSIONS**

Home » Administration » People » Permissions   Permissions   Roles

Roles allow you to fine tune the security and administration of Drupal. A role defines a group of users that have certain privileges as defined on the permissions page. Examples of roles include: anonymous user, authenticated user, moderator, administrator and so on. In this area you will define the names and order of the roles on your site. It is recommended to order your roles from least permissive (anonymous user) to most permissive (administrator). To delete a role choose "edit role".

By default, Drupal comes with two user roles:

- Anonymous user: this role is used for users that don't have a user account or that are not authenticated.
- Authenticated user: this role is automatically granted to all logged in users.

Show row weights

NAME	OPERATIONS	
✛ anonymous user *(locked)*		edit permissions
✛ authenticated user *(locked)*		edit permissions
✛ administrator	edit role	edit permissions

[   ] (Add role)

(Save order)

There are two locked roles, which we can't edit (though we can edit the permissions of them), these are **anonymous user** and **authenticated user** roles. The reason for this is that all users who access the site, who are not logged in, are regarded by Drupal as anonymous users. All users who are logged in are regarded as authenticated users (though they may have other roles too, to grant them more permission).

Modules

The **Modules** section lists all of the modules that we have available to use, which by default is all of the core modules. When we download new modules and extract the files into our Drupal folder, they show up in the **Modules** section, from where we can install them so that we can make use of their functionality:

Modules can be enabled or disabled, simply by ticking or unticking the box next to their name. Some modules require other modules to work, which is indicated by the **Requires** and **Required by** notes as part of the description.

Where appropriate, we can manage the permissions of a module by clicking the **Permissions** link next to it, which will take us to the appropriate modules' permissions within the permissions section of the administration area. If a module has configuration options, these can be altered through the **Configure** link.

Configuration

We looked at the important aspects of the **Configuration** tab in *Chapter 1, Drupal and Social Networking*. There are a number of areas of this section which we will need to alter throughout the course of this book; however it is best for us to wait until we need to, before we do that.

Reports

The **Reports** section provides useful information about our site:

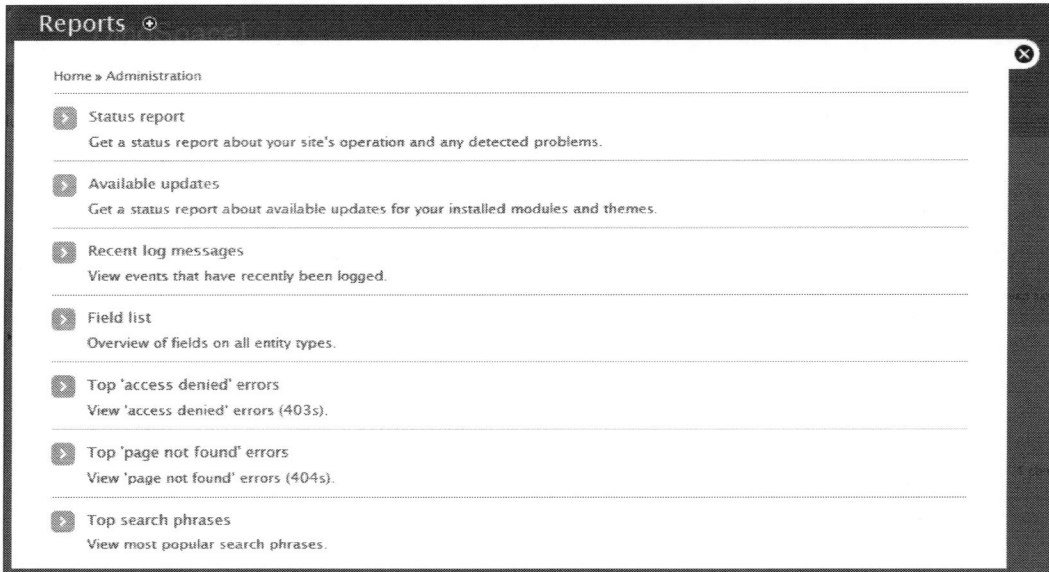

From here we can view a **Status report**, which gives us an overview of our site, including various server settings, ensuring everything is configured to allow Drupal to run properly. There is an **Available updates** report which lists any modules or themes which may be out of date. As we are working with a version of Drupal we have recently downloaded, we should be all up to date!

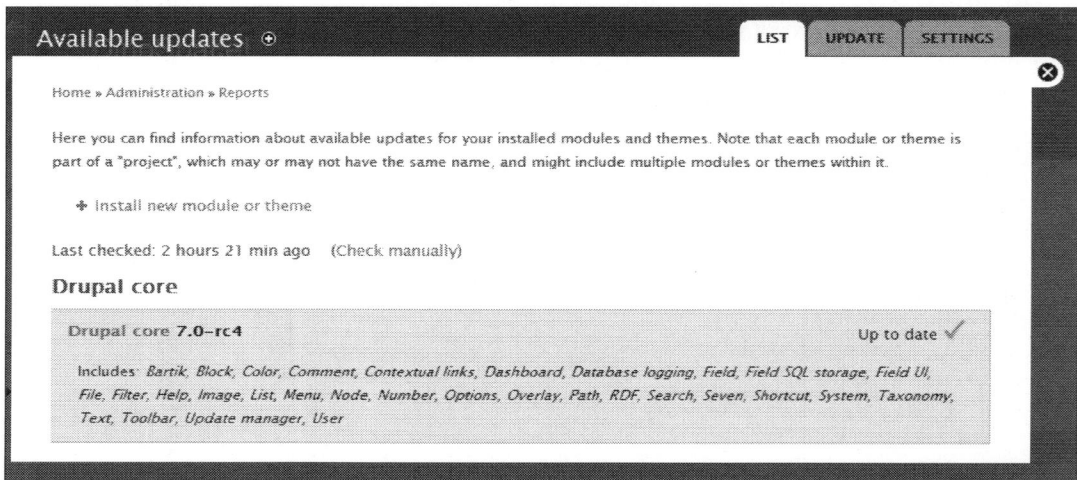

It is important to check this regularly, to see if any modules have new releases, especially if there are security vulnerabilities which have been fixed in the new update. Updates to Drupal core are generally made clear throughout the administration area to ensure that we are up to date.

Help

Finally, we have the **Help** section. This provides us with some basic help information, and links to a range of **Help topics** which may be of use to us:

Help ⊕

Home » Administration

Follow these steps to set up and start using your website:

1. **Configure your website** Once logged in, visit the administration section, where you can customize and configure all aspects of your website.
2. **Enable additional functionality** Next, visit the module list and enable features which suit your specific needs. You can find additional modules in the Drupal modules download section.
3. **Customize your website design** To change the "look and feel" of your website, visit the themes section. You may choose from one of the included themes or download additional themes from the Drupal themes download section.
4. **Start posting content** Finally, you can add new content for your website.

For more information, refer to the specific topics listed in the next section or to the online Drupal handbooks. You may also post at the Drupal forum or view the wide range of other support options available.

Help topics

Help is available on the following items:

- Block
- Color
- Comment
- Contextual links
- Dashboard
- Database logging
- Field
- Field SQL storage
- Field UI
- File
- Filter
- Help
- Image
- List
- Menu
- Node
- Number
- Options
- Overlay
- Path
- RDF
- Search
- Shortcut
- System
- Taxonomy
- Text
- Toolbar
- Update manager
- User

Content types and taxonomy: A detailed look

In the previous versions of Drupal, there was a very popular suite of modules called CCK (Content Construction Kit), the main purpose of which was to make it easier for administrators to create new customized content types, with more options and fields available to them. Much of the Content Construction Kit code has now been brought into the core Drupal 7 installation, negating the need to install the module. As a result of this, the core taxonomy module has been updated to make use of this feature, to make it easier to define how content can be categorized.

> **What is taxonomy?**
>
> Taxonomy is a powerful module which makes it easy for us to group and categorize our content. This could be by entering a keyword, a series of keywords, or selecting a category from a drop-down list. Categorized content can then be aggregated and displayed together through useful lists of content.

Let's have a look at customizing content types and how taxonomy links into it.

Creating a new content type

If we go **to Structure | Content types | Add content type**, we can start creating a new content type. At this stage we don't have a genuine need to create a new content type other than to look at the feature in more detail, so we will use test data.

The first half of the form asks us to enter a name and a description for the content type. Drupal automatically generates a "machine name" for this content type based on its name. This is a reference it uses, which must be formatted in a certain way:

Content types ⊕

Home » Administration » Structure » Content types

Individual content types can have different fields, behaviors, and permissions assigned to them.

Name *

Test content type   Machine name: test_content_type [Edit]

The human-readable name of this content type. This text will be displayed as part of the list on the *Add new content* page. It is recommended that this name begin with a capital letter and contain only letters, numbers, and spaces. This name must be unique.

Description

Describe this content type. The text will be displayed on the *Add new content* page.

The second half of the form provides us with options to set the name of the Title field, and also other customizable information, including:

- If the user creating content of this type must first be shown a preview before the content is saved
- **Explanation or submission guidelines** to explain how to create or edit content of this type

- If the content should be published, promoted, or sticky (although Administrators can override this when creating content of this type)
- If the author's name and publication date should be displayed with the content
- If comments are permitted, and various settings to go with that
- Which menus it will be possible for this content to automatically go in, and the default parent item for it

The following screenshot shows the submission form settings option and the other setting groups which can be configured:

Once we have completed the form, we should click the **Save and add fields** button.

Adding fields to the content type

Now, the content type is saved, and we are presented with the **MANAGE FIELDS** screen, from which we can edit the fields associated with the content type, and associate new fields with it. These fields are what the user will be asked to complete when creating an element of this content or instance. If we wanted to create a directory of physiotherapists who work with dinosaurs, we might add fields for address, contact number, website, and a list of breeds they work with (taxonomy). Then when the user creates a record of that content type, they are prompted to enter information for all of those fields we have created:

If we wanted to add an address field to the content, we would simply call the field address, put **address** in the name field, select **Long text** as the field, and select **Text area (multiple rows)** from the **Widget** drop down:

The types of field we can create are:

- Boolean
- Decimal
- File upload
- Float
- Image upload
- Integer
- List (of floats, integers, or text)
- Long text
- Long text and a summary
- Term reference
- Text

Linking taxonomy to the content type

If we now wish to link a taxonomy vocabulary to our content type, we need to select **Term reference** from the field drop-down list. With that selected, we have three options for **Widget**:

- **Select list**: A list of the options which can be selected
- **Checkboxes / radio buttons**: If only one can be selected, then radio will be used; if more than one, checkboxes will be used
- **Autocomplete term widget**: Allowing the user to type part of the work to associate with the content, and select the actual word from a list, or enter a new word they wish to associate with the content:

Add new field			
Keywords	field_ keywords	Term reference ▾	Autocomplete term widget (tagging) ▾
Label	Field name (a-z, 0-9, _)	Type of data to store.	Form element to edit the data.

Once we have added our taxonomy field to the content type, we need to click the **Save** button at the bottom of the page.

Customizing how the taxonomy works with the content type

After clicking **Save,** the field will be created and saved so that it can be used with other content types in the future. We can now select the taxonomy vocabulary we wish to use, and then click on the **Save field settings** button to save the field:

FIELD SETTINGS

These settings apply to the *Keywords* field everywhere it is used. These settings impact the way that data is stored in the database and cannot be changed once data has been created.

Vocabulary *

Tags ▾

The vocabulary which supplies the options for this field.

Save field settings

Finally, we are taken to more detailed settings about the field, where we can indicate if the field is required, provide help text to the user, and even provide a default value, and select the maximum number of terms which the content can be associated with.

Test content in action!

If we now go to **Content | Add content | Test content type**, we can create a new element of this content type and see the options in action!

The first thing which is noticeable is that the Title field is showing up as **Heading** (as we named it in the settings):

Heading *

Beneath the content field, we have our **Address** field, and our taxonomy field of **Keywords**:

Address

Keywords

keyword

Planning our site

We now have a basic understanding of how Drupal works, and what the various aspects of its administration section do. So let's now start planning our site!

When working on new, interesting, and exciting projects, such as a new website like this one, it is often tempting to jump right in at the deep end and start building the site. But that would be a bad idea. If we planned our website and its content carefully, then we should be able to offer our visitors a much better social network than we would if we just went straight into creating the site.

Let us first focus on the content we create for our site, as opposed to the content our users will create for us. This way we can prepare the site and its preliminary content and structure, and then begin to think about how our users are going to interact and contribute. This also allows us to try and contain the non-community aspect of the site. We set up this content now, so that we can focus on our users and build a true social network in the rest of the book!

Static content

Content which isn't going to change very often is generally referred to as **static content**, and might include content such as a page describing the history of a company. For our site, a social network for dinosaur owners, the following can almost certainly be classified as static content:

- **Contact us**: A postal address and e-mail address to get in touch with us, the owners of the website
- **About us**: About the website and the people behind it
- **Legal information**: Terms and conditions, privacy policy, copyright notice, and so on

> It is now difficult to categorize any other content for this particular site as static content. We may wish to provide some generic information on dinosaurs, but since this is a social network, and our users are the experts, we should let them contribute to the site. So I think it is best to leave the static content limited to the information mentioned earlier.

Grouping content

We looked at taxonomy earlier when we had a brief tour of Drupal's administration features and observed that it was a great way to classify content. Certain content can be clearly classified with our DinoSpace site, such as forum posts, pages, or generic content about specific breeds of dinosaurs. We can create tags for each specific breed such as:

- T-Rex
- Pterodactyl
- Triceratops

These terms would be grouped together as Dinosaur breed.

Starting to build our site

Now that we have a basic plan of our site's static content, we can start to build the static elements of our site.

Using taxonomy

Let's start with taxonomy. Since this is a way of categorizing content, it makes sense to set this up before we start creating content.

Creating the vocabulary

We need to go to **Structure | Taxonomy | Add vocabulary** to define a group of terms to categorize our content with. Enter a name of **Dinosaur Breed** and a description of **specific breed of dinosaur**, before clicking the **Save** button. We will use this to categorize content which relates to specific breeds of dinosaur:

With the vocabulary created, we now need to add terms to it, using the **add terms** link:

Here we can add the various breeds of dinosaur to the vocabulary using the create term form:

Now that we have a new vocabulary with terms associated with it, we need to link it to the appropriate content types. We need to go to **Structure | Content types | Basic page | Manage fields**.

From here, we enter Dinosaur Breed as the field **label**, dinosaur_breed as the **field name**, **Term reference** as the **field** type, and **Select list** as the **Widget**:

Add new field

| Dinosaur Breed | field_ dinosaur_breed | Term reference ▾ | Select list ▾ |
| Label | Field name (a-z, 0-9, _) | Type of data to store. | Form element to edit the data. |

Next, we select **Dinosaur Breed** as the vocabulary to use:

Dinosaur Breed ⊕   EDIT   **FIELD SETTINGS**   WIDGET TYPE   DELETE   ⊗

Home » Administration » Structure » Content types » Basic page » Manage fields » Dinosaur Breed

FIELD SETTINGS

These settings apply to the *Dinosaur Breed* field everywhere it is used. These settings impact the way that data is stored in the database and cannot be changed once data has been created.

Vocabulary *

| Dinosaur Breed ▾ |

The vocabulary which supplies the options for this field.

Save field settings

Finally, we ensure the field is set as required, and that the maximum **number of values** is set to **1**:

Dinosaur Breed ⊕   EDIT | FIELD SETTINGS | WIDGET TYPE | DELETE

Home » Administration » Structure » Content types » Basic page » Manage fields

✓ Updated field *Dinosaur Breed* field settings.

BASIC PAGE SETTINGS

These settings apply only to the *Dinosaur Breed* field when used in the *Basic page* type.

Label *

Dinosaur Breed

☐ Required field

Help text

Select the breed of dinosaur this content relates to.

Instructions to present to the user below this field on the editing form.
Allowed HTML tags: `<a> <b> <big> <code> <del> <em> <i> <ins> <pre> <q> <small> <span> <strong> <sub> <sup> <tt> <ol> <ul> <li> <p> <br> <img>`

DEFAULT VALUE

The default value for this field, used when creating new content.

Dinosaur Breed

- None -

DINOSAUR BREED FIELD SETTINGS

These settings apply to the *Dinosaur Breed* field everywhere it is used.

Number of values

1

Maximum number of values users can enter for this field.

Now, if we go to create a page, we can select the breed of dinosaur it relates to:

Dinosaur Breed

T-Rex

Select the breed of dinosaur this content relates to.

Now we have a new page created, related to T-Rex:

DinoSpace!

My account   Log out

Home

✓ Basic page *T-Rex related content* has been created.

Home

🔍

Navigation

▸ Add content

T-Rex related content

View Edit

This is some T-Rex related content

Dinosaur Breed:
T-Rex

If we click the taxonomy term, we are taken to a page listing content which has been categorized as T-Rex related:

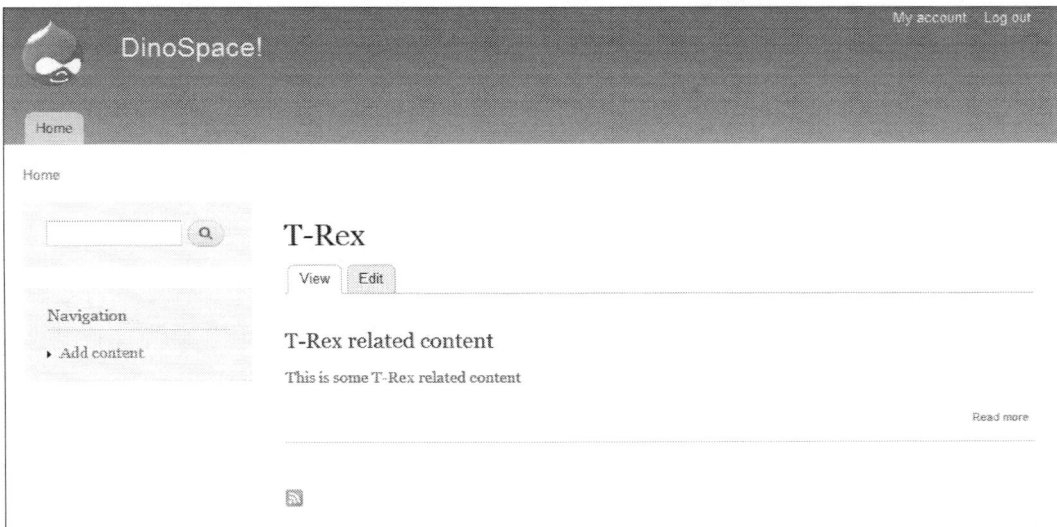

> **Try it yourself**
>
> Now that you have an understanding of how to create content, why not create all of the static content we planned earlier. Make sure you select a menu for the pages to appear in. Once you have done that, why not create a Frequently Asked Questions page; use taxonomy to tag pages as FAQ answers and use the Drupal link to all content tagged with FAQ answers as the link to the FAQs pages in the menu.

Summary

In this chapter, we looked at Drupal in more detail, particularly at how to use its administration options, which should help us in building our site. This should prove to be a useful reference point in future. We also planned some of the static content for our site, and started to create this content for it.

Our Drupal site is now ready to become a social networking site! We can now move forward with more interactive and dynamic features.

3
User Content: Contributions, Forums, and Blogs

We now have our Drupal installation ready to become a social networking site! One key element of social networking sites is user-generated content and that is what we will look at in this chapter. Drupal contains a number of core modules (modules which come with Drupal as opposed to modules written by others which we need to download and install), which allow our site to support user-generated content. In this chapter, you will learn the following:

- About user comments
- Enabling and managing user contributions as well as uploaded files
- Setting up and managing discussion forums
- Giving each of your users a blog with the Blog module
- Facilitating wiki-based collaborative writing with the Book module
- Running polls with the Polls module

We are also going to plan the types of user we are going to have on our site, and plan the roles and permissions they will have. Let's start by having a look at how these relate to our site.

Our site

We are going to look at a range of modules in this chapter, but it is important to understand how these relate to our site. A number of websites and discussion forums are now leveraging the power of **syndicated** content from other websites. Various websites make some of their content, such as news or blog posts, available as RSS feeds. We can make use of the aggregator module to import this content into our site, providing our users with additional resources to keep them on our site, instead of seeking news and information from elsewhere.

Provided we set up the permissions accordingly, any type of content such as pages, forums, and blogs, can be commented on by other users. We will look at how to use the comment system to allow users to comment on contributions, which helps promote discussion and communication.

Users can also contribute to our site by posting other forms of content, we will look at how to enable this, and also how to enable users to upload files with their contributions, creating a more content and media rich experience.

With blogging becoming more and more popular, we can offer our users a blog direct from our site. This could be supplementary to a blog they may already have (such as to track issues specific to their dinosaur) or as their primary blog. By allowing users to have their own area of the site, they will be more inclined to continue to visit the site, as they will have spent time and energy to create their own blog and contributions.

By allowing users to work together to build up the content of the site, they will be more inclined to continue to use the site (as with their own blog) but they can also work together to contribute to the content of our site. The collaborative book module provides an excellent way for different groups of users to work together, building up the content of the site, making them feel part of the running of the site, and making our site a better and more useful place for the other users as well.

Polls can allow us to gauge user feedback about our site, and also as a bit of fun to find out information such as favorite breed of dinosaur, or the average age of our users, or just for fun.

User roles: An important note

Different actions, such as posting a comment, posting on a forum, or uploading files, require appropriate permissions. It is easier to set up all of these features first, and then configure the permissions later, so for the course of this chapter we will test these features with our own administrative user account.

In this chapter, we will think about the different roles which might be appropriate, so that in the next chapter we will know the appropriate permissions and roles needed to allow our users to contribute to the site. We won't focus too much on the detail of how these permissions and roles work, as we will look at that in detail in the next chapter. However, at the end of this chapter we will have a site complete with collaborative features for our users, as well as permissions in place for users to be able to use the site as we have planned.

Drupal modules

All of the features we are going to look at in this chapter are provided via modules, which we need to enable. Let's enable all of these modules now to save us some time later, so we don't need to come back and forth to this section.

> Modules which are not included with Drupal need to be both downloaded and then installed. These are called contributed modules. Since the modules we wish to use are part of the Drupal core, they only need enabling; we don't have to download anything at this stage.
>
> Installing a module simply involves extracting it into the Drupal `modules` folder. From here Drupal automatically detects the module and allows us to enable it, which will allow the module to perform any configuration necessary for it to work on our installation. It is also possible to install a module from the module's web address using the **Install new module** link.

Modules are managed from the **Modules** tab on the administration bar. This page lists all modules which are installed, regardless of whether they are enabled or disabled.

We need to enable the following modules from the **Core** group of modules (for our default installation, this is the only group we have), some of which are illustrated in the following screenshot:

Ensure the following modules are ticked, so that they will install:

- **Blog**: Allows users to have their own blog
- **Book**: Enables collaborative writing
- **Comment** (should already be enabled): Allows users to comment on content
- **Forum**: Enables discussion board features
- **Poll**: Enables user polls

Once ticked, we click **Save configuration** at the bottom of the page.

Once the modules have been enabled, we are shown a confirmation message at the top of the page to confirm that those modules have been enabled:

> ✓ The configuration options have been saved.

Now, we can configure and use these newly-enabled modules.

As a result of these newly-enabled modules, we now have a range of content types available to us when creating new content for our site:

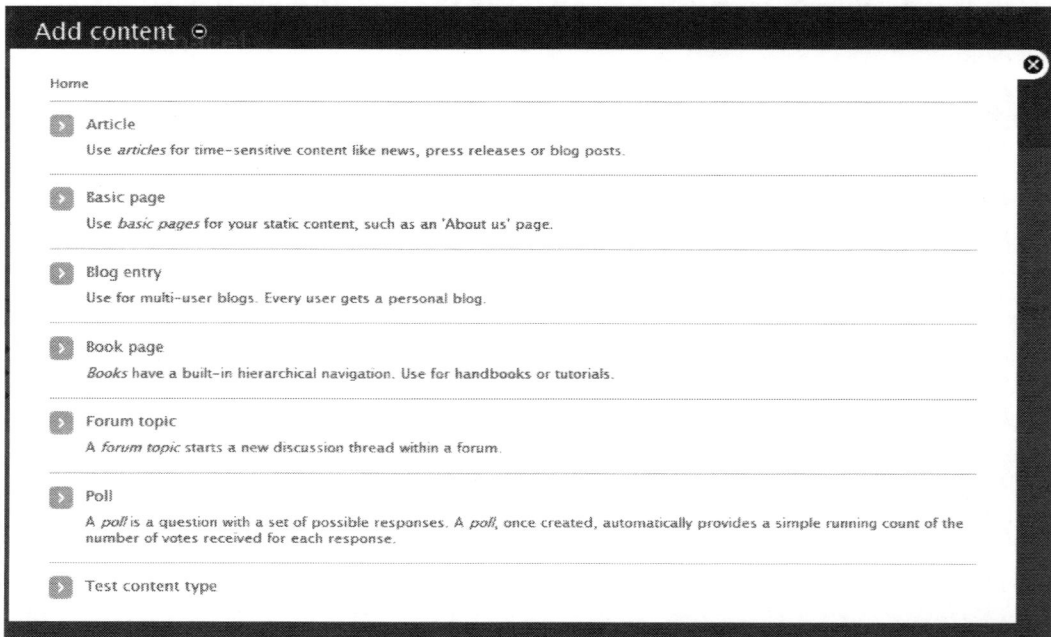

Add content ⊖

Home

> **Article**
> Use *articles* for time-sensitive content like news, press releases or blog posts.

> **Basic page**
> Use *basic pages* for your static content, such as an 'About us' page.

> **Blog entry**
> Use for multi-user blogs. Every user gets a personal blog.

> **Book page**
> *Books* have a built-in hierarchical navigation. Use for handbooks or tutorials.

> **Forum topic**
> A *forum topic* starts a new discussion thread within a forum.

> **Poll**
> A *poll* is a question with a set of possible responses. A *poll*, once created, automatically provides a simple running count of the number of votes received for each response.

> **Test content type**

Managing comments

In *Chapter 2, Preparing Drupal for a Social Networking Site*, we briefly looked at all aspects of Drupal's administration area, including **comments** and their **moderation**. Now, let us look at how we can enable comments, and how they are created.

When creating content for our site (currently, either through the **Add content** shortcut in the administration bar, or via **Content | Add content**) there is a section entitled **Comment settings**. Clicking this brings the comment settings for the content into focus:

Menu settings Not in menu	⊙ Open
	Users with the "Post comments" permission can post comments.
Book outline	⊙ Closed
Revision information No revision	Users cannot post comments.
URL path settings No alias	
Comment settings Closed	
Authoring information By Michael	
Publishing options Published	

From here we can enable comments by selecting **Open**, or leave them disabled by selecting **Closed**. If comments are enabled, users still require the appropriate permission (**Post comments**) to post comments. The default option for **Comment settings** for creating new content is defined by the settings for the content type.

Because social networking sites rely on user contributions, collaboration, and communication, for most user created content we would want to enable comments for that content. Once comments have been enabled for a particular content element, the **Add new comment** form is displayed.

As we are logged in, the comment form picks up our username, and has options for providing a subject for the comment and the comment itself. Because of our permissions, we can also select the format of the text we are posting; this allows us to change the format if we want to include additional HTML tags which are not allowed by default:

Add new comment

Your name   Michael

Subject

> This is a comment

Comment *

> Once we post this, the comment should go to the page|

Text format   [Filtered HTML ▾]   More information about text formats ⓘ

- Web page addresses and e-mail addresses turn into links automatically.
- Allowed HTML tags: <a> <em> <strong> <cite> <blockquote> <code> <ul> <ol> <li> <dl> <dt> <dd>
- Lines and paragraphs break automatically.

Comments are threaded within Drupal, which allows our users to comment on other comments, hopefully leading to a more interesting discussion among our users. Comments can be marked as a reply to another comment by clicking the **reply** link within the comment in question. Replies are clearly indented to make it obvious that they are in reply to a specific comment. This is illustrated in the following screenshot:

Comments

Michael
Thu,
01/06/2011 -
18:22
permalink

This is a comment

Once we post this, the comment should go to the page

delete   edit   reply

Michael
Thu,
01/06/2011 -
18:24
permalink

The comment was posted to the

The comment was posted to the page, and this is a threaded reply!

delete   edit   reply

Comments within DinoSpace!

Comments are clearly a fundamental communication feature for any site which facilitates user interaction; however, these features can easily be abused by spammers. To help protect us against spam, we should only allow logged in users to post comments.

> While this will help to reduce spam, there are some more effective methods which we will cover in *Chapter 10, Deploying and Maintaining Our Social Network*.

By requiring users to sign up and log in before allowing them to comment, we can hopefully also encourage them to visit the site again, as they can receive e-mail notifications to further comments and also receive e-mails from us as site administrators, welcoming them to the site, or updating them about goings on within our site.

Forums

Discussion forums are a great way to allow users to discuss various topics with other users on the site. Forums themselves act as containers for topics and any child forums within them.

Within Drupal discussion forums, **topics** are similar to pages with comments. A user creates a topic containing a subject and some content, and other users can then write comments on the topic. These comments are threaded in style so that replies to specific comments are clearly grouped, showing the conversation which takes place within the comments.

Planning our forum structure

Before we start creating forums for our site, it is a good idea to think about the sort of discussions we would like to have. Initially, we would probably want to have discussions on the following:

- Dinosaur health
- Dinosaur care
- Places to visit with your dinosaur
- Dinosaur-friendly hotels
- General discussion amongst users
- Stories from our users

While this initial list is helpful, it isn't structured. We now need to think about those topics, and decide how to group them within our forums. Based on the initial list, we could build a structured discussion area with the following categories and sub-forums:

- General
  - Site news and announcements
  - New member introductions
  - General (Dinosaur related)
  - General (Non-dinosaur related)

- Health and care
  - Dinosaur health issues
  - Caring for your dinosaur

- Out and about
  - Places to visit
  - Dinosaur friendly hotel reviews
  - Help and advice

Now that we know how we are going to structure our forums, we can create them!

Creating and managing forums and containers

In the administration toolbar, under **Structure** we have a new option called **Forums**:

> **Forums**
> Control forum hierarchy settings.

From here we can control the hierarchy of our discussion forums, change the settings for how forums are displayed, and edit and delete forums and their containers:

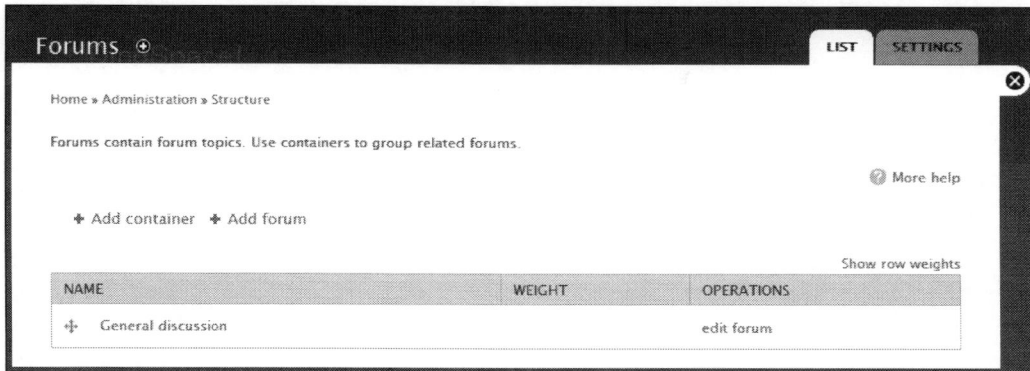

If we want to group a number of forums together, we can either create a container for them or a forum for them. If we create a container, topics can only be posted in the forums within the container. If we use a forum, topics can be posted in there or in one of the forums within it.

Let's click **Add container** to create our first container. The forum's module already includes a general discussion forum, so let's start with the health and care container. From here we must enter a name for the container (**Health & Care**) and select a **Parent** for it, so Drupal knows where the container is within the structure. Selecting **<root>** as the **Parent** will ensure that the category is shown on the main forums page; the **Weight** option indicates the order of the container when there are other forums or containers with the same parent. Selecting an alternative parent would mean that users need to select the parent container or forum first, before they see the container.

We can also provide a description for the container:

Once we have created our container (by completing the form and clicking the **Save** button!), we can now create our forum which will be part of this category.

The options for creating our forum are the same as when we created the container, this is because, in terms of data and configuration, they are the same. However, they act slightly different when used (as discussed earlier).

Let's create a **Health and Illness** forum, to go within our newly created **Health and Care** container:

The ordering and structure of our forums and containers can be modified from the **Forums** screen by clicking the icon next to the forum name and dragging it to reorder. Once changes are made, we are reminded that we need to use the **Save** button before the changes are applied:

Viewing our forums

Within the **Navigation** menu on our site, we have a **Forums** link, which lists the forums and allows our users to view and create topics within them. We can rename and reposition this menu item, if we wish, from the **Structure | Menus** section within the administration area:

Creating a forum topic

From within the **Forums** section, there is a link to **Add new Forum topic**, and we can click this to create a new topic. Alternatively, we can click **Add content** and select **Forum topic** as the content type, or we can go into a forum and click **Add a new Forum topic** to create a topic for that specific forum:

Topics need to have a subject, which will be displayed as part of a list when we view a forum, a forum to be part of, and the description of the topic itself.

Taxonomies

In *Chapter 2, Preparing Drupal for a Social Networking Site*, we created a vocabulary of dinosaur breeds in order to help us categorize our content. The reason that we were not asked to select a dinosaur breed when creating a forum topic is because we have not assigned the vocabulary to this type of content.

To associate the vocabulary with forum topics, from the administration toolbar we need to select **Structure | Content types | Forum topic | Manage fields**:

Forum topic (Machine name: forum)		manage	manage
A *forum topic* starts a new discussion thread within a forum.	edit	fields	display

Now, we can select our vocabulary. Because we have already associated the vocabulary with one type of content, we can select it from the **Add existing field** section:

Add existing field		
dino_breed	Term reference: field_dinosaur_breed (Dinosaur Breed) ▾	Select list ▾
Label	Field to share	Form element to edit the data.

Once we click the **Save** button, we are taken to a page of settings for the field **dino_breed** when it is used within a **Forum topic**. This allows us to have the vocabulary behave differently with different types of content, for instance, making the field required:

FORUM TOPIC SETTINGS

These settings apply only to the *dino_breed* field when used in the *Forum topic* type.

Label *

dino_breed

☐ Required field

Once saved, our users can now select a dinosaur breed to categorize their forum topics with.

Planning: How will roles fit in?

Now, let us take a step back to think about how our users will use the forums. While we wouldn't want users who haven't logged in to create topics and forum posts (as this could encourage spam, and makes communication less personal), we would want them to be able to read topics. We would want all of our registered users to be able to contribute through the forums. If we have a selection of very helpful and trustworthy users, we may wish to allow them to edit and delete topics, to help moderate the discussions. We may find that as the community grows, there are some users who would be well suited to help restructure the forums, to introduce new forums and categories as the site grows.

Here, we can see that we may have the need for different levels of permission, with all registered users being able to contribute, and a small subset of users having additional privileges to help moderate and curate the site.

Setting up and using blogs

The blogs module doesn't provide a great deal of configuration options, apart from user permissions, as it is a very straightforward module. Each user (with permissions) is given their own blog. This provides users with their own area to post their own content.

Blogs can be a great way to engage communities; for our DinoSpace site we could use it as a platform for our members to record what they are doing with their dinosaurs on a day-to-day basis, or to share in more detail what they are up to in general.

> In *Chapter 4, Users and Profiles*, we will be looking at giving our users the ability to change the design of their blogs, allowing them to select designs which better reflect their personality or interests.

Viewing blogs and the blog menu

Despite the blog module being enabled, by default it isn't very clear where it is. At the moment, we need to click the **My account** link, and from here click the **View recent blog entries** link to see your own personal blog:

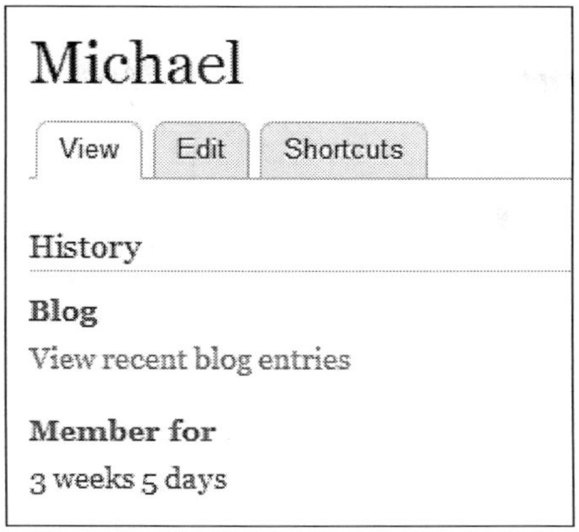

Michael

| View | Edit | Shortcuts |

History

Blog
View recent blog entries

Member for
3 weeks 5 days

To make this more intuitive, we should enable the blog menu links in the navigation menu. These links have automatically been created; however, they are currently disabled. From the **Administrative** toolbar we need to go to **Structure | Menus | Navigation:**

| ✛ | Blogs (disabled) | ☑ | edit |
| | ✛   My blog | ☑ | edit |

From here we can enable the **Blogs** menu link, which in turn will allow the **My blog** link to be displayed. We simply need to select the **Enabled** checkbox, and click the **Save configuration** button at the bottom of the screen.

We now have a blogs link in our menu, which (if we had any blog entries in our site) would list recent entries. Within the blogs section there would be a link to our own blog, and to **Create a new blog entry**:

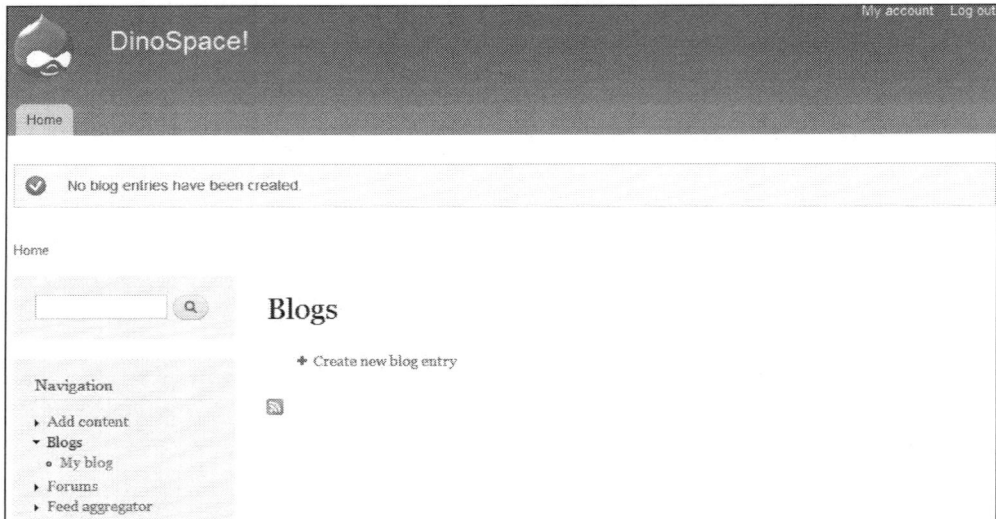

Once we have a range of users signed up, this link will provide an interesting list of recent blog entries for our users to browse, and hopefully find new users they want to follow or connect with. If we click the username of a user who has posted an entry, we will be taken to their blog page.

Using the blog

To create blog entries, we can either use the **Create new blog entry** link from within the blog module itself, or click **Blog entry** from the **Add content** screen.

At this stage, it would be useful to create a page informing users about the blog feature and how they can use their own personal blog to share detailed entries with other users. A link to this could be included as part of a user's welcome e-mail.

Collaborative writing

Drupal's book module provides our users with a wiki-based collaboration platform, wherein they can create structured, multi-page content on our site, for things such as the following:

- Resources and guides
- Manuals

- Frequently asked questions
- An online book

A suitable use for this module for our site would be to allow our users to create and contribute to a book about looking after a dinosaur throughout its lifetime. In turn, this would provide other users with a valuable resource, which they too can collaborate on if they have advice or information to share. Of course, as our site grows it would be better to have more books related to specific breeds of dinosaur, which is something we can work to accommodate as our social network starts to grow.

Creating a book

The first stage in creating a new collaborative book is to create a new book page; this will serve as the contents page, and the primary page for the book. We can create this page from the **Add content** screen:

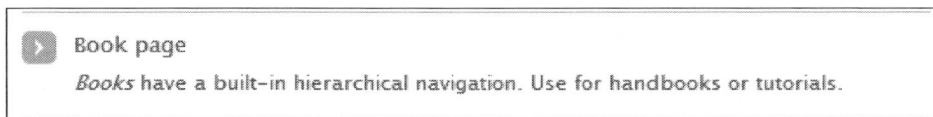

> Book page
>
> *Books* have a built-in hierarchical navigation. Use for handbooks or tutorials.

As with all content, we need to enter a title for the book, and the body content for the page. To create a new book, we need to go to the **Book outline** section at the bottom of the page for creating a new book, and select **<create a new book>** from the **Book** section. This will make the page the top level page within the book. The screenshot is as follows:

Menu settings Not in menu	**Book**
	<create a new book> ▾
Book outline	Your page will be a part of the selected book.
Revision information No revision	*This will be the top-level page in this book.*
	Weight
URL path settings No alias	0 ▾
Comment settings Open	Pages at a given level are ordered first by weight and then by title.
Authoring information By Michael	
Publishing options Published	

Once we click the **Save** button we have a new book on our site.

Creating pages in the book

Now that we have a new book, we need to put pages in it. After we created the book, we were taken to its front page, and on this page is a link to **Add child page**:

Caring for our dinosaur: From egg to adult

View	Edit	Outline

published by Michael on Wed, 01/12/2011 - 20:17

A practical guide to looking after your dinosaur throughout its lifetime.

Add child page   Printer-friendly version

This will open the new Book page screen, and preselect the book to use as its parent, saving us the need to select this, which would have happened if we went direct from the **Add content** screen:

Menu settings
Not in menu

Book outline

Revision information
No revision

URL path settings
No alias

Comment settings
Open

Authoring information
By Michael

Publishing options
Published

Book

Caring for our dinosaur: From egg to adult ▼

Your page will be a part of the selected book.

Parent item

Caring for our dinosaur:... ▼

The parent page in the book. The maximum depth for a book and all child pages is 9. Some pages in the selected book may not be available as parents if selecting them would exceed this limit.

Weight

0 ▼

Pages at a given level are ordered first by weight and then by title.

As we start to create pages within our book, it starts to take shape. The book's front page lists the sections of the book, and each page contains a link to the next page, the previous page and any child pages, making navigation through the book easy:

Caring for our dinosaur: From egg to adult

View   Edit   Outline

published by Michael on Wed, 01/12/2011 - 20:17

A practical guide to looking after your dinosaur throughout its lifetime.

  ▸ Egg care
  ∘ Hatched

Egg care ›

Add child page   Printer-friendly version

Outline

Clicking the **Outline** tab on a page brings up information about the page's location within a book, allowing us to quickly reposition a page elsewhere if we need to:

Caring for our dinosaur: From egg to adult ⊕   VIEW   EDIT   OUTLINE

Home » Caring for our dinosaur: From egg to adult

The outline feature allows you to include pages in the Book hierarchy, as well as move them within the hierarchy or to reorder an entire book.

BOOK OUTLINE

Book

Caring for our dinosaur: From egg to adult ▾

Your page will be a part of the selected book.

This is the top-level page in this book.

Weight

0 ▾

Pages at a given level are ordered first by weight and then by title.

Update book outline

As well as providing the ability to quickly move the page, it also provides links which allow us to easily reorder the contents of an entire book. Let's click the **reorder an entire book** link to see how this works. This lists all of the books within our site, with a link **edit order and titles** next to each book for editing orders and titles:

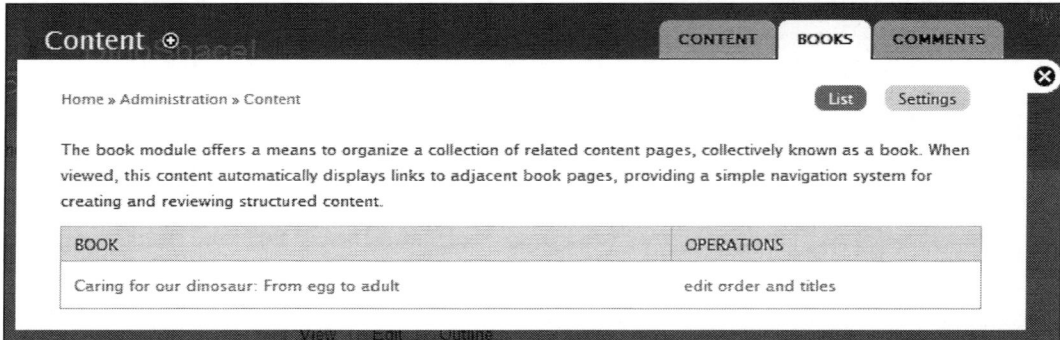

BOOK	OPERATIONS
Caring for our dinosaur: From egg to adult	edit order and titles

We are now presented with the reorder screen, which uses the drag-and-drop system we are already familiar with, allowing us to reorder the pages. We can also change the titles from here:

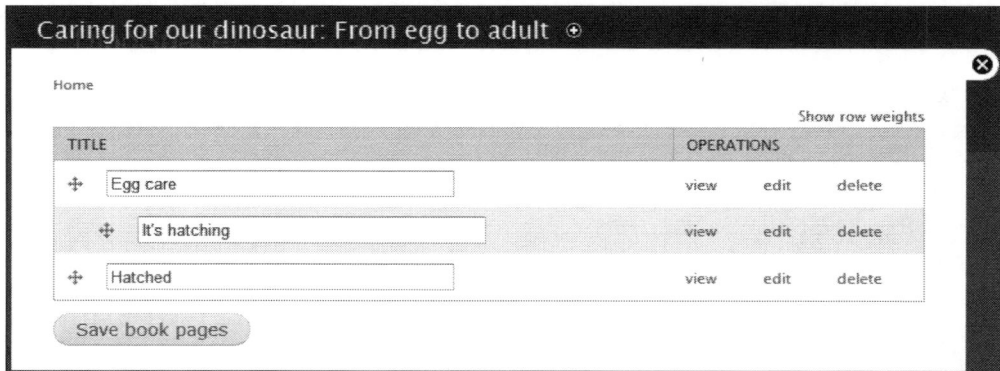

TITLE	OPERATIONS		
Egg care	view	edit	delete
It's hatching	view	edit	delete
Hatched	view	edit	delete

Permissions and roles

The book module provides a great opportunity for our community members to come together and share their knowledge on a collaborative project. There is scope for three different levels of community involvement, which would require three different roles:

- **Reader**: A reader is a user who just reads the content within a book
- **Contributor**: A contributor is a user who contributes to existing books

- **Commissioner / Contributor**: This is a user who not only contributes to existing books, but who also creates new books

Why not grant all permissions?

One reason why it isn't a good idea to give all of these permissions to our users is to prevent new users, who have just signed up, from diving in and reordering and restructuring content. A more democratic system can work by encouraging the community, and giving respected and trusted members of the community more permissions to help curate the site. Once a new user has established himself/herself as responsible, we could grant them more permissions to contribute more within the site.

Polls

Polls enable users to post and vote on simple questions. Sometimes these can be for fun, or purely for general information. However, we could also use them to improve the site. For instance, if we created a poll asking about the most popular area of the site, or which are needed more improvement, we would gain a general picture of which areas of the site need more attention and could be improved. Alternatively, we could ask what breed of dinosaurs our users have, giving us statistics on the more popular breeds. This could either help us curate more content and discussion around those breeds, or prompt us to try and get more keepers of other breeds signed up to the site, to make the discussions more varied.

Polls are created from the **Add content** section where, unlike with most other content, we don't provide a title and body of content. Instead, we provide a question (which is really the title renamed!) and a number of possible answers:

Question *

What breed of dinosaur do you look after?

Show row weights

	CHOICE	VOTE COUNT
✛	T-Rex	0
✛	Pterodactly	0
✛	Tricerotops	0
✛	Other	0

More choices

We can also set the poll **Active** or **Closed** (that is, if users can vote on it) as it is a new poll (we are not changing an existing one) we should make sure this is active, and also for how long the poll should remain active:

▾ POLL SETTINGS

Poll status

◯ Closed

◉ Active

When a poll is closed, visitors can no longer vote for it.

Poll duration

Unlimited ▾

After this period, the poll will be closed automatically.

Once created, we are taken to the page with the poll on it. We could either link this up through the menu, or from an existing page, or we could enable the latest poll block (from the **Structure | Blocks** section of the administration toolbar) to display the latest poll on a number of our pages. The options from the poll are displayed so that our users can vote on their selection:

What breed of dinosaur do you look after?

| View | Edit | Outline | Results | Votes |

published by Michael on Wed, 01/12/2011 - 20:59

◉ T-Rex

◯ Pterodactly

◯ Tricerotops

◯ Other

(Vote)

Once a user has voted, they are shown the results graph that shows the percentage of votes for each option:

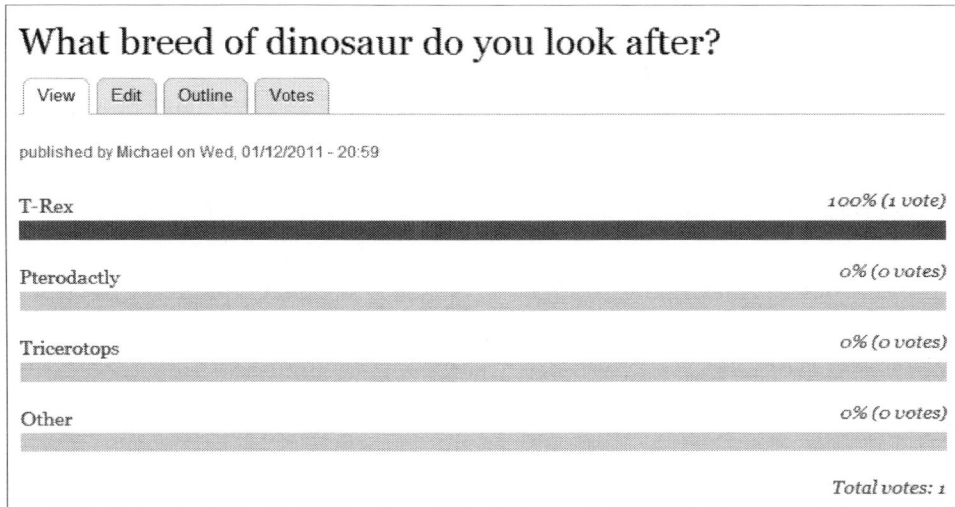

What breed of dinosaur do you look after?

| View | Edit | Outline | Votes |

published by Michael on Wed, 01/12/2011 - 20:59

T-Rex — *100% (1 vote)*

Pterodactly — *0% (0 votes)*

Tricerotops — *0% (0 votes)*

Other — *0% (0 votes)*

Total votes: 1

The **Votes** tab lists all of the users who voted in the poll, along with what they voted for and the time they placed their vote. If anonymous users vote (provided their permissions allow), they are shown by their computer's IP address:

What breed of dinosaur do you look after?

| View | Edit | Outline | Votes |

This table lists all the recorded votes for this poll. If anonymous users are allowed to vote, they will be identified by the IP address of the computer they used when they voted.

Visitor	Vote	Timestamp
Michael	T-Rex	Wed, 01/12/2011 - 21:03

Adding roles

For the polls feature, we should allow registered users to create new polls, and all users (registered or not) should be allowed to vote. We may also wish to allow another group of users the permissions to edit or remove polls, should any inappropriate polls be posted on the site.

Contributions in the form of pages

So far, we have looked at a range of different user-contributed content, except for the most fundamental aspect, that is, the pages themselves. We can allow page contributions based on the permissions of our users (which we will discuss in *Chapter 4, Users and Profiles*).

Permissions and roles

We might want to allow a number of our users to create new pages for the site (though we probably wouldn't want these pages to appear in the menu, or be promoted to the front page!), so we may wish to create a suitable group that can promote useful or interesting content to the front page.

Uploaded files

Since enabling the File module, we can allow our users to upload and attach files or images to content. It is good that it allows users to share additional media and make their posts more interesting, but it causes problems with regards to what they can share. In particular, we wouldn't want users sharing large files, nor would we want users sharing files of certain types, such as program files, which could contain viruses. Thankfully, there are settings available for this module which allow us to restrict the types of files our users can upload, as well as the sizes of the files they can upload.

File and image uploads are set up through additional fields on our content types. Let's look at allowing file uploads on our forum topics. We do this from **Structure | Content types | Forum topic | Manage fields**.

The field we need to select is **File**, which automatically selects the **File** widget:

LABEL	NAME	FIELD	WIDGET	OPERATIONS	
⊕ Subject	title	Node module element			
⊕ Forums	taxonomy_forums	Term reference	Select list	edit	delete
⊕ Body	body	Long text and summary	Text area with a summary	edit	delete
⊕ dino_breed	field_dinosaur_breed	Term reference	Select list	edit	delete

⊕
Add new field

File	field_ [file]	[File ▼]	[File ▼]
Label	Field name (a–z, 0–9, _)	Type of data to store.	Form element to edit the data.

⊕
Add existing field

[ ]	- Select an existing field - ▼	- Select a widget - ▼
Label	Field to share	Form element to edit the data.

(Save)

After clicking **Save** we can select if users should have the option to display a file when viewing the topic, and also if that should be enabled by default:

FIELD SETTINGS

These settings apply to the *File* field everywhere it is used. These settings impact the way that data is stored in the database and cannot be changed once data has been created.

☑ Enable *Display* field
The display option allows users to choose if a file should be shown when viewing the content.

☑ Files displayed by default
This setting only has an effect if the display option is enabled.

Upload destination

◉ Public files

Select where the final files should be stored. Private file storage has significantly more overhead than public files, but allows restricted access to files within this field.

After clicking **Save field settings,** we are taken back to the Manage field list. Click **Edit** (next to the field we just created); then we have further options which we can configure, including the following:

- If the field is required
- Help text for the field, that is, instructions for our users
- A list of allowed file extensions; this should be used with caution
- Directory to store the files
- The maximum upload size
- If a description field should be available

The following screenshot shows the options which can be edited and managed:

FORUM TOPIC SETTINGS

These settings apply only to the *File* field when used in the *Forum topic* type.

Label *

File

☑ Required field

Help text

Instructions to present to the user below this field on the editing form.
Allowed HTML tags: <a> <b> <big> <code> <del> <em> <i> <ins> <pre> <q> <small> <span> <strong> <sub> <sup> <tt> <ol> <ul> <li> <p>
 <img>

Allowed file extensions *

txt

Separate extensions with a space or comma and do not include the leading dot.

File directory

Optional subdirectory within the upload destination where files will be stored. Do not include preceding or trailing slashes.

Maximum upload size

Enter a value like "512" (bytes), "80 KB" (kilobytes) or "50 MB" (megabytes) in order to restrict the allowed file size. If left empty the file sizes will be limited only by PHP's maximum post and file upload sizes (current limit *4 MB*).

☑ Enable *Description* field

The description field allows users to enter a description about the uploaded file.

The maximum file sizes available depend entirely on the amount of space and resources the site has made available. If you are going to run your social network from a shared host web server, you may want to ensure these sizes are relatively low. If you are planning on using dedicated or virtual servers, you may wish to increase some of the limits, depending on how many users are active on the site. These facts need to be considered carefully when deploying the site.

> The maximum size for uploaded files is often also limited by the server's PHP settings. If we were to increase our limit to 5 MB, we might still be limited to 2 MB because of the default PHP configuration. This can be altered via the PHP configuration file. For more information, contact your web host about limits they might impose, and for information regarding editing the PHP.ini file.

Now if we create a new forum topic, we have the option to upload a file:

File

Choose File | No file chosen | Upload

Files must be less than **4 MB**.
Allowed file types: **txt**.

Roles

As previously discussed, we have two roles by default:

- Anonymous user: The anonymous user is the one who has not logged into our site
- Authenticated user: The authenticated user is the one who has logged into our site

We shouldn't need to change the anonymous user role a great deal, as by default permissions are not granted to that role, though features such as search should be enabled for guests. We will need to significantly modify the authenticated user role to allow our users to contribute more to our site. A number of new roles will also need to be created for moderators and power contributors.

> We will be looking at users, roles, and permissions in great detail in the next chapter; this is just a brief look at the changes we will need to make, and roles we will need to create. Return to this list once you are more comfortable with editing permissions and creating roles, to make the changes.

Anonymous role permissions

For the anonymous user role, we need to ensure that permissions are granted for the view content and view comment options.

Authenticated users

We need to check the following permissions for the authenticated user role, so they can use these new features:

- **Blog module**: This has the permissions to create blog entries, delete own blog entries, and edit own blog entries
- **Comment module**: This has the permissions to access comments, post comments, skip comments, and edit own comments
- **Forum module**: This has the permissions to create forum topics and edit own forum topics
- **Node module**: This has the permissions to access content, create article content, and create page content
- **Poll module**: This has the permission to vote on polls

Additional roles

From the modules we have enabled in this chapter, the following additional roles would be beneficial for our community:

- **Contributors**: These are the users who are going to be a little more active in the running of the site
- **Moderators**: These are the users who will be able to edit and remove inappropriate content
- **Power contributors**: These are the users who can add additional major content elements to the site

At a minimum, they would need the following permissions:

Contributors

Contributors need to be able to do the following:

- Add content to books
- Create books
- Create pages
- Create polls

Moderators

Moderators need to be able to do the following:

- Delete or edit any blog entry, page, or forum topic
- Administer comments
- Revert content to previous versions

Power contributors

Power contributors need to be able to do the following:

- Administer book outlines and create new books
- Administer forums

Summary

The focus of this chapter was very much on content; with these features in place we can now look at users, their profiles, and allowing them to connect with one another to create a powerful social network.

In this chapter, we have enabled various core modules enabling user contributions to our site, including comments, blog entries, forum topics and forum posts, contributions through pages and collaborative books, basic file sharing with the File module, and the ability for users to vote on topics with the poll module.

In the process of setting up these modules, we have also thought about the various user roles which we might consider in our site. This is a very important aspect to consider, as without the correct setup of roles and permissions, we may end up with a social networking website where our users cannot do anything (with our current setup, unless they are assigned the administrator role), or have a site where all users could do anything to the site, resulting in chaos.

Now, we can look towards our users, their profiles, their permissions, and their interaction on our site.

4
Users and Profiles

Now that DinoSpace is ready to accept user content, and with our planned roles for the site, we can now focus on our users and their profiles. We need to set up our user roles, look at managing users, the settings associated with them, and provide them with tools and options to improve their experience on the site. In this chapter, you will learn:

- How to manage users, roles, and their permissions
- About Gravatars and how to enable them
- How users can track the activity of each other
- How to extend user profiles
- About settings and rules for users
- How to give authenticated users a more relevant home page

What are we going to do and why?

Before we get started, let's take a closer look at what we are going to do in this chapter and why. At the moment, our users can interact with the website and contribute content, including through their own personal blog. Apart from the blog, there isn't a great deal which differentiates our users; they are simply a username with a blog! One key improvement to make now is to make provisions for customizable user profiles. Our site being a social network with a dinosaur theme, the following would be useful information to have on our users:

- Details of their pet dinosaurs, including:
  - Name
  - Breed
  - Date of birth
  - Hobbies

- Their details for other social networking sites; for example, links to their Facebook profile, Twitter account, or LinkedIn page

- Location of the user (city / area)

- Their web address (if they have their own website)

Some of these can be added to user profiles by adding new fields to profiles, using the built in Field API; however we will also install some additional modules to extend the default offering.

Many websites allow users to upload an image to associate with their user account, either a photograph or an avatar to represent them. Drupal has provisions for this, but it has some drawbacks which can be fixed using Gravatar. Gravatar is a social avatar service through which users upload their avatar, which is then accessed by other websites that request the avatar using the user's e-mail address. This is convenient for our users, as it saves them having to upload their avatars to our site, and reduces the amount of data stored on our site, as well as the amount of data being transferred to and from our site. Since not all users will want to use a third-party service for their avatars (particularly, users who are not already signed up to Gravatar) we can let them upload their own avatars if they wish, through the Upload module.

There are many other social networking sites out there, which don't complete with ours, and are more generalized, as a result we might want to allow our users to promote their profiles for other social networks too. We can download and install the Follow module which will allow users to publicize their profiles for other social networking sites on their profile on DinoSpace.

Once our users get to know each other more, they may become more interested in each other's posts and topics and may wish to look up a specific user's contribution to the site. The tracker module allows users to track one another's contributions to the site. It is a core module, which just needs to be enabled and set up.

Now that we have a better idea of what we are going to do in this chapter, let's get started!

Getting set up

As this chapter covers features provided by both core modules and contributed modules (which need to be downloaded first), let's download and enable the modules first, saving us the need for continually downloading and enabling modules throughout the chapter.

The modules which we will require are:

- Tracker (core module)
- Gravatar (can be downloaded from: `http://drupal.org/project/gravatar`)
- Follow (can be downloaded from: `http://drupal.org/project/follow`)
- Field_collection (can be downloaded from: `http://drupal.org/project/field_collection`)
- Entity (can be downloaded from: `http://drupal.org/project/entity`)
- Trigger module (core module)

These modules can be downloaded and then the contents extracted to the `/sites/all/modules` folder within our Drupal installation. Once extracted they will then be ready to be enabled within the **Modules** section of our admin area.

Users, roles, and permissions

In *Chapter 3, User Content: Contributions, Forums, and Blogs*, we discussed the permissions and roles we would like to set up for our site, but we didn't look at how to actually set them up. Let's take a detailed look at users, roles, and permissions and how they all fit together.

Users, roles, and permissions are all managed from the **People** section of the administration area:

User management

Within the **People** section, users are listed by default on the main screen. These are user accounts which are either created by us, as administrators, or created when a visitor to our site signs up for a user account. From here we can search for particular types of users, create new users, and edit users—including updating their profiles, suspending their account, or delete them permanently from our social network.

Once our site starts to gain popularity it will become more difficult for us to navigate through the user list. Thankfully there are search, sort, and filter features available to make this easier for us. Let's start by taking a look at our user list:

	USERNAME	STATUS	ROLES	MEMBER FOR ▼	LAST ACCESS	OPERATIONS
☐	Michael2	active	• temp	2 days 15 hours	2 days 15 hours ago	edit
☐	Michael	active	• administrator	1 month 1 week	1 sec ago	edit

This user list shows, for each user:

- Their username
- If their user account is active or blocked (their status)
- The roles which are associated with their account
- How long they have been a member of our community
- When they last accessed our site
- A link to edit the user's account

Users: Viewing, searching, sorting, and filtering

Clicking on a username will take us to the profile of that particular user, allowing us to view their profile as normal. Clicking one of the headings in the user list allows us to sort the list from the field we selected:

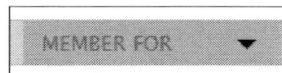

MEMBER FOR ▼

This could be particularly useful to see who our latest members are, or to allow us to see which users are blocked, if we need to reactivate a particular account.

We can also filter the user list based on a particular role that is assigned to a user, a particular permission they have (by virtue of their roles), or by their status (if their account is active or blocked). This is managed from the **SHOW ONLY USERS WHERE** panel:

SHOW ONLY USERS WHERE

role	any ▾	Filter
permission	any ▾	
status	active ▾	

Creating a user

Within the **People** area, there is a link **Add user**, which will allow us to create a new user account for our site:

```
 + Add user
```

This takes us to the new user page where we are required to fill out the **Username**, **E-mail address**, and **Password** (twice to confirm) for the new user account we wish to create. We can also select the status of the user (**Active** or **Blocked**), any roles we wish to apply to their account, and indicate if we want to automatically e-mail the user to notify them of their new account:

This web page allows administrators to register new users. Users' e-mail addresses and usernames must be unique.

Username *

```
Emma
```

Spaces are allowed; punctuation is not allowed except for periods, hyphens, apostrophes, and underscores.

E-mail address *

```
emma@test.com
```

A valid e-mail address. All e-mails from the system will be sent to this address. The e-mail address is not made public and will only be used if you wish to receive a new password or wish to receive certain news or notifications by e-mail.

Password *

```
·········
```
Password strength: **Strong**

Confirm password *

```
·········
```
Passwords match: yes

Provide a password for the new account in both fields.

Status

⊙ Blocked

◉ Active

Roles

☑ authenticated user

☐ administrator

☐ temp

☐ Notify user of new account

(Create new account)

Editing a user

To edit a user account we simply need to click the **edit** link displayed next to the user in the user list. This takes us to a page similar to the create user screen, except that it is pre-populated with the users details. It also contains a few other settings related to some default installed modules. As we install new modules, the page may include more options.

> **Inform the user!**
>
> If you are planning to change a user's username, password, or e-mail address you should notify them of the change, otherwise they may struggle the next time they try to log in!

Suspending / blocking a user

If we need to block or suspend a user, we can do this from the edit screen by updating their status to **Blocked**:

Status

◉ Blocked

◯ Active

This would prevent the user from accessing our site. For example, if a user had been posting inappropriate material, even after a number of warnings, we could block their account to prevent them from accessing the site.

> **Why block? Why not just delete?**
>
> If we were to simply delete a user who was troublesome on the site, they could simply sign up again (unless we went to a separate area and also blocked their e-mail address and username). Of course, the user could still sign up again using a different e-mail address and a different username, but this helps us keep things under control.

Canceling and deleting a user account

Also within the edit screen is the option to cancel a user's account:

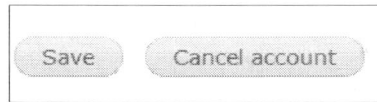

Save	Cancel account

On clicking the **Cancel account** button, we are given a number of options for how we wish to cancel the account:

When cancelling the account

- ⦿ Disable the account and keep its content.
- ⦾ Disable the account and unpublish its content.
- ⦾ Delete the account and make its content belong to the *Anonymous* user.
- ⦾ Delete the account and its content.

- ☐ Require e-mail confirmation to cancel account.
    When enabled, the user must confirm the account cancellation via e-mail.

Select the method to cancel the account above. This action cannot be undone.

Cancel account	Cancel

The first and third options will at least keep the context of any discussions or contributions to which the user was involved with. The second option will unpublish their content, so if for example comments or pages are removed which have an impact on the community, we can at least re-enable them. The final option will delete the account and all content associated with it.

Finally, we can also select if the user themselves must confirm that they wish to have their account deleted. Particularly useful if this is in response to a request from the user to delete all of their data, they can be given a final chance to change their mind.

Bulk user operations

For occasions when we need to perform specific operations to a range of user accounts (for example, unblocking a number of users, or adding / removing roles from specific users) we can use the **Update options** panel, in the user list to do these:

	USERNAME	STATUS	ROLES	MEMBER FOR ▼	LAST ACCESS	OPERATIONS
☑	Emma	active		14 min 22 sec	never	edit
☐	Michael2	active	• temp	2 days 15 hours	2 days 15 hours ago	edit
☐	Michael	active	• administrator	1 month 1 week	7 min 40 sec ago	edit

UPDATE OPTIONS

Block the selected users ▾   Update

From here we simply select the users we want to apply an action to, and then select one of the following options from the **UPDATE OPTIONS** list:

- **Unblock the selected users**
- **Block the selected users**
- **Cancel the selected user accounts**
- **Add a role to the selected users**
- **Remove a role from the selected users**

Roles

As we discussed briefly in *Chapter 3, User Content: Contributions, Forums, and Blogs*, users are grouped into a number of roles, which in turn have permissions assigned to them. By default there are three roles within Drupal:

- Administrators
- Anonymous users
- Authenticated users

The anonymous and authenticated roles can be edited but they cannot be renamed or deleted. We can manage user roles by navigating to **People | Permissions | Roles**.

The **edit permissions** link allows us to edit the permissions associated with a specific role. To create a new role, we simply need to enter the name for the role in the text box provided and click the **Add role** button.

Permissions

The permissions section provides us with a grid view for roles and the available permissions. This allows us to see at a glance which roles can do what, and also allows us to quickly change the permissions of multiple roles:

Home » Administration » People   Permissions   Roles

Permissions let you control what users can do and see on your site. You can define a specific set of permissions for each role. (See the Roles page to create a role). Two important roles to consider are Authenticated Users and Administrators. Any permissions granted to the Authenticated Users role will be given to any user who can log into your site. You can make any role the Administrator role for the site, meaning this will be granted all new permissions automatically. You can do this on the User Settings page. You should be careful to ensure that only trusted users are given this access and level of control of your site.

Hide descriptions

PERMISSION	ANONYMOUS USER	AUTHENTICATED USER	ADMINISTRATOR	TEMP
Aggregator				
Administer news feeds	☐	☐	☑	☐
View news feeds	☐	☐	☑	☐
Block				
Administer blocks	☐	☐	☑	☐
Book				
Administer book outlines	☐	☐	☑	☐
Create new books	☐	☐	☑	☐
Add content and child pages to books	☐	☐	☑	☐
View printer-friendly books View a book page and all of its sub-pages as a single document for ease of printing. Can be performance heavy.	☐	☐	☑	☐

This screen is particularly useful once new modules are installed; we can simply visit this page and select which roles should have permissions related to that module.

Permissions work on a "granted" basis; if a user is a member of a role which has a particular permission, then they have that permission. If they are members of other roles as well which don't have that permission, it won't make any difference.

Creating customizable user profiles

The provisions within Drupal for dynamically extending the fields available for content aren't just limited to content; we can also change the fields related to a users profile. These fields can be set up to allow the user to add another instance of the field. If for example, we have a field for the name of their dinosaur, they could duplicate this to add one for each of their dinosaurs. However, it doesn't support duplicating a group of fields (such as dinosaur's name, breed, date of birth, and hobbies), so we will use a field collection (a module we downloaded) for that.

From our initial planning earlier in this chapter, there are two fields we can create using the default field functionality — location of the user, and their web address:

- To manage the fields associated with a user's profile, we need to go to **Configuration | People | Account settings** and then click the **MANAGE FIELDS** tab:

- From here we can add fields just as we did to content types earlier in the book; let's start with adding the user's web address — we will make it a field which can be duplicated in case they wish to list more than one website they have.

- We start by adding the label for the field, the name for the field, and selecting **Text** as the type of data to be stored in the field:

✛ **Add new field**

| Web address | field_ | web_address | | Text | ▼ | | Text field | ▼ |
| Label | | Field name (a-z, 0-9, _) | | Type of data to store. | | | Form element to edit the data. | |

- Once we click the **Save** button to save the field, we are prompted to supply the maximum length of the field:

Web address ⊕   EDIT   **FIELD SETTINGS**   WIDGET TYPE   DELETE

                                                                                                    ✖

Home » Administration » Configuration » People » Account settings » Manage fields » Web address

FIELD SETTINGS

These settings apply to the *Web address* field everywhere it is used. These settings impact the way that data is stored in the database and cannot be changed once data has been created.

Maximum length *

255

The maximum length of the field in characters.

(Save field settings)

- After clicking **Save field settings**, we are then taken to the screen to edit the field in more detail. On this screen, we should select that the field is to be displayed on the registration form:

USER SETTINGS

These settings apply only to the *Web address* field when used in the *User* type.

Label *

Web address

☐ Required field

☑ Display on user registration form.
   This is compulsory for 'required' fields.

- We also want to change the number of values to **Unlimited**, which allows the user to enter as many of their web addresses as they wish.

WEB ADDRESS FIELD SETTINGS

These settings apply to the *Web address* field everywhere it is used.

Number of values

Unlimited ▼

Maximum number of values users can enter for this field.
'Unlimited' will provide an 'Add more' button so the users can add as many values as they like.

Maximum length *

255

The maximum length of the field in characters.

- We should then repeat this process for the user's location, except we should leave the **Number of values** option as **1**.

Listing your dinosaurs

To allow our users to enter multiples of a group of fields, we need to create a field collection, thanks to our newly downloaded module:

⊹ **Add new field**

| Your dinosaurs | field_ | your_dinosaurs | Field-collection ▼ | Hidden ▼ |
| Label | Field name (a-z, 0-9, _) | | Type of data to store. | Form element to edit the data. |

After entering the new field details and clicking **save**, we are taken to a confirmation screen (as there are no specific settings, such as field length) to set. After clicking **Save field settings** (a confusingly named button in light of the lack of settings) we are taken to the edit field screen, where we can select it as a field to be displayed on the registration form, and as a field we want the user to be able to enter multiple values of.

The field collection we have created is simply a container for a group of fields; we now need to go and setup the fields for our field collection. These can be managed from **Structure | Field-collections**, this screen lists all field-collections which have been created and allows us to manage their fields:

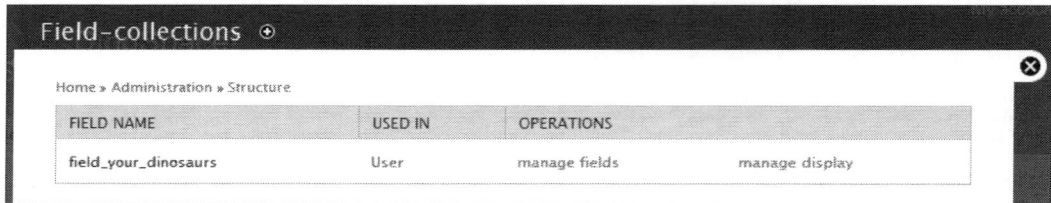

If we click the **manage fields** link, we are taken to the standard screen for adding and managing fields for a content type or for user profiles, which we are already familiar with. From here we should create fields for:

- Name of the dinosaur
- Breed of dinosaur
- Date of birth
- Hobbies

All of the fields should have their **Number of values** setting set to **1**, except for the **Hobbies** box, which we would want to allow any number of.

> Unfortunately at the time of writing, field collections don't display on the registration page, and instead only work on the users profile itself, and are added and managed by the user viewing their own profile.

Linking to other social network profiles

The **Follow** module which we downloaded and installed allows our users to enter their profiles for various social networks; this includes the following social networks out of the box:

- Twitter
- Facebook
- Virb
- MySpace
- Picasa

- Flickr
- YouTube
- Vimeo
- Blip.tv
- Last.fm
- LinkedIn
- Delicious
- Tumblr

The actual links to these social networking sites are displayed in a block, which needs to be enabled. We need to go to **Structure | Blocks**, and from here we need to find the **Follow User** block, and select it to be part of the **Sidebar second** region (remember to click **Save** at the bottom of the page to save the changes):

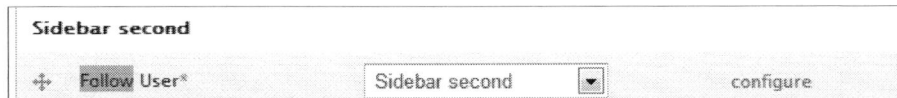

Sidebar second		
✛ Follow User*	Sidebar second ▼	configure

Profile in action

If we now take a look at a profile with these new fields and options, you can see the web addresses, location, links to follow the user on other social networking sites, and their pet dinosaurs:

Michael

View | Edit | My follow links | Shortcuts

Web address:
http://www.michaelpeacock.co.uk
http://www.peacockcarter.co.uk
Location:
Chester-le-Street, UK
Your dinosaurs:

Name: Mr Glen
Date of birth: 01/01/2005
Breed: T-Rex
Hobbies: Running

Edit Delete

✚ Add

History

Blog
View recent blog entries

Member for
1 month 1 week

Follow Michael on:
- Twitter
- Facebook
- Flickr
- LinkedIn
- Delicious
- last.fm

Additional dinosaurs can be added using the **Add** link, from which the details can be added and any number of hobbies listed:

Add new your dinosaurs

Name

Stu Fishman

Breed

Stegosaurus

Date of birth

2/5/2001

Show row weights

Hobbies:

+ Walking

+ Hiding

+

Add another item

Save

Finally, the social networking links can be edited from the **My follow links** tab:

Michael

| View | Edit | My follow links | Shortcuts |

Please copy and paste the url for your public profile or page for each service you would like to display in the block. Links need to match the domain of the service in question.

Show row weights

Follow Michael on:

- Twitter
- Facebook
- Flickr
- LinkedIn
- Delicious
- last.fm

Name	URL	Customized Name
+ Twitter	http://www.twitter.com/michaelpeacock	
+ Facebook	http://www.facebook.com/michaelpeacock	
+ Flickr	http://www.flickr.com/photos/26701119@N04/	
+ LinkedIn	http://www.linkedin.com/in/michaelkeithpeacock	
+ Delicious	http://www.delicious.com/michaelpeacock	
+ lastfm	http://www.last.fm/user/mkpeacock	

Globally recognized avatars: Enabling Gravatars

Gravatars are globally recognized avatars (an avatar being a small picture used to represent a user when making comments or posts), and are very popular among blogs and forums, with many blog and forum systems supporting Gravatars. Gravatars enable users to use the same avatar across all socially-oriented sites they use, should they wish to.

The settings for this module are accessed through **Configuration | People | Gravatar**. Configuration options available include:

- What default image should be used if a user doesn't have a Gravatar
- The preferred size for Gravatars to be displayed within the site
- Which sort of images are permitted (based off Gravatars maturity filter)

The following screenshot shows these configuration options:

Default image

- Global default user image

  There currently is not a global default user picture specified. This setting can be adjusted in the user pictures settings.

- Module default image (white background)
- Module default image (transparent background)
- Gravatar.com mystery man
- Gravatar.com logo
- Gravatar.com identicon (generated)
- Gravatar.com monsterid (generated)
- Gravatar.com wavatar (generated)
- Gravatar.com retro 8-bit arcade-style pixelated faces (generated)

Specifies an image that should be returned if either the requested e-mail address has no associated gravatar, or that gravatar has a rating higher than is allowed by the maturity filter.

Gravatar size

100

The preferred image size for Gravatars (maximum 512 pixels).

Image maturity filter

G

- G: Suitable for display on all websites with any audience type.
- PG: May contain rude gestures, provocatively dressed individuals, the lesser swear words, or mild violence.
- R: May contain such things as harsh profanity, intense violence, nudity, or hard drug use.
- X: May contain hardcore sexual imagery or extremely disturbing violence.

Now when a user edits their profile they are presented with an option to either upload an avatar or if they have a valid Gravatar associated with their e-mail address, whether to use that instead:

PICTURE

Upload picture

Choose File   No file chosen

Your virtual face or picture. Pictures larger than 1024x1024 pixels will be scaled down. Only upload photographs you have permission to post, and which are suitable for the age-range of the audience of this website.

☑ If you have a valid Gravatar associated with your e-mail address, use it for your user picture.

Your Gravatar will not be shown if you upload a user picture.

Tracking user activity

The tracker module allows users to view the recent contributions of a user to the site, by clicking the **Track** tab on their profile:

Michael

| View | Edit | My follow links | Shortcuts | Track |

Type	Title	Author	Replies	Last updated
Poll	What breed of dinosaur do you look after?	Michael	0	2 weeks 2 days ago
Book page	Hatched	Michael	0	2 weeks 2 days ago
Book page	It's hatching	Michael	0	2 weeks 2 days ago
Book page	Egg care	Michael	0	2 weeks 2 days ago
Book page	Caring for our dinosaur: From egg to adult	Michael	0	2 weeks 2 days ago

This is particularly useful if a user finds another user's posts interesting; they can use this to find other contributions the user made in the hope that they too will be interesting. This however, is primitive user interaction, as it is only one-way; we will look at full user interaction later in the book.

User centric home page

Once a user has logged into the site we will want to redirect them to a stream of user activity, to truly take them into the social network. We can do this using actions and triggers. At the moment we don't have a stream of activity, so we will set it up to take them to their own profile page for now.

Triggers are events on our site, such as a user logging in. Through the trigger settings we can assign an **action** to happen when the event is triggered. Actions are managed from **Configuration | System | Actions**. To redirect the user when they log in we need to create an advanced action, **Redirect to URL**:

> **CREATE AN ADVANCED ACTION**
>
> Redirect to URL... ▾   Create

To redirect the user to their profile page, we should enter user as the **URL**, and click **Save**:

> **Configure an advanced action** ⊕
>
> ❌
>
> Home » Administration » Configuration » System » Actions
>
> An advanced action offers additional configuration options which may be filled out below. Changing the *Description* field is recommended, in order to better identify the precise action taking place. This description will be displayed in modules such as the Trigger module when assigning actions to system events, so it is best if it is as descriptive as possible (for example, "Send e-mail to Moderation Team" rather than simply "Send e-mail").
>
> **Label**
>
> Redirect to URL
>
> A unique label for this advanced action. This label will be displayed in the interface of modules that integrate with actions, such as Trigger module.
>
> **URL** *
>
> user
>
> The URL to which the user should be redirected. This can be an internal URL like node/1234 or an external URL like http://drupal.org.
>
> Save

Once we have created our action we can associate it with a trigger. Triggers are managed in **Structure | Triggers**, and we need to select the **User** tab to list triggers related to user events.

From here we select the newly created **Redirect to URL** action from the **TRIGGER: AFTER A USER HAS LOGGED IN** section:

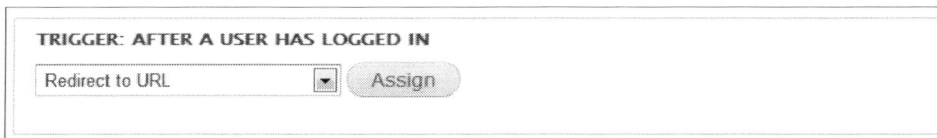

TRIGGER: AFTER A USER HAS LOGGED IN

| Redirect to URL | ▾ | Assign |

Once we click **Assign**, the action is bound to the user login trigger.

Working with login blocks

These instructions for redirecting the user won't work when you try logging in through a login block on the page. There are two ways around this:

1. remove the login block and force the user to use the login page
2. update the login block HTML to match the HTML on the main login page. More information can be found on the Drupal website, including a patch around the issue and HTML to replace the login block, at http://drupal.org/node/286668.

Account settings

The final user and profile related feature we have left is the user account settings area, which is managed from **Configuration | People | Account settings**, though we did cover this briefly in *Chapter 1, Drupal and Social Networking*. From here we can:

- Change the name given to users who are not logged in
- Change the administrator role
- Set who can register user accounts, and if e-mail or administrator verification is required
- Set the default action when a user opts to cancel their own account
- Enable or disable user signatures
- Enable, disable, and configure user pictures

- Configure e-mails which are sent out to users when:
  - Their account is created by an administrator
  - Their account is pending approval
  - Their account has been created
  - Their account has been activated
  - Their account has been blocked
  - To confirm their account cancelation
  - Their account has been canceled
  - They have forgotten their password

From here we should ensure signatures and pictures are enabled.

Summary

We have now expanded our social networking site to allow users to sign up and customize their experience on the site. This included custom user profiles complete with links to their profiles on other social networking sites and details of their pet dinosaurs. We used globally recognized avatars to automatically pull in our user's Avatar if they have one. A custom home page was set for our logged in users, and we enabled the viewing of recent contributions from other members.

We also looked through features to make it possible for us, as administrators, to manage our users, including creating and editing user profiles, deleting and canceling user accounts, updating the e-mails sent to our users on key events (registration, forgotten password, and so on), as well as the management of user roles and permissions.

With these features in place, and our knowledge of Drupal expanding, we can now look at enabling user interaction on our site, making it a truly social experience!

5
Enabling User Interaction

Our social network is really starting to take shape, with a range of collaboration features allowing our users to get active with and contribute to the site. At this stage, however, we don't have a true network; we need to let our users build relationships with one another, as well as communicate and collaborate as a whole and in smaller groups. In this chapter, you will learn how to do the following:

- Use the user relationships module to create a range of relationship types, allowing users to mark each other as friends, colleagues, and acquaintances
- Stream social activity from a user's network of connections with the heartbeat module, using rules to stream custom information
- Enable user communication
- Facilitate tighter user collaboration with organic groups

DinoSpace!: A review

So far, our users could contribute to our site using some of the user-centric modules built into Drupal. Our members can also extend their user profile and enhance their experience on the site.

If we look back at *Chapter 1, Drupal and Social Networking*, we can see that one of the most fundamental concepts of a social networking website is the building of connections with other users, which together with the connections of even more users with the same interests help build up a network of social links between our users.

Preparation: Installing the modules

This chapter requires a range of modules to be downloaded and installed, many of which are simply installed because another module requires them to function. Let's download these modules now, and install them all in one go to save us time during the chapter:

- Contact (built-in, just needs enabling)
- Entity (`http://drupal.org/project/entity`)
- Flag (`http://drupal.org/project/flag`)
- Heartbeat (`http://drupal.org/project/heartbeat`)
- Rules (`http://drupal.org/project/rules`)
- Chaos tool suite (`http://drupal.org/project/ctools`)
- User relationships (`http://drupal.org/project/user_relationships`)
- Panels (`http://drupal.org/project/panels`)
- Views (`http://drupal.org/project/views`)
- Guestbook (`http://drupal.org/project/guestbook`; the Drupal 7 version is still in development and can be downloaded from the **All releases** page: `http://drupal.org/node/5460/release`)
- Organic Groups (`http://drupal.org/project/og`)

Once installed, we will need to set appropriate permissions, in particular for our heartbeat and user relationship modules to indicate which users can create, manage, and have relationships within our network.

Relationships

We are going to use the user relationships module to allow our users to connect with each other and build a range of relationships with each other. One of the great things about the module is that we as administrators can define the types of relationships we want our site to support. For instance, we could have friends, family, and co-workers if we wanted. The module also allows users to save a note to **elaborate** on the relationship and describe how they know the user.

Naturally, the first stage for setting this feature up within our site successfully is planning.

Planning user relationships

Relationships with this module can either be one-way or two-way, where the relationship is reciprocal. Most social networking sites make use of friendship relationships and this is usually a two-way relationship. Obviously, some users may wish to connect with other users who don't want to classify them as "friends"; perhaps they just find their contribution to the site interesting, and want to continue to stay up-to-date with their progress through the site. Here, we have the option to indicate that one user is "following" another, and it can be a one-way relationship. A co-workers relationship may also be useful, though it may be more suited to a site focused on business activities, where other relationships are set up to help define job titles and roles within a company, for example, User A manages User B.

For DinoSpace we will set up relationship types for the following:

- Friends
- Followers

We will also set it up so that one of our own user accounts is automatically friends with new users on the site. Let's get started!

Managing and creating relationships

Relationships are defined and managed within **Administration | Configuration | People | Relationships**:

Relationships ⊙   LIST   SETTINGS

Home » Administration » Configuration » People

This page lets you setup user relationship types.

✦ Add relationship type   ✦ Add default relationship

RELATIONSHIP TYPES

NAME	TYPE	REQUIRES APPROVAL	OPERATIONS
No relationships available.			

DEFAULT RELATIONSHIPS

RELATIONSHIP TYPE	USER	OPERATIONS
No default relationships available.		

From here we can create and manage types of relationships, and also any default relationships which new users have (we will discuss default relationships shortly).

Creating a relationship type

To create a new relationship type, we first click the **Add relationship type** link; this takes us to the new relationship type form.

Creating a two-way relationship which requires approval

Let's first start by creating our friends relationship type. Within the form we need to enter a name for the type, which for our friends relationship type is `friend`; we then enter a plural name, which is `friends`, select if relationships of this type require approval, and if so when the request expires, and if the relationship is one-way:

We can also specify how the relationships of this type are listed, including if we want to do the following:

- Hide this relationship type from the relationships list
- Create a separate tab (and path) for this relationship type

There is also a group of settings for which roles are permitted to request and permitted to receive relationship requests of this type:

Listings

Allowed Roles

Role request access

☐ authenticated user

☐ administrator

You may choose which roles are allowed to request this relationship. If none are selected, all roles are allowed.

Role receive access

☐ authenticated user

☐ administrator

You may choose which roles are allowed to receive this relationship. If none are selected, all roles are allowed to receive the relationship.

Creating a one-way relationship

Our follower relationship type doesn't need approval and is a one-way relationship. Unchecking the **Requires Approval** option removes the **Request Expires In** box automatically, which is nice. When we tick the one-way option a new option is presented to us, allowing us to select if the **one-way relationship can be reciprocated**:

Name *

follower

Example: buddy, friend, coworker, spouse.

Plural name *

followers

Example: buddies, friends, coworkers, spouses.

☐ Requires Approval

    Check this if the requestee must approve the relationship

☑ This is a one-way relationship

    Check this if this relationship should only go one way (ex Manager, Subscriber)

☑ This one-way relationship can be reciprocated

    Check if this one-way relationship can go either way

The implied relationships section is enabled when we select a one-way relationship. This allows us to set it so that one relationship implies another. Optionally we can specify that the requestee / requester roles in the relationship are reversed, and that the relationship is strict, and would be removed if this relationship is deleted.

This could allow us to create a one-way "manages" relationship, which would automatically create a "subordinate" or "is managed by" relationship with the roles being reversed from the original relationship. Making this strict would mean that removing the manages relationship would subsequently remove the "is managed by" relationship too:

Creating default relationships

With the User Relationships module we can also create default relationships which apply to all users on our site automatically. There are a few reasons we might want to do this, including:

- As part of a sponsorship package, our sponsor is automatically friends with all of our users, so they can see what the sponsor is up to

- All users are automatically friends with one of our own user accounts, helping to increase our own popularity on the site

- All users are automatically friends with a user account of a mascot for our social network

Let's create a default relationship for a new user account called DS T-Rex, the DinoSpace T-Rex mascot. First we click **Add default relationship** on the relationships page, and then we enter the **username** we wish to relate all users to, and the type of **relationship** to create:

Username *

DS T-Rex

Start typing the name of a user to automatically create a relationship to

Relationship *

friend

Start typing the name of a relationship to use

Submit

Once we are done, we click the **Submit** button to save the default relationship. Now we have our relationship types and our default relationship all set up and ready to go:

RELATIONSHIP TYPES

NAME	TYPE	REQUIRES APPROVAL	OPERATIONS
friend	Mutual	Yes (within 10 days)	edit | delete
follower	Reciprocal	No	edit | delete

DEFAULT RELATIONSHIPS

RELATIONSHIP TYPE	USER	OPERATIONS
friend	DS T-Rex	delete

Settings

The User Relationships module also comes with a wealth of settings which we can configure. These settings are accessed from the **Settings** tab within **Administration | Configuration | People | Relationships**. Let's look through the most useful ones now.

General settings

The general settings for the module allow us to set:

- If a user is permitted to have more than one relationship (of different types) with another user
- If each type of relationship between two users should show a separate link
- If users pictures should be displayed along with their name on relationships lists
- If users' can opt to auto-approve relationship requests
- How many relationships should be listed on a page (more than this number, and it is broken down into multiple pages)

General	
E-mail Notification	☑ **Allow multiple relationships**
	If checked, a user may create multiple relationships (each relationship of a different type) with another user.
Elaborations	☑ **Show a separate link per relationship type**
Custom Screen Messages	On a user's page, show a separate link for each available relationship type (instead of the generic 'Create a relationship' link).
AJAX Popup Positioning	☐ **Show user pictures on relationship pages**
Share content	Show a picture next to each user's name on 'My relationships' pages.
	☐ **Allow users to auto approve**
	Provide users with an option to automatically approve all requested relationships.
	Relationships per page
	16
	Number of relationships to show per page. If set to 0 all will be shown.

Customizing e-mail notifications

This module sends out e-mail notifications at key points including:

- When a new relationship request is made
- When a request is canceled, approved, or declined
- When a relationship is deleted
- When a relationship is pre-approved

Each of these notifications can be turned on or off, and the contents of the e-mail and the e-mail subject can be configured. We can also set if we wish to allow users to turn off receiving some of these notifications if they so wish:

Customizing on-screen messages

When actions such as a relationship being created or approved happen on the site, as well as users being e-mailed (as discussed previously) the user is informed of the result of the action through an on-screen message.

The contents of these messages can be configured too:

Sharing content

With the User Relationships module we have the ability to allow our users to share and promote content which they have created or edited with their network of contacts. The share content settings area allows us to define which content types we want to be "shareable":

Enabled content types

☑ Article

☑ Basic page

Add a check mark next to each content type that users should be allowed to share with their established relationships. Only these content types will have "Share content" options on their content creation and edit forms.

Other settings

There are also settings and options for:

- Turning off the elaborations UI
- Changing the position and usage of AJAX confirmation dialogues

Permissions

As with the majority of Drupal modules, the User Relationships module introduces a range of permissions which we will need to assign to the appropriate user groups; these permissions are:

- UR-UI
  - Maintain own relationships
  - View own user relationships
- User relationships
  - Can have relationships

These permissions will need to be granted to users who we want to be able to have and maintain relationships with other users on our site.

Relationships in action

Now that we have set up the module, let's see it in action!

Befriending users

To add another user as a friend, we simply visit their profile page; on the page, it lists our relationship with them (at the moment, that is an empty list), and lists relationships which we could create.

Let's select **Become Emma's friend**:

Now, we can elaborate on the relationship, and provide a comment or detail which both users will be able to see. When we are ready, we simply click **Send** to initiate the relationship request:

We then see a visual notification that the friend request has been sent. Now we have to wait for the other user to respond to the friend request:

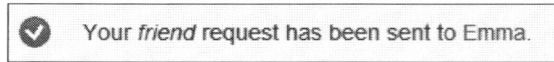

> ✓ Your *friend* request has been sent to Emma.

Approving requests

When we log in as a user with pending friend requests, we see a visual notification of any users who have requested to be our friend (or other relationship type), along with a link **pending relationship requests** to view our pending requests. Let's click this link:

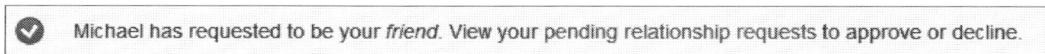

> ✓ Michael has requested to be your *friend*. View your pending relationship requests to approve or decline.

Now, we see a list of our received requests, along with the **User** who initiated the request, the type of **Relationship**, their **Comments**, and the option to **Approve** or **Decline** the request. Let's click on **Approve**:

My relationships (received requests)

Current	Received requests (1)	Sent requests	friends

User	Relationship	Comments	Operations
Michael	friend	Here I can add more details to elaborate on the relationship	Approve Decline

The approval screen provides us with the ability to edit the comments the other user supplied to elaborate on the relationship. When we are happy with that, we simply click **Yes** to approve the request:

Approve relationship

Are you sure you want to approve the *friend* relationship request from Michael?

Comments

Here I can add more details to elaborate on the relationship

Add more details about your relationship. Both parties will be able to view these comments.

Yes   No

Now we have a friend!

My *friends*

| View | Edit | Relationships | My guestbook |

| Current | Received requests | Sent requests | followers | friends |

User	Relationship	Comments		Operations
Michael	friend	Here I can add more details to elaborate on the relationship		Remove

Related user activity stream

Now that our users can connect with other users, and start to build a truly social network, we need to provide streams of information which relate to these connections. The heartbeat module can help us with just that; it's an extensible module which provides useful streams of activity, and comes with basic support, out of the box, for the User Relationships module.

Depending on the relationship type, we would want the stream to display a different message, for example:

- Jack and Jill are now friends
- Jack is now following Jill

This will involve us:

- Creating a template for heartbeat to inform users of the relationship in their stream
- Creating a new rule to detect when a relationship is approved (we don't want to add the relationship to the stream until it has been approved) and to send notification to heartbeat

A template for each relationship type

Let's start by creating a heartbeat template for the friend relationship; we need to go to **Administer | Structure | Heartbeat | Heartbeat templates** and click the **Add** link. The first stage is to enter a name (**Message ID**) for the message, and a brief **Description of the message**. Let's fill those in and click the **Access** link:

The **Access** settings allow us to disable the message, select who can see the message, and also which users (based on their roles) see the message:

The **Content** section allows us to enter the text that will be displayed on the stream. Within the text we can add variables (prefixed with an exclamation mark) which will be dynamically inserted with data via the rules module. Let's enter the following:

`!requestee and !requester are now friends.`

Later, when we create a rule to notify heartbeat of an approved friend request, it will send with it the name of the requesting user and the requestee:

Add a new Heartbeat template ⊙

Home » Administration » Structure » Heartbeat » Heartbeat templates

Message ID *

Heartbeat Approve Relationship 1

The unique ID for this Heartbeat template.

Definition	**Single message** *
Access	!requestee and !requester are now friends
Examples	"!" is available to interpret words as variables.
Content	Note that the actor variable of the message should be **!username**.
Attachments	**Type of message** *
	Single: Treat all activity instances as standalone messages

Type of message when it comes to grouping messages together.
Single is when you want to repeat messages without merging them together. These messages are standalone and they dont take notice on previous and upcoming messages.
Count means you want to merge the messages together so you know the occurrency. Only one message in its single format will be displayed.
A **summary** is when you want to group the same instance of several messages together. For this you will summarize a part of the message and use it as substitional variables (with separators) to form the merged messages. The occurrency of the message instance is also known as the count.

Save

The final option, **Attachments**, allows us to enable comments on heartbeat stream messages and lets users indicate if they like a particular update:

Add a new Heartbeat template ⊙

Home » Administration » Structure » Heartbeat » Heartbeat templates

Message ID *

Heartbeat Approve Relationship 1

The unique ID for this Heartbeat template.

Definition	☑ Enable comments for this activity template
Access	☐ Enable node comments for this activity template if a node is available
Examples	☐ Enable flag count for this activity message
Content	**Add flags to this activity message**
Attachments	☑ I like

Save

With the template created, we can now create the rule to communicate with heartbeat.

A rule for each relationship type

Let's start with a rule for the friends relationship type; the steps required for the rule are as follows:

1. Set to react on the event: A user relationship has been approved.
2. Be conditional upon the relationship type being friend.
3. Add the action "Log activity for Heartbeat Approve Relationship 1", the template we created earlier.
4. Send the name of the requester and requestee.

To create the rule we need to navigate to **Administration | Configuration | Workflow | Rules**, and click **Add new rule**. The first stage is to enter a name, such as Users are now friends, and select the type of event the rule is in reaction to; we should select A user relationship has been approved:

Rules ⊕

Home » Administration » Configuration » Workflow » Rules

Name *

Users are now friends   Machine name: users_are_now_friends [Edit]

React on event

A user relationship has been approved

Whenever the event occurrs, rule evaluation is triggered.

Save

Clicking **Save** then creates a basic rule which detects when a user relationship has been created. From this screen we need to click **Add condition** under the **Conditions** section:

Editing reaction rule "Users are now friends" ⊕

Home » Administration » Configuration » Workflow » Rules

✓   Your changes have been saved.

Events

EVENT	OPERATIONS
A user relationship has been approved	delete
✛ Add event	

Conditions

ELEMENTS	WEIGHT	OPERATIONS
None		
✛ Add condition ✛ Add or ✛ Add and		

Actions

ELEMENTS	WEIGHT	OPERATIONS
None		
✛ Add action ✛ Add loop		

▸ SETTINGS

(Save changes)

From the **Add a new condition** screen we can restrict the rule to only take effect
when the relationship type is **friend**. Under **Select the condition to add** we need to
select relationship as type:

Add a new condition ⊕

Home » Administration » Configuration » Workflow » Rules » Editing reaction rule "Users are now friends"

Select the *condition* to add

| Data comparison ▾ |

(Continue)

From here we simply select **friend** from the **RELATIONSHIP TYPE** section, and click **Save**:

Now, the rule only takes affect when a friend request is approved. The next stage is to notify heartbeat.

Under the actions section we click **Add action**.

The type of action we want to take when the rule is triggered is to **Log activity for User Approves Relationship 1**, so let's select that:

We need to enter 0 as the Entity ID value so that an ID is automatically generated, and under **USER ID** we need to enter [requester:uid] so that the ID of the user making the relationship request is stored. The **REPLACEMENT PATTERNS** link provides a list of dynamic variables (in this instance, related to the website, the user making the request, or the user approving the friend request):

ENTITY ID

Value *

0

▸ REPLACEMENT PATTERNS

Switch to data selection

USER ID

Value *

[requester:uid]

▸ REPLACEMENT PATTERNS

Switch to data selection

Under **Entity Target ID** and **User Target ID** we should enter **0**:

ENTITY TARGET ID

Value

0

▸ REPLACEMENT PATTERNS

Switch to data selection

USER TARGET ID

Value

0

▸ REPLACEMENT PATTERNS

Switch to data selection

Finally, there are two options, one for **!REQUESTEE** and one for **!REQUESTER**. These two options are detected from the contents of the heartbeat template we created earlier. In these we want the name of the user, and a link to their profile for the user who accepted the request, and the user who initiated the request. So we enter [requestee:link] and [requester:link] respectively:

```
!REQUESTEE

Value *
[requestee:link]

▸ REPLACEMENT PATTERNS

Switch to data selection


!REQUESTER

Value *
[requester:link]

▸ REPLACEMENT PATTERNS

Switch to data selection
```

After saving this we have our heartbeat module set up, with new records added when users connect with one another.

Activity stream in action

If we now create a new friend relationship with one of our users (the heartbeat and rules modules can't work retroactively), and then view the **User relations activity**, we see the new relationship in the stream:

User relations activity

Bill and **Doug** are now friends 7 sec ago · Delete · I like this

Doug has added page Doug. 4 min ago · Delete · I like this · Comment

DS T-Rex has added page DS T-Rex. 9 hours ago · Delete · I like this · Comment

The user relations activity only includes the activity of users whom we are connected to, providing a useful and informative stream of information. Within the stream is also a record of activity from the user **DS T-Rex**, who we didn't add as a friend; however this user was automatically befriended with us as we set up a default relationship earlier in the chapter.

Contacting users

The built-in contact module allows us to give each user their own contact form, allowing users to get in touch directly with other users if they wish. As usual, we need to set the permissions for the module, so that authenticated users can use the site-wide contact form and also the per-user contact forms:

Contact			
Administer contact forms and contact form settings	☐	☐	☑
Use the site-wide contact form	☐	☑	☑
Use users' personal contact forms	☐	☑	☑

Now, when we look at a user's profile, we have a tab called **Contact**, containing a contact form allowing users to communicate with other users:

Contact Bill

| View | Edit | My follow links | Relationships | Shortcuts | My guestbook | Contact |

Your name *

Bill

Your e-mail address *

mkpeacock@gmail.com

To
Bill

Subject *

Message *

Groups

Groups, courtesy of the organic groups module, can enhance our community by providing an area for groups of users to communicate and work together. Users can create groups, join groups, contribute to groups, and subscribe to groups, thus creating a series of smaller communities within the site.

Groups for DinoSpace!

Why might we want to provide groups in our DinoSpace network? Let's take a look at some potential groups:

- T-Rex owners groups
- New users group: Help and support for new users with the site
- UK dinosaur owners group: Related discussion and comments specific to dinosaur owners residing in the UK

Groups support a number of different membership options, including:

- **Open membership**: Where requests for memberships are automatically approved
- **Moderated**: Where new requests must be approved first
- **Invite only**: New members can only join the group on invitation by a group administrator
- **Closed**: All memberships are managed by an administrator

This allows us to have private groups should we wish to use that option. Of course, as these are organic groups, users can create new groups as the need for them arises.

Using the organic groups module

The organic groups module needs some simple configuration; to get it up and running we need to do the following:

- Create a new content type to act as a group
- Configure group settings
- Configure the page content type to allow it to be contributed to a group
- Configure the relevant content blocks

> There are two types of content for the Organic Groups module: **Group content type**, a content type which acts as a group and **Group content**, content which can be posted to a group.

Creating a group content type

The first thing we need to do is create a new content type to act as a group, we do this from **Administration | Structure | Content types**. Let's call the new content type Group, so we know what we are creating when we use this content type in the future:

Individual content types can have different fields, behaviors, and permissions assigned to them.

Name *

| Group | Machine name: group [Edit] |

The human-readable name of this content type. This text will be displayed as part of the list on the *Add new content* page. It is recommended that this name begin with a capital letter and contain only letters, numbers, and spaces. This name must be unique.

Description

Describe this content type. The text will be displayed on the *Add new content* page.

At the bottom of the page, there is a new section called **Group** (since we have installed the organic groups module), which allows us to set group specific settings for the content type. We need to select that the content type is a **Group type**, and that it is **Not a group content type**. This means creating content of this type will create a new organic group:

Submission form settings Title	Specify how Group should treat content of this type. Content may behave as a group, as group content, or may not participate in Group at all.
Publishing options Published , Promoted to front page	**Group**
Display settings Display author and date information.	○ Not a group type ● Group type
Addthis settings	
Comment settings Open, Threading , 50 comments per page	**Group content** ● Not a group content type
Menu settings	○ Group content type
Group	

Once we click **Save content type**, we have the ability to create groups!

Configuring content types

With the group content type created, we now need to create content which can be posted within a group. To do this, we can either create new content types, or edit existing content types and select them as **Group content type** under the **Group content** section:

Submission form settings Title	Specify how Group should treat content of this type. Content may behave as a group, as group content, or may not participate in Group at all.
Publishing options Published	**Group**
Display settings Don't display post information	● Not a group type ○ Group type
Addthis settings	
Comment settings Hidden, Threading , 50 comments per page	**Group content** ○ Not a group content type
Menu settings	● Group content type
Group	

Now we have a content type which can be posted into a group.

Formatting groups

Out of the box, the groups module visually looks like any other page on the site. It is up to us to change that. This will involve:

1. Adding some user context to the group.
2. Using panels to structure the page.
3. Using views to pull in group content.

Adding some user context to the group

The next stage for us is to add a little bit of context to groups, something which tells the user how they are related to the group; that is, if they are a member, or an administrator, or the option to allow them to join the group. Once we have done that, we can take a look at our groups in action, and start to make them more feature rich.

To do this, we need to edit the fields for the group content type, from **Administration | Structure | Content types | Group | manage display**. From here we select **Group subscription** as the **Group type** field and save:

FIELD	LABEL	FORMAT
⊹ Group type	Above ▾	Group subscription ▾
⊹ Body	<Hidden> ▾	Default ▾

Hidden

No field is hidden.

Using panels to structure the group page

We can use the panel's module to structure the layout of the groups page, splitting the page up into a number of sections, one to describe the group, and another to pull in the group content.

This module will be used to detect if the page the user is viewing is a group, and if so to display it differently. The first stage is to go into **Administration | Structure | Pages** and **Enable** the **node_view** page. Once enabled, we should edit it to structure it, by clicking the **Edit** link. This allows us to edit how pages are displayed:

System	node_view	Node template	/node/%node	In code	Edit Enable

The following screenshot lists any variants of this page; let's add one by clicking the
Add a new variant link:

Home

| | Enable | Add variant |

Summary ▶	**Summary**
Variants	Get a summary of the information about this page.
No variants	When enabled, this overrides the default Drupal behavior for displaying nodes at *node/%node*. If you add variants, you may use selection criteria such as node type or language or user access to provide different views of nodes. If no variant is selected, the default Drupal node view will be used. This page only affects nodes viewed as pages, it will not affect nodes viewed in lists or at other locations. Also please note that if you are using pathauto, aliases may make a node to be somewhere else, but as far as Drupal is concerned, they are still at node/%node.
	This page has no variants and thus no output of its own.
	» Add a new variant

We should give the variant a name, such as Group, select **Panel** as the **Variant
type**, and check the **Selection rules** and **Contexts** optional features, before clicking
Create variant:

Home

| | Enable | Add variant |

Summary	**Add variant**
Variants	Add a new variant to this page.
No variants	

Title

Group

Administrative title of this variant. If you leave blank it will be automatically assigned.

Variant type

Panel ▾

Optional features

☑ Selection rules

☑ Contexts

Check any optional features you need to be presented with forms for configuring them. If you do not
check them here you will still be able to utilize these features once the new page is created. If you
are not sure, leave these unchecked.

(Create variant)

The next stage is to specify a selection rule, so that the panel only takes effect if the node is a group. We do this by selecting **OG: Node is a group**, and then clicking the **Add** button:

	Enable	Add variant	Configure

Summary

Variants

No variants

Configure   *Changed* 🔒

Configure a newly created variant prior to actually adding it to the page.

✅ Before this variant can be added, it must be configured. When you are finished, click "Create variant" at the end of this wizard to add this to your page.

Selection rules » Contexts » Choose layout » Panel settings » Panel content

If there is more than one variant on a page, when the page is visited each variant is given an opportunity to be displayed. Starting from the first variant and working to the last, each one tests to see if its selection rules will pass. The first variant that meets its criteria (as specified below) will be used.

TITLE	DESCRIPTION	

No criteria selected, this test will pass.

OG: Node is a group ▾	Add

⦿ All criteria must pass.
○ Only one criteria must pass.

Continue

You have unsaved changes to this page. You must select Save to write them to the database, or Cancel to discard these changes. Please note that if you have changed any form, you must submit that form before saving.

Save   Cancel

The criteria for this section rule should be when the node is being viewed, and the node **Is "Group content"**, then we click **Save**:

Add criteria   Close Window ⊠

Node   Node being viewed ▾

⦿ Is "Group content"

○ Is not "Group content"

Check to see if the node is of type "Group content".

☐ Reverse (NOT)

Save

We then click **Continue** to move onto the next section.

Next, under relationships we select **Group from node**, and click **Add relationship**:

RELATIONSHIPS	OPERATION
Group from node ▾	Add relationship

We can leave the settings for the relationship as they are, and click **Finish**:

Add relationship "Group from node"   Close Window ⊗

Get the group context from a node.

Node   Node being viewed ▾

Identifier   Group from node

Enter a name to identify this context on administrative screens.

Keyword   og_group

Enter a keyword to use for substitution in titles.

Finish   Cancel

Next we can choose the layout for our page; let's select the two column stacked layout:

Selection rules » Contexts » **Choose layout** » Panel settings » Panel content

Category
Columns: 2 ▾

Columns: 2

Two column   Two column bricks   Two column stacked

Back   Continue

To save this, we click **Continue**, then **Continue** again, then **Create variant**, and then **Update and save**. We now have our new panel set up. What we don't yet have is any group specific information being imported into our Panel. After saving the variant, we are shown the different parts of the two column stacked layout. Next to the **Left side** block, we need to click the little cog icon and then click **Add content**:

> **Left side**

Under the **Node** section we should select the **body field**. This will first display the description we entered when we created the group:

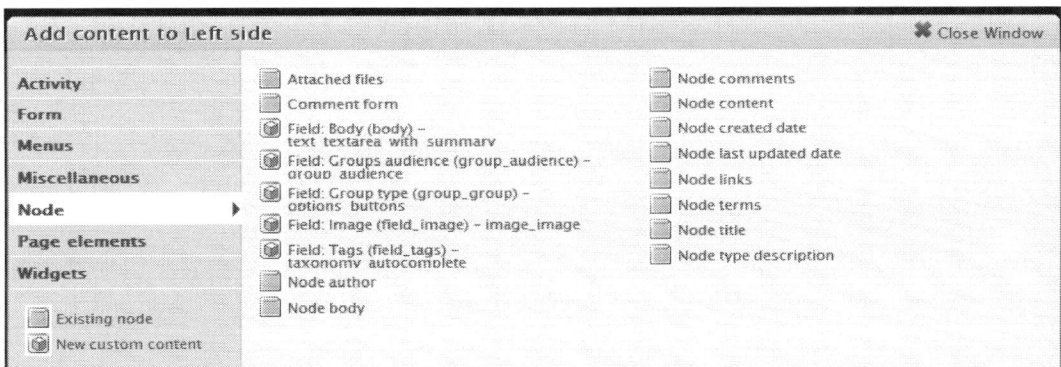

Add content to Left side   ✖ Close Window

Activity

Form

Menus

Miscellaneous

Node ▶

Page elements

Widgets

Existing node

New custom content

Attached files
Comment form
Field: Body (body) – text textarea with summary
Field: Groups audience (group_audience) – group audience
Field: Group type (group_group) – options buttons
Field: Image (field_image) – image_image
Field: Tags (field_tags) – taxonomy autocomplete
Node author
Node body

Node comments
Node content
Node created date
Node last updated date
Node links
Node terms
Node title
Node type description

Under Formatter Options, we can provide a heading if we wish, then click **Continue** to save the formatter options, **Finish** to add the pane to the panel, and then **Update and save** to save the panel:

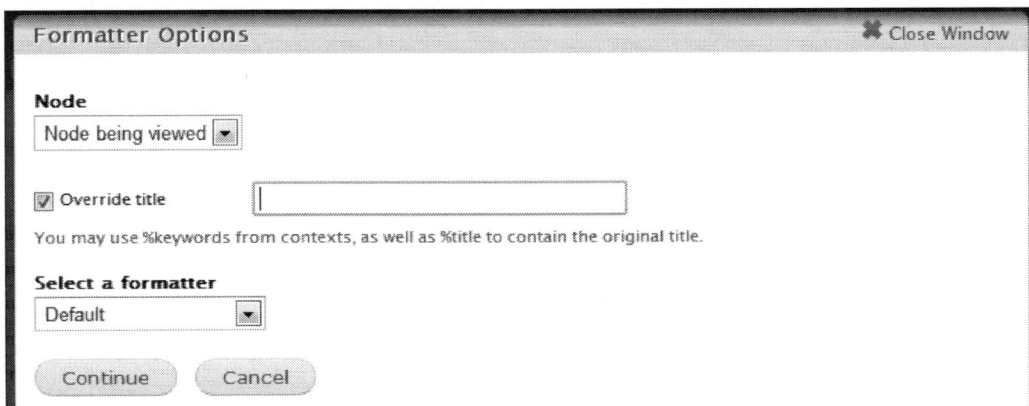

Formatter Options   ✖ Close Window

Node

Node being viewed ▾

☑ Override title [   ]

You may use %keywords from contexts, as well as %title to contain the original title.

Select a formatter

Default ▾

(Continue) (Cancel)

We should then repeat this process, selecting **Group type** as the field, which will pull in the users' membership status:

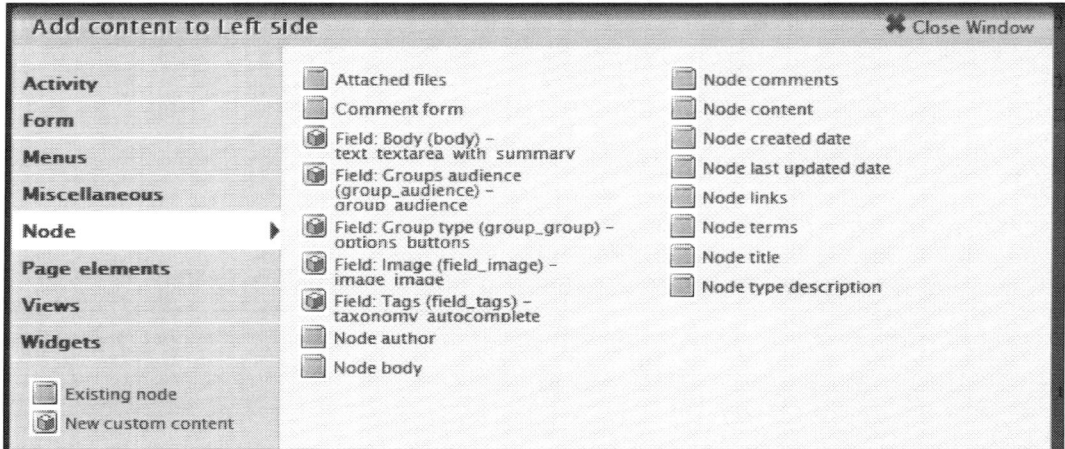

We should override the title with `Membership` and select the formatter of **Group subscription**:

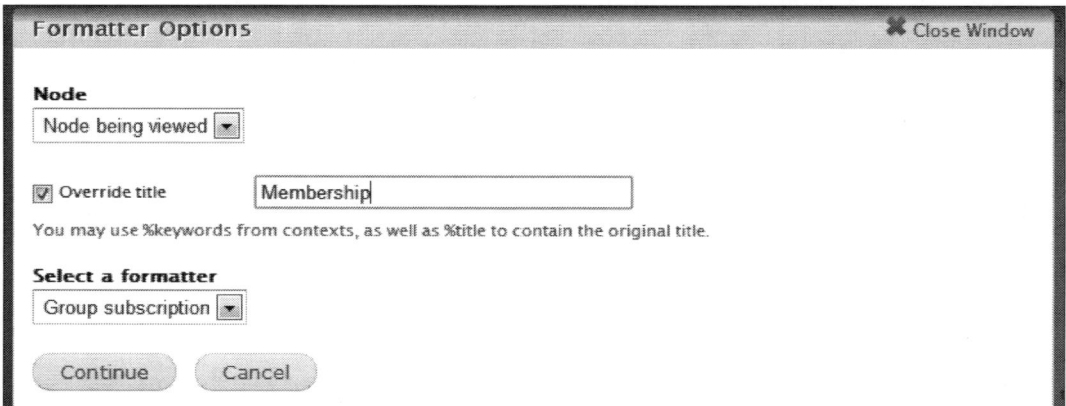

Click **Continue**, **Finish**, and **Update and save** to update the panels once again.

Using views to pull in group content

Now we need to pull the default Organic Group views into our group panel. On the right-hand side block, let's click **Add content**, and this time select **og_members** from views to add a list of group members to the page:

Add content to Right side   ✖ Close Window

Activity
Form
Menus
Miscellaneous
Node
Page elements
Views   ▶
Widgets

☐ Existing node
☐ New custom content

flag_bookmarks   og_members
flag_bookmarks_tab   og_nodes
og_list   rules_scheduler

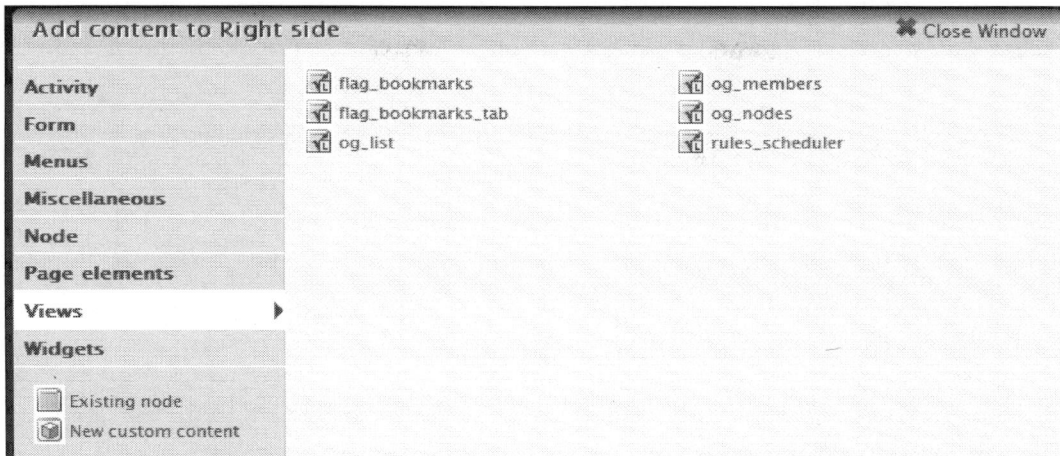

After selecting it, we should select **Block** as the display:

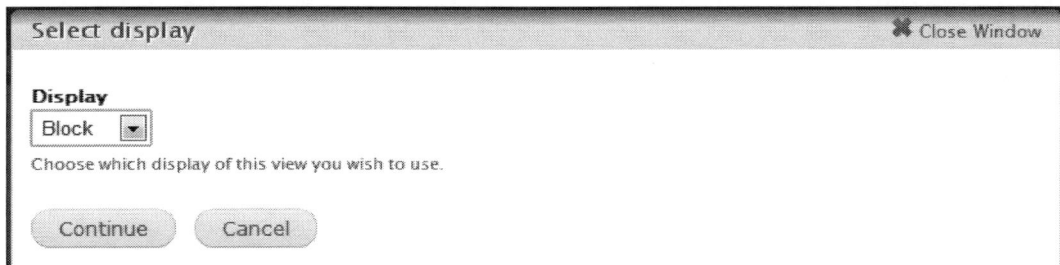

Select display   ✖ Close Window

Display
Block ▾

Choose which display of this view you wish to use.

(Continue)   (Cancel)

Let's override the title, and link it using the **Group ID** field:

Configure view og_members (Block)   ✖ Close Window

☑ Override title   Group Members

You may use %keywords from contexts, as well as %title to contain the original title.

Fields: Groups audience (group_audience) – gid
Group ID ▾

Please choose which context and how you would like it converted.

☑ Link title to view

To save this pane, we click **Finish** then **Update and save** once again.

Finally, let's add a list of group content to the left-hand side of the page; after clicking **Add content**, we need to select **og_nodes** from views and configure the block to link onto the **Group ID** field again:

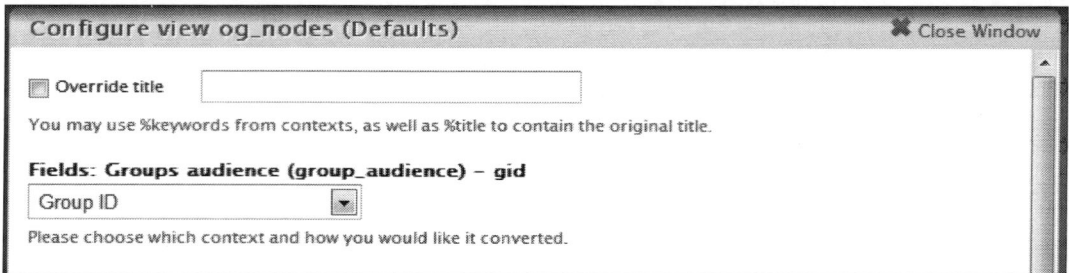

Configure view og_nodes (Defaults)   ✖ Close Window

☐ Override title

You may use %keywords from contexts, as well as %title to contain the original title.

Fields: Groups audience (group_audience) – gid

Group ID ▾

Please choose which context and how you would like it converted.

Now we have the organic groups, views, and panels modules working together to display a suitable page for each group.

Creating a group

To create a group, we simply add content and click the group content type, and supply a **Title** and **Body** content as usual:

Title *

T-Rex Owners Group

Group type *

◯ Not a group type

◉ Group type

Body (Edit summary)

Group for the support of T-Rex owners

Text format | Filtered HTML ▾ | More information about text formats ❓

- Web page addresses and e-mail addresses turn into links automatically.
- Allowed HTML tags: <a> <em> <strong> <cite> <blockquote> <code> <ul> <ol> <li> <dl> <dt> <dd>
- Lines and paragraphs break automatically.

Adding content to a group

Any content types which we created which are marked as group content can be added to our new group; we simply create the content as normal, and select the group on the create screen:

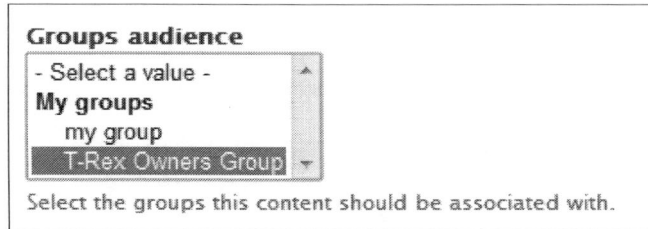

Groups audience

```
- Select a value -
My groups
   my group
   T-Rex Owners Group
```

Select the groups this content should be associated with.

Viewing our group

Now that we have the panels all set up, a new group created, and some content in that group, let's view the group and see what it looks like:

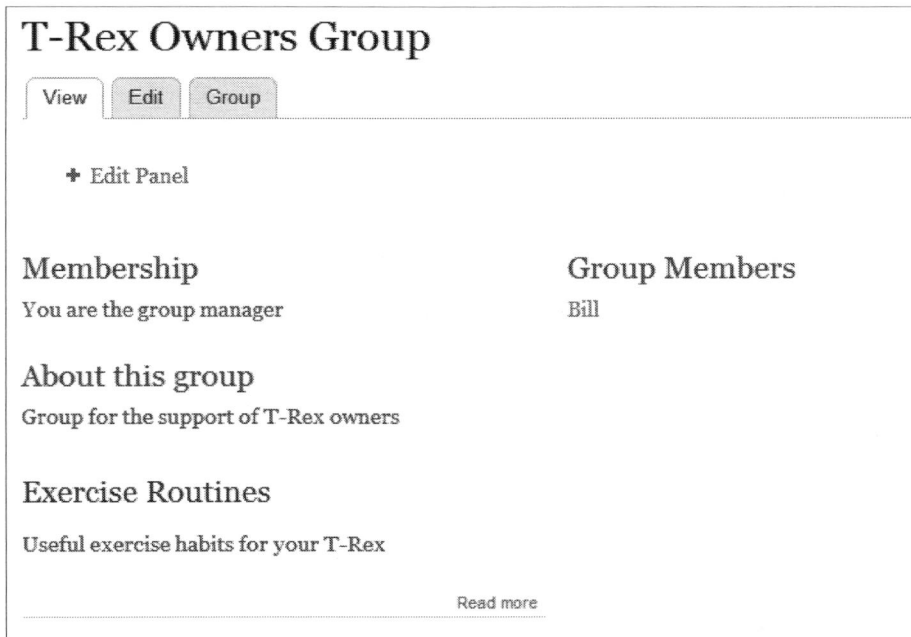

T-Rex Owners Group

| View | Edit | Group |

✦ Edit Panel

Membership
You are the group manager

About this group
Group for the support of T-Rex owners

Exercise Routines
Useful exercise habits for your T-Rex

Group Members
Bill

Read more

We have a list of group members on the right, our membership status at the top, followed by a description of the group, followed by recent content additions to the group. There is also a very handy link at the top to allow us to quickly edit the panel.

Commenting on user profiles

Unfortunately development on modules which allow users to comment on profiles of other users is still very much ongoing.

The guestbook module

At the moment, the most suitable working module is the guestbook module, as this provides each user with their own guestbook as part of their profile which other users can comment on. At the time of writing, this module is still very much "in development", but is still the most suitable for now.

Bill

| View | Bookmarks | Edit | My follow links | Relationships | Shortcuts | My guestbook | Contact |

Add guestbook entry

Message *

---

* No HTML tags allowed.
* Web page addresses and e-mail addresses turn into links automatically.
* Lines and paragraphs break automatically.

(Send)

What to look out for

There are however a number of other modules under development which are more suited to this type of feature. The most promising is a Facebook-style statuses (microblog) module (`http://drupal.org/project/facebook_status`). There is no Drupal 7 version available, however there is a discussion about how this is going to work at `http://drupal.org/node/671822`.

> **Get involved**
>
> Why not consider getting involved with module development? Even by simply providing feedback, and reporting issues to the developers to help them progress their modules.

Summary

In this chapter, we have really been able to develop our site into something social. Our users can connect with one another and build relationships thanks to the User Relationships module, and as a result they can keep up-to-date with what their connections are doing thanks to the heartbeat module. Users can communicate with one another, and thanks to the organic groups module, along with views and panels, they can collaborate in separate groups within our site.

With our site starting to take on a more social feel the next step is for us to add some social seasoning to our site.

6
Social Seasoning

With DinoSpace! starting to take shape in terms of social features, let's take a look at some of the various third-party social features which we can easily add to our site, to sprinkle in some additional "social seasoning". In this chapter you will learn how to:

- Encourage user discussion on pages using Disqus
- Enable users to share content on our site with users from other social networks using AddThis
- Leverage various Facebook and Twitter integration features, including:
    ° Like this page on Facebook
    ° Tweet this page on Twitter
    ° Find us on Facebook
    ° My latest tweets

Let's start seasoning our site with third-party social features.

Let's prepare our modules

Drupal already has support to integrate with some of these features thanks to some of the existing modules available. Let's start by first downloading and installing these modules now to save us time later. The two available modules are:

- Disqus module: `http://drupal.org/project/disqus`
- AddThis module: `http://drupal.org/project/addthis`

Encouraging discussion with Disqus

Disqus is a feature rich commenting system, which also helps reduce the barrier by preventing anonymous users from registering and commenting on our site. Features of the Disqus comment system include:

- Social integration allowing users to use their credentials from third-party social networks to log in and then share their comment
- Discussions continually updated in real time
- Comments can be posted through e-mail and mobile devices
- Comments and discussions can be followed over a range of different websites; our users won't be restricted to just ours
- Comments can be rated, and poorly rated comments can be hidden from the conversation if they don't add value

Register for Disqus

To use the Disqus module we need to register our site to use Disqus:

1. This can be done from the registration page: `http://disqus.com/admin/register/`.
2. Here we simply enter a few short details about our website, and a few details about us as the primary moderator, and click **Continue**:

Register your site to use Disqus (it's free)

Site URL	http:// localhost/drupal7/	ex. http://example.com
Site Name	Dino Space	ex. My Example Blog
Site Shortname	dinospace	Used to uniquely identify your site on Disqus. No spaces; only letters, numbers, and hyphens. You can log in at **dinospace**.disqus.com

Primary Moderator

Create a new Disqus account below in order to manage this site. This account will be the primary moderator. *Already have a profile?*

Username	dinospace	Your commenter profile will be at disqus.com/dinospace
Password	••••••••	At least 6 characters.
Email address	mkpeacock+dinospace@gmail.com	Must be valid. No spam from us, promise.

Continue ➡

3. The next stage of the process presents us with a range of features which we can enable for our site. These include:

   ° The language of our site
   ° Our Twitter username, this is for any comments which are tweeted
   ° Allowing media to be attached to a comment
   ° If a user is not logged in, we can select which login buttons to display, including Facebook, Twitter, OpenID, and Yahoo!
   ° Trackbacks
   ° Spam protection
   ° Reactions

Quick Setup

You can always change these settings later, so no problem if you just skip this step and continue.

Language [English ▼]

Optional Features

Twitter @Replies
Optional: Set a Twitter username for tweeted comments to @reply.
[dino_space]

☐ **Disable Like Buttons**

☑ **Media Attachments**

☑ Trackbacks

☐ Akismet

☑ Reactions
[Select all services] [Reset]
  ☑ FriendFeed
  ☑ Twitter
  ☑ Digg
  ☑ Reddit
  ☑ Hacker News

< You may choose to enable a feature by clicking on it.

Hovering over will display detailed information in this spot.

☑ **Display login buttons with comment box**

☑ Facebook   ☑ Twitter   ☑ OpenID

☑ Yahoo!

---

4. Once we have our Disqus account setup, we can configure the module. Configuration options for the module can be accessed from **Configure | Disqus**. Here we need to enter the **Shortname** for our site, which we entered when registering our site with Disqus:

The following provides the general configuration options for the Disqus comment web service.

Shortname
[dinospace]

The website shortname that you registered Disqus with. If you registered http://example.disqus.com, you would enter "example" here.

---

5. Next we can select which node types we want to enable Disqus on, where we want the comments to be displayed (either in a block or in the main content area), and the weight of the comments with respect to other page elements:

Visibility		

Behavior

Node Types

☑ Blog entry

☑ Poll

☐ Forum topic

☑ Article

☑ Book page

☑ Basic page

☐ Simplenews newsletter

☐ Test content type

Apply comments to only the following node types.

Location

Content Area ▾

Display the Disqus comments in the given location. When "Block" is selected, the comments will appear in the Disqus Comments block.

Weight

50 ▾

When the comments are displayed in the content area, you can change the position at which they will be shown.

Why not forum topics?

Comments posted with Disqus are stored on the Disqus servers, so when we do a search comments won't be included in the results. For most content this won't be a problem, but for discussion topics the comments form an integral part of the topic, and our users will want to search the comments when searching the site.

6. Next we need to enter our Disqus API Key, and, since our Drupal install is running on our local computer, select the **Testing** checkbox. The API key can be found at the following website: `http://disqus.com/api/get_my_key/`. Simply copy it and paste it into the appropriate form on our Drupal install:

Visibility	**User API Key**
Behavior	My-API-Key

The API key of the administrator account on Disqus. You can get yours here.

☑ Testing

When enabled, uses the disqus_developer flag to tell Disqus that you are in a testing environment. Threads will not display on the public community page with this set.

7. The final option we need to set is the permissions for our users. We need to go to **People | Permissions** and select the appropriate options from within **Disqus**:

Disqus

Administer Disqus Perform administrative actions with Disqus.	☐	☐	☑	☐
View Disqus comments Allows access to view Disqus comments.	☑	☑	☑	☑
Disqus comments in profile When enabled, will display Disqus comments on the profiles of users belonging to this role.	☐	☑	☑	☑

8. Now we have Disqus set up and enabled for our site, if we view some of our content we can see the Disqus comment options:

👍 Like 💬   🔒 ⚙ DISQUS ▾

Add New Comment   Logout

Type your comment here.

+ Image | Post as dinospace

Showing 0 comments   Sort by popular now ▾

✉ Subscribe by email 🔊 RSS

Now our users can comment using the Disqus platform, which provides a range of additional features out of the box, acting as a big improvement on the standard comments within Drupal.

Sharing content with AddThis

AddThis is a service which makes it easy for website visitors to share content they like with others using a range of social networking and social bookmarking websites. To use AddThis with our site, we simply need to sign up for an account, install the module, enter our username, and place the AddThis block in a suitable part of our site:

Once we have registered at `addthis.com`, we need to keep a note of our AddThis username, as we will need it for the next stage. Configuration options for the module can be found through the administration area within **Configuration | Add This**. Here, we simply enter our AddThis username, select the **Display on node pages** checkbox, and the module is set up and configured:

GENERAL SETTINGS

Username

dinospace

Your username for addthis.com. Example: my-username

☑ Display on node pages

Display an AddThis button always on a node page's links section.

☐ Display in node teasers

Display an AddThis button in the node teasers.

The final stage is to enable the **Add this button block** by selecting the region of the page we want to display it on. **Sidebar second** will place it on the right-hand side of the page:

Sidebar second

✛ Add this button*   Sidebar second ▾   configure

Now when we visit a node page on our site we have the **Addthis** button on the right-hand side. Hovering over the button will show the various sites we can quickly share this page with at the click of a button:

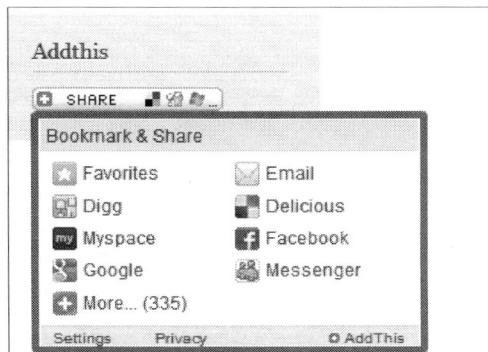

Addthis

❶ SHARE

Bookmark & Share

⭐ Favorites   ✉ Email
🔲 Digg   ◼ Delicious
my Myspace   f Facebook
🔳 Google   👥 Messenger
➕ More... (335)

Settings   Privacy   ⚙ AddThis

With this feature in place, our users can easily share our quality content with their friends, and hopefully bring new members to our site over time.

Leverage other features

Established social networks such as Facebook and Twitter provide additional nuggets of social interaction which we can integrate on our own site, including:

- Like this page on Facebook
- Tweet this page on Twitter
- Find us on Facebook
- Embedding our latest tweets

Let's look at how we can integrate these into our site.

Like this on Facebook

Many websites now display a link to allow users to indicate that they like a particular page and notify their friends on Facebook of this page. This feature also indicates the total number of users who like the page, and if any of those are the user's friends, it will display their names and / or photographs.

Enabling PHP in content blocks

We will embed the Facebook like button in the Drupal footer; however we need to make use of PHP in the block for this to work. By default, Drupal 7 does not allow PHP code to be entered into blocks, so we need to enable this module from the module list:

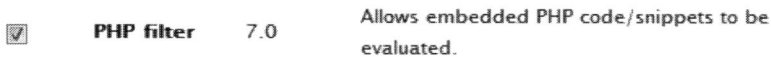

☑	**PHP filter**	7.0	Allows embedded PHP code/snippets to be evaluated.

Once enabled (by clicking **Save**), we now have a link to view permissions associated with the module, which we need to view so that we can allow administrators to use the new filter:

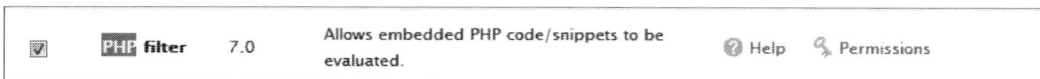

☑	**PHP filter**	7.0	Allows embedded PHP code/snippets to be evaluated.	ⓘ Help	🔑 Permissions

We need to ensure that administrators and only administrators can use the PHP code text format from the permission screen:

> Use the PHP code text format
> *Warning: This permission may have security implications depending on how the text format is configured.*

Once saved, we can now add PHP to our content blocks.

Like this page

The Facebook developer website contains a list of various tools and APIs which are available to developers and website owners. There is a section for the like feature at `http://developers.facebook.com/docs/reference/plugins/like/`. This page provides a tool for generating the code we need to allow our users to like a particular page. You should use this tool with a test web address to get the latest code direct from Facebook. Where the URL appears in the code we will dynamically insert the URL of the page the user is currently viewing.

Creating the block

Now that we can use PHP in our content blocks and we have the code from the Facebook developer website, we need to create a new content block for our site. The contents of the block are as follows:

```
<iframe src="http://www.facebook.com/plugins/like.php?href=
  <?php

    $path = isset($_GET['q']) ? $_GET['q'] : '<front>';
    $link = url($path, array('absolute' => TRUE));

    echo urlencode( $link );
  ?>
  &amp;layout=standard&amp;show_faces=true&amp;width=450&amp;
    action=like&amp;font&amp;colorscheme=light&amp;height=80"
    scrolling="no" frameborder="0" style="border:none;
    overflow:hidden; width:450px; height:80px;"
    allowTransparency="true"></iframe>
```

Downloading the example code

You can download the example code files for all Packt books you have purchased from your account at http://www.PacktPub.com. If you purchased this book elsewhere, you can visit http://www.PacktPub.com/support and register to have the files e-mailed directly to you.

As you can see, where the page URL goes, we tell our Drupal installation to build a URL equivalent to the page the user is currently on. The URL is then URL encoded so that it can form part of a valid web address.

We probably won't want to enter a title for the block as we will just want the Facebook like button on its own. We need to remember to select a section of the page for the block to appear on; I recommend **Triptych first**, which is just above the footer.

> **Some themes don't call it a footer...**
>
> Take a look at the block area options for the theme you are using and select a name and location to use.

Block description *

```
Like this on Facebook
```

A brief description of your block. Used on the Blocks administration page.

Block title

```

```

The title of the block as shown to the user.

Block body *

```
<iframe src="http://www.facebook.com/plugins/like.php?href=<?php

$path = isset($_GET['q']) ? $_GET['q'] : '<front>';
$link = url($path, array('absolute' => TRUE));

echo urlencode( $link );
?
>&amp;layout=standard&amp;show_faces=true&amp;width=450&amp;action=like&amp;font&amp;colorscheme=light&amp;height=80" scrolling="no" frameborder="0" style="border:none; overflow:hidden; width:450px; height:80px;" allowTransparency="true"></iframe>
```

Text format `PHP code` ▾   More information about text formats ⊘

• You may post PHP code. You should include <?php ?> tags.

Now if we look at the bottom of our pages we see the Facebook like button, and as we have just added it, a message asking us to be the first of our friends to like the page:

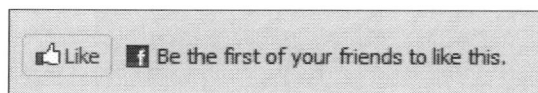

👍 Like   f Be the first of your friends to like this.

Tweet this

Similar to Facebook's Like this page, Twitter has a tool for building a Tweet button. Unlike the Facebook method this doesn't require the URL of the page to be included in the code. We can simply go to their Tweet button generator and select the type of button we want to use. This can be found at `http://twitter.com/about/resources/tweetbutton`:

Tweet Button

Add this button to your website to let people share content on Twitter without having to leave the page. Promote strategic Twitter accounts at the same time while driving traffic to your website.

1 Choose your button. Customize it (optional).

Button	Tweet text	URL	Language

○ Vertical count ○ Horizontal count ○ No count

6,314

🐦 Tweet   🐦 Tweet 6,314   🐦 Tweet

2 Recommend people to follow (optional).

Recommend up to two Twitter accounts for users to follow after they share content from your website. These accounts could include your own, or that of a contributor or a partner.

1. dino_space — This user will be @ mentioned in the suggested Tweet
2. Related account — Related account description

Preview your button, grab your code. Done!

Your Tweet Button will look like this. Click on it to try it out!

24.8K

🐦 Tweet

55px x 62px

Copy and paste this code into the HTML for your website wherever you want the button to appear.

```
<a href="http://twitter.com/share" class="twitter-share-button" data-count="vertical" data-via="dino_space">Tweet</a><script type="text/javascript" src="http://platform.twitter.com/widgets.js"></script>
```

The code generated will be similar to the following code, we simply copy it and create a new block (using Full HTML as the filter type):

```
<a href="http://twitter.com/share" class="twitter-share-button" data-count="vertical" data-via="dino_space">Tweet</a><script type="text/javascript" src="http://platform.twitter.com/widgets.js"></script>
```

Once saved and inserted into the block and the block is positioned into our site, we have a Tweet button installed on our site too! When a user clicks this, it will allow them to tweet about the current page of our site which they are on:

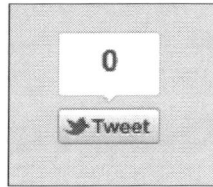

Find us on Facebook

Facebook also has a Like Box plugin, which can be added to a block on our site. This plugin would give the user a snippet of information about our Facebook profile and encourage them to link up with us through Facebook too.

The use of this feature will depend greatly on the type of social network you are setting up; if sites like Facebook compete directly with you then you won't want to encourage your visitors to use it. On the other hand, you might want to encourage your users to promote your social network to their friends through other existing social networks.

More information on the plugin is available at `http://developers.facebook.com/docs/reference/plugins/like-box/`, along with a tool to build the code needed to go into a block on the site.

Latest tweets

Twitter also has a widget generator which will allow us to embed our latest tweets into our own website, which is available at `http://twitter.com/about/resources/widgets/widget_profile`. This code could be put into a block on our site to list the latest tweets we have made to our DinoSpace! official Twitter account.

Summary

With the features discussed in this chapter we can now easily leverage a range of third-party tools and features to add a range of simple social features to our social network, and to any other Drupal site we build in the future. These features included use of the Disqus comments system, sharing content with AddThis, and integration with some social nuggets from Twitter and Facebook.

7
Module Development: Rapidly Improve your Social Network

During the course of this book, we have seen just how powerful Drupal's modular structure is by downloading and installing new modules to extend our site. Until now, we have almost exclusively used existing modules to extend our site. In this chapter, we will look into the module system in more detail and create new functionality for the site following a "crash course" in module development. In this chapter, you will learn the following:

- The basics of how Drupal's modular system works
- How to create new custom content types
- How to rapidly develop a module
- How to create new custom content types as part of the module installation process
- How to use Google Maps within our module
- About other useful APIs which are available for us

An important disclaimer

Drupal's module system contains a huge wealth of features, and to fully explain it and provide a tutorial for it would require a book in its own right. As such, the main focus of this chapter is to illustrate how the module system can be used to rapidly extend our social network. This chapter certainly isn't an example of how modules should be created, and many best practices are ignored for the sake of speed. If you would like to know more about module development, see the *Useful resources* section of this chapter.

Let's get started by discussing what we are going to develop in this crash course learning chapter.

Dinosaur-friendly venues

We will develop a customizable, map-based directory of dinosaur-friendly places / venues, as recommended by users on our site. This will involve creating two new content types as follows:

- **Dinosaur-friendly venues**: These contain details of a dinosaur-friendly venue, including new fields for the latitude and longitude of the venue, so that we can plot it on a map.

- **Map of dinosaur friendly venues**: This is a map, centred at a specific latitude and longitude, with a specific width, height, and zoom level to act as a container for some of the dinosaur-friendly venues.

Useful resources

The following are some useful resources for us to further our learning and understanding of the Drupal module system:

- Drupal 7 Module Development: `https://www.packtpub.com/drupal-7-module-development/book`

- Beginner's Guide to Drupal 7 Fields: `https://www.packtpub.com/drupal-7-fields-cck-beginners-guide/book`

- Drupal 7 API: `http://api.drupal.org/api/drupal`

Building our module

Modules are built up of a number of different files:

- **Installation files**: These files contain code which is executed when a module is installed and uninstalled
- **Info files:** These files contain basic information about the module, including the name and Drupal core they are compatible with
- **Module files**: These files contain the logic behind the module
- **Optional templates**: These files are used to override the layout and design of the pages (suggestions)

For each module we want to create we need to create some, if not all of these files. Detailed documentation for them is available on the Drupal website:

- Install files: `http://drupal.org/node/876250`
- Info files: `http://drupal.org/node/542202`
- Template suggestions: `http://drupal.org/node/1089656`

Let's get started with building our modules, and begin by creating the relevant `.install` files.

Installation files

When we enable our modules, Drupal will automatically look for an `.install` file to run as part of the module installation process. We can use these files to automatically create new types of content within our site.

As part of the Drupal API documentation, there is an `example` module which illustrates how we can create modules which implement their own type of node. We can make use of this as a basis for our own module, and follow their approach to the installation process. Documentation can be viewed on the Drupal website along with the source code for the `example` file at `http://api.drupal.org/api/examples/node_example--node_example.install/7`.

Within the install file we need to implement two hooks as follows:

- `hook_install`: This is called as part of the install process, and will house our code for setting up the appropriate content types
- `hook_uninstall`: This is called as part of the uninstall process, and will house code for removing information when the module is uninstalled

There are a number of functions we need to make use of within our install hooks, these will allow us to create the content type, create new fields, and to associate them with our new content types:

- `node_type_save`: This saves the content type; documentation for the function is on the Drupal API web page: `http://api.drupal.org/api/drupal/modules--node--node.module/function/node_type_save`.

- `field_create_field`: This creates a new field within Drupal; documentation for the function is on the Drupal API web page: `http://api.drupal.org/api/drupal/modules--field--field.crud.inc/function/field_create_field/7`.

- `field_create_instance`: This creates a new instance of a field, and binds it to a bundle, which for us means binding it to our new content type. Documentation for the function is on the Drupal API web page: `http://api.drupal.org/api/drupal/modules--field--field.crud.inc/function/field_create_instance/7`.

Let's start creating our install files for our modules.

Map installer: dino_friendly_places/dfp_map.install

The map installer needs to create a new content type for our map, and needs to support the following new fields:

- Position to center the map
  - Longitude
  - Latitude

- Zoom level of the map
- Size of the map
  - Width
  - Height

The install file needs to be created as `dfp_map.install` within the `sites/all/modules/dino_friendly_places` folder:

```php
<?php

function dfp_map_install() {
  $t = get_t();
```

The first aspect of the install function is to create the new content type; we need to set the properties of the content type, including the type itself, name, and description.

```php
$dino_friendly_places_map = array(
  'type' => 'dino_friendly_places_map',
  'name' => $t('Map of Dinosaur Friendly Places'),
  'base' => 'node_content',
  'description' => $t('A map listing dinosaur friendly places.'),
  'body_label' => $t('Map Description')
);
```

Any properties which we haven't set, we then need to lookup the defaults for using the node_type_set_defaults function:

```php
$content_type = node_type_set_defaults($dino_friendly_places_map);
node_add_body_field($content_type);
```

Then we save the content type:

```php
node_type_save($content_type);

$body_instance = field_info_instance('node', 'body', 'dino_friendly_places_map');

$body_instance['display']['example_node_list'] = array(
  'label' => 'hidden',
  'type' => 'text_summary_or_trimmed',
);

field_update_instance($body_instance);
```

For all of the fields we have, we need to then create the field, using the field_create_field function and then create an instance and associate it with the content type using the field_create_instance field. The details of these fields are to be defined later within the file:

```php
foreach (_dfp_map_installed_fields() as $field) {
  field_create_field($field);
}

foreach (_dfp_map_installed_instances() as $instance) {
  $instance['entity_type'] = 'node';
  $instance['bundle'] = $dino_friendly_places_map['type'];
  field_create_instance($instance);
}
}
```

We need to define the actual fields we are going to create and associate with the content type. Some of these fields need to be numeric; we can find the details of what we need to set the type property to from the documentation at `http://api.` `drupal.org/api/drupal/modules--field--modules--number--number.module/` `function/number_field_info/7`.

For each field, we define a name, the number of them to be displayed on the content create/edit form (cardinality), the type, and any additional settings including the maximum length of the field:

```
function _dfp_map_installed_fields() {
  $t = get_t();
  return array(
    'dfp_map_longitude' => array(
      'field_name' => 'dfp_map_longitude',
      'cardinality' => 1,
      'type'        => 'number_float',
      'settings'    => array(
        'max_length' => 60,
      ),
    ),
    'dfp_map_latitude' => array(
      'field_name' => 'dfp_map_latitude',
      'cardinality' => 1,
      'type'        => 'number_float',
      'settings'    => array(
        'max_length' => 60,
      ),
    ),
    'dfp_map_zoom' => array(
      'field_name' => 'dfp_map_zoom',
      'cardinality' => 1,
      'type'        => 'number_integer',
      'settings'    => array(
        'max_length' => 60,
      ),
    ),
    'dfp_map_width' => array(
      'field_name' => 'dfp_map_width',
      'cardinality' => 1,
      'type'        => 'number_integer',
      'settings'    => array(
        'max_length' => 60,
      ),
```

```
    ),
    'dfp_map_height' => array(
      'field_name' => 'dfp_map_height',
      'cardinality' => 1,
      'type'        => 'number_integer',
      'settings'    => array(
        'max_length' => 60,
      ),
    ),
  );
}
```

The field definition process is repeated; however, this defines how the content is displayed, created, and edited, and how it interacts with the field's API:

```
function _dfp_map_installed_instances() {
  $t = get_t();
  return array(
    'dfp_map_longitude' => array(
      'field_name' => 'dfp_map_longitude',
      'label'      => $t('The longitude for the central point of the
map.'),
      'widget'     => array(
        'type'     => 'text_textfield',
      ),
      'display' => array(
        'example_node_list' => array(
          'label' => 'hidden',
          'type' => 'hidden',
        ),
      ),
    ),

    'dfp_map_latitude' => array(
      'field_name' => 'dfp_map_latitude',
      'label'      => $t('The latitude for the central point of the
map.'),
      'widget'     => array(
        'type'     => 'text_textfield',
      ),
      'display' => array(
        'example_node_list' => array(
          'label' => 'hidden',
          'type' => 'hidden',
        ),
```

```
      ),
    ),

    'dfp_map_zoom' => array(
      'field_name' => 'dfp_map_zoom',
      'label'      => $t('The zoom level for the map.'),
      'widget'     => array(
        'type'     => 'text_textfield',
      ),
      'display' => array(
        'example_node_list' => array(
          'label' => 'hidden',
          'type' => 'hidden',
        ),
      ),
    ),

    'dfp_map_width' => array(
      'field_name' => 'dfp_map_width',
      'label'      => $t('The width of the map.'),
      'widget'     => array(
        'type'     => 'text_textfield',
      ),
      'display' => array(
        'example_node_list' => array(
          'label' => 'hidden',
          'type' => 'hidden',
        ),
      ),
    ),

    'dfp_map_height' => array(
      'field_name' => 'dfp_map_height',
      'label'      => $t('The height of the map.'),
      'widget'     => array(
        'type'     => 'text_textfield',
      ),
      'display' => array(
        'example_node_list' => array(
          'label' => 'hidden',
          'type' => 'hidden',
        ),
      ),
```

```
        ),

    );
}
```

The uninstall process then removes any content we have created which is of this content type:

```
function dfp_map_uninstall() {

  $sql = 'SELECT nid FROM {node} n WHERE n.type = :type';
  $result = db_query($sql, array(':type' => 'dino_friendly_places_
map'));
  $nids = array();
  foreach ($result as $row) {
    $nids[] = $row->nid;
  }

  node_delete_multiple($nids);

  foreach (array_keys(_dfp_map_installed_fields()) as $field) {
    field_delete_field($field);
  }

  $instances = field_info_instances('node', 'dino_friendly_places_
map');
  foreach ($instances as $instance_name => $instance) {
    field_delete_instance($instance);
  }

  node_type_delete('dino_friendly_places_map');

  field_purge_batch(1000);
}
```

Venue installer: dino_friendly_places/dfp_venue. install

The venue installer is structured in the same way as the map installer. The additional fields we need to create with the content type are as follows:

- The longitude coordinate of the venue
- The latitude coordinate of the venue

The following code saved as our install file will set up the venue content type for us:

```php
<?php

function dfp_venue_install() {

  $t = get_t();

  $dino_friendly_places_venue = array(
    'type' => 'dino_friendly_places_venue',
    'name' => $t('Dinosaur friendly place'),
    'base' => 'node_content',
    'description' => $t('A dinosaur friendly place.'),
    'body_label' => $t('Venue Description')
  );

  $content_type = node_type_set_defaults($dino_friendly_places_venue);
  node_add_body_field($content_type);

  node_type_save($content_type);

  $body_instance = field_info_instance('node', 'body', 'dino_friendly_
places_venue');

  $body_instance['display']['example_node_list'] = array(
    'label' => 'hidden',
    'type' => 'text_summary_or_trimmed',
  );

  field_update_instance($body_instance);

  foreach (_dfp_venue_installed_fields() as $field) {
    field_create_field($field);
  }

  foreach (_dfp_venue_installed_instances() as $instance) {
    $instance['entity_type'] = 'node';
    $instance['bundle'] = $dino_friendly_places_venue['type'];
    field_create_instance($instance);
  }
}

function _dfp_venue_installed_fields() {
  $t = get_t();
```

```
    return array(
      'dfp_venue_longitude' => array(
        'field_name' => 'dfp_venue_longitude',
        'cardinality' => 1,
        'type'        => 'number_float',
        'settings'    => array(
          'max_length' => 60,
        ),
      ),
      'dfp_venue_latitude' => array(
        'field_name' => 'dfp_venue_latitude',
        'cardinality' => 1,
        'type'        => 'number_float',
        'settings'    => array(
          'max_length' => 60,
        ),
      ),
    );
}


function _dfp_venue_installed_instances() {
  $t = get_t();
  return array(
    'dfp_venue_longitude' => array(
      'field_name' => 'dfp_venue_longitude',
      'label'        => $t('The longitude for the central point of the
map.'),
      'widget'       => array(
        'type'      => 'text_textfield',
      ),
      'display' => array(
        'example_node_list' => array(
          'label' => 'hidden',
          'type' => 'hidden',
        ),
      ),
    ),

    'dfp_venue_latitude' => array(
      'field_name' => 'dfp_venue_latitude',
      'label'        => $t('The latitude for the central point of the
map.'),
      'widget'       => array(
```

```
        'type'    => 'text_textfield',
      ),
      'display' => array(
        'example_node_list' => array(
          'label' => 'hidden',
          'type' => 'hidden',
        ),
      ),
    ),


  );
}


function dfp_venue_uninstall() {

  $sql = 'SELECT nid FROM {node} n WHERE n.type = :type';
  $result = db_query($sql, array(':type' => 'dino_friendly_places_
venue'));
  $nids = array();
  foreach ($result as $row) {
    $nids[] = $row->nid;
  }

  node_delete_multiple($nids);

  foreach (array_keys(_dfp_venue_installed_fields()) as $field) {
    field_delete_field($field);
  }

  $instances = field_info_instances('node', 'dino_friendly_places_
venue');
  foreach ($instances as $instance_name => $instance) {
    field_delete_instance($instance);
  }

  node_type_delete('dino_friendly_places_venue');

  field_purge_batch(1000);
}
```

Module information files

The module information files define the name and description of the module, as well as the Drupal core version they are compatible with. As we are creating two related modules, we should also define a package for them, and ensure this is the same for both modules. This will group them together in the modules list. Full details of these files are available on the Drupal website: `http://drupal.org/node/542202`.

Map information file

The map information file (containing the following) will be called `dfp_map.info` and saved in the `sites/all/modules/dino_friendly_places` folder.

```
name = DFP Map
description = A map of various dinosaur friendly places
core = 7.x
package = "Dinosaur Friendly Places"
```

Venue information file

The venue information file (containing the following) will be called `dfp_venue.info` and saved in the `sites/all/modules/dino_friendly_places` folder:

```
name = DFP Venue
description = A dinosaur friendly venue
core = 7.x
package = "Dinosaur Friendly Places"
```

Module files

Any functionality we wish to associate with our new modules and content types need to be put into a `.module` file. These module files then implement various Drupal hooks to extend the default functionality of the content type and of Drupal.

Create the map module file

The module file for the map needs to be called `dfp_map.module` and saved in the `sites/all/modules/dino_friendly_places` folder. The first bit of code within this file provides a description for the module within the Administration help section:

```php
<?php

function dfp_map_help( $path, $arg ) {
    switch( $path )
    {
```

```
        case 'admin/help#dino_friendly_places':
            return '<p>' . t("Maps dinosaur friendly places created by
users") . '</p>';
            break;
    }
}
```

To add functionality to the view page of a node of this content type, we need to implement the `node_view` hook, which is executed when a node of that type is viewed:

```
function dfp_map_node_view( $node )
{
```

Within this hook, we need to add Google Maps JavaScript to our Drupal installation, to do this we can use the `drupal_add_js` function which will add JavaScript within the page's head tag.

```
    drupal_add_js('http://maps.google.com/maps/api/js?sensor=false',
'external');
```

Once the JavaScript has been added, we need to build a list of venues which we will populate into the map. This can be done by executing a query, which looks for nodes that are of type `dino_friendly_places_venue` and joining the nodes onto their appropriate longitude and latitude coordinates:

```
    $points = "";
    $sql = "SELECT
            n.nid, v.title, lat.dfp_venue_latitude_value as latitude,
lon.dfp_venue_longitude_value as longitude
            FROM node n LEFT JOIN node_revision v ON ( n.vid=v.vid )
            LEFT JOIN field_revision_body b ON ( n.vid=b.revision_id )
            LEFT JOIN field_revision_dfp_venue_latitude lat ON (
n.vid=lat.revision_id )
            LEFT JOIN field_revision_dfp_venue_longitude lon ON (
n.vid=lon.revision_id )
            WHERE n.type='dino_friendly_places_venue' ";
    $result = db_query( $sql );
    foreach( $result as $row )
    {
```

For each node we find in the database, we then build some JavaScript code which will add the point to the map; the point is set to pop up an "InfoWindow" which contains a link to allow the user to click through to view the venue detail page:

```
        $points .= "

        var location = new google.maps.LatLng( {$row->latitude}, {$row-
>longitude} );
```

```
        var marker = new google.maps.Marker({position: location, map:
map });
        var infowindow = new google.maps.InfoWindow({ content:
\"<strong><a href='node/{$row->nid}'>{$row->title}</a></strong>\"  });
        google.maps.event.addListener(marker, 'click', function() {
          infowindow.open(map,marker);
        });
      ";
    }
```

We then take the details from the map node itself, including the longitude and latitude of the coordinates to centre the map on, and the zoom level, to build the JavaScript to generate the map itself. We then combine the JavaScript of points we generated earlier and the result is the completed JavaScript which we need:

```
    $longitude = $node->dfp_map_longitude['und'][0]['value'];
    $latitude = $node->dfp_map_latitude['und'][0]['value'];
    $zoom = $node->dfp_map_zoom['und'][0]['value'];

    $js = "
    function initialize() {
        var latlng = new google.maps.LatLng({$latitude}, {$longitude});
        var myOptions = {
          zoom: {$zoom},
          center: latlng,
          mapTypeId: google.maps.MapTypeId.ROADMAP
        };
        var map = new google.maps.Map(document.getElementById('map_
canvas'), myOptions);
        " . $points . "
    }


    jQuery(document).ready(function () { initialize(); });

    ";
```

Finally, we add the JavaScript to the page, allowing the map to display:

```
    drupal_add_js( $js , 'inline');
}
```

Venue: no module file required

To view a venue, we only need to display details related to the venue itself; as such we don't need any custom module code since we don't need to perform any additional logic.

Template files

To override the display of the map page and the venue page we can use a suggestion (more on that in *Chapter 8, Themes*); this is a special template which is used when viewing a node of a particular content type. We can do this by creating the following template files in the `/themes/bartik/templates` folder:

`node--dino_friendly_places_map.tpl.php`

`node--dino_friendly_places_venue.tpl.php`

Map: node--dino_friendly_places_map.tpl.php

Within the map template we need to extract the page content / map description, the width of the map, and the height of the map from the node itself, and use this information to display a `<div>` to contain our map. All of the logic to generate the map is part of the module file itself:

```
<div id="node-<?php print $node->nid; ?>" class="<?php print $classes;
?> clearfix"<?php print $attributes; ?>>

  <?php print render($title_prefix); ?>
  <?php if (!$page): ?>
    <h2<?php print $title_attributes; ?>>
      <a href="<?php print $node_url; ?>"><?php print $title; ?></a>
    </h2>
  <?php endif; ?>
  <?php print render($title_suffix); ?>

  <?php if ($display_submitted): ?>
    <div class="meta submitted">
      <?php print $user_picture; ?>
      <?php print $submitted; ?>
    </div>
  <?php endif; ?>

  <div class="content clearfix"<?php print $content_attributes; ?>>
    <?php
```

```php
    // We hide the comments and links now so that we can render them
later.
    hide($content['comments']);
    hide($content['links']);

    $bodycontent =  $node->body['und'][0]['value'];
    $width = $node->dfp_map_width['und'][0]['value'];
    $height = $node->dfp_map_height['und'][0]['value'];
  print render( $bodycontent );
 ?>
 <div id="map_canvas" style="width:
 <?php print $width; ?>px; height:
 <?php print $height; ?>px"></div>
</div>

<?php
    // Remove the "Add new comment" link on the teaser page or if the
comment
    // form is being displayed on the same page.
    if ($teaser || !empty($content['comments']['comment_form'])) {
      unset($content['links']['comment']['#links']['comment-add']);
    }
    // Only display the wrapper div if there are links.
    $links = render($content['links']);
    if ($links):
 ?>
   <div class="link-wrapper">
     <?php print $links; ?>
   </div>
 <?php endif; ?>

 <?php print render($content['comments']); ?>

</div>
```

Venue: node--dino_friendly_places_venue.tpl.php

The template for a venue simply needs to display a static map, which shows the location of the venue, along with the description of the venue:

```php
<div id="node-<?php print $node->nid; ?>" class="<?php print $classes;
?> clearfix"<?php print $attributes; ?>>

  <?php print render($title_prefix); ?>
  <?php if (!$page): ?>
```

```
    <h2<?php print $title_attributes; ?>>
      <a href="<?php print $node_url; ?>"><?php print $title; ?></a>
    </h2>
  <?php endif; ?>
  <?php print render($title_suffix); ?>

  <?php if ($display_submitted): ?>
    <div class="meta submitted">
      <?php print $user_picture; ?>
      <?php print $submitted; ?>
    </div>
  <?php endif; ?>

  <div class="content clearfix"<?php print $content_attributes; ?>>
    <?php
      // We hide the comments and links now so that we can render them
later.
      hide($content['comments']);
      hide($content['links']);
```

Google provides a static maps API which allows us to pass coordinates and a size, and Google will return a static image of that area of the map with the point selected. The highlighted code below builds the static map image:

```
      $bodycontent =  $node->body['und'][0]['value'];
      $longitude = $node->dfp_venue_longitude['und'][0]['value'];
      $latitude = $node->dfp_venue_latitude['und'][0]['value'];
      print "<img src='http://maps.google.com/maps/api/
staticmap?center=" . $latitude . "," . $longitude . "&zoom=14&size=51
2x512&maptype=roadmap&markers=color:blue|label:X|" . $latitude . "," .
$longitude . "&sensor=false' alt='Location' />";
       print render( $bodycontent );
      ?>

  <?php
    // Remove the "Add new comment" link on the teaser page or if the
comment
    // form is being displayed on the same page.
    if ($teaser || !empty($content['comments']['comment_form'])) {
      unset($content['links']['comment']['#links']['comment-add']);
    }
    // Only display the wrapper div if there are links.
    $links = render($content['links']);
    if ($links):
    ?>
```

```
    <div class="link-wrapper">
      <?php print $links; ?>
    </div>
  <?php endif; ?>

  <?php print render($content['comments']); ?>

</div>
```

Module in action

Now that we have our module created, let's have a look at it in action.

Install the module

Within **Administration | Modules** we now have two new modules which we can install **DFP Map** and **DFP Venue**:

Let's enable the modules so that we can try them out.

If we try to create content, we now have two new options:

- **Dinosaur Friendly place**
- **Map of Dinosaur Friendly places**

The following screenshot shows these new options:

Creating a map

Let's create a new map of dinosaur friendly places. The form has provisions for us to add the name of the map, the coordinates of the center point, the zoom level, and the size of the map.

Title *

Venues North East England

Body (Edit summary)

Text format | Filtered HTML ▾ | More information about text formats

- Web page addresses and e-mail addresses turn into links automatically.
- Allowed HTML tags: <a> <em> <strong> <cite> <blockquote> <code> <ul> <ol> <li> <dl> <dt> <dd>
- Lines and paragraphs break automatically.

The longitude for the central point of the map.

1.614

The latitude for the central point of the map.

54.974

The zoom level for the map.

8

The width of the map.

500

The height of the map.

350

Creating a venue

Let's also create a venue. We have the option to specify the coordinates of the venue:

Title *

> Some venue

Body (Edit summary)

Text format | Filtered HTML ▼   More information about text formats ⑦

- Web page addresses and e-mail addresses turn into links automatically.
- Allowed HTML tags: <a> <em> <strong> <cite> <blockquote> <code> <ul> <ol> <li> <dl> <dt> <dd>
- Lines and paragraphs break automatically.

The longitude for the central point of the map.

> -1.61774

The latitude for the central point of the map.

> 54.9693

Viewing a map

Now if we view the newly created map, we can see it covers the location we defined; it also shows the newly created venue within there, and if we click the venue, it pops up with the name of the venue as a link to view more details:

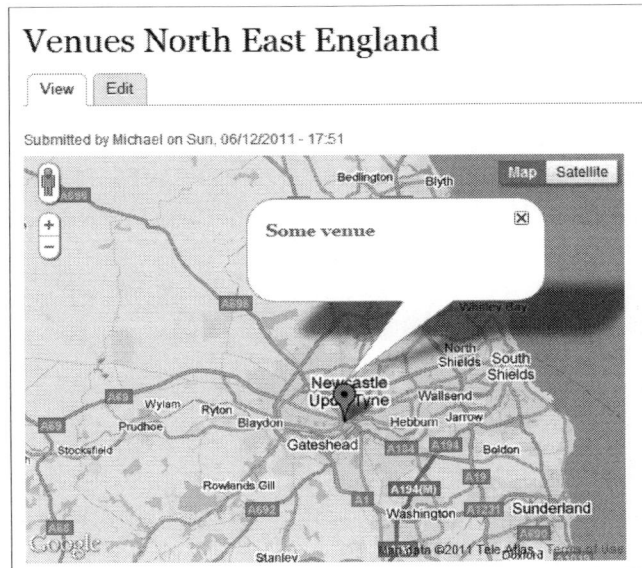

Venues North East England

View | Edit

Submitted by Michael on Sun, 06/12/2011 - 17:51

Some venue

Viewing   a venue

If we click to view the venue, we see a map containing only the venue, as well as the name and any description of the venue itself:

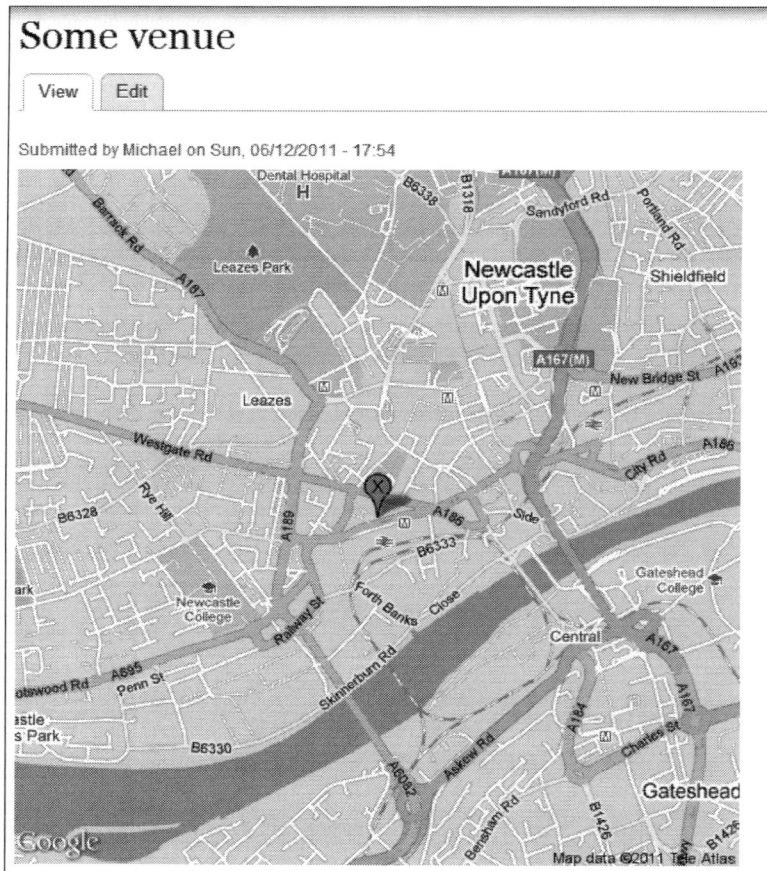

Summary

In this chapter, we have quickly explored some of Drupal's modular system and used it to create two modules (as part of the same package) which added some additional functionality to our site and will add value to our social network. This included the following:

- Creating `.install` files to allow the module to be installed and uninstalled, automatically creating the new content types and their fields
- Creating the `.info` files to define the name, compatibility, package, and description of the modules
- Creating `.module` files to add functionality to viewing maps and venues
- Overriding some of the default Drupal output using theme suggestions

Now that we can see how powerful the modular system is within Drupal, we can investigate the system further and leverage it to add any custom functionality which we need to our site.

8
How We Can Design Our Site

Our social network is now, finally, feature complete, but at the moment it resembles any other default Drupal installation, as it uses the default theme. Let's take a look at themes within Drupal and how we can change the design of our site to something more appropriate.

In this chapter you will learn how to:

- Customize the default theme
- Make use of other themes and learn more about Drupal themes
- Go about creating a custom theme

Let's get started and customize our site's design.

Drupal themes

The design (or the "look and feel") of our site is controlled by the **theme**. Drupal provides us with a small number of themes out of the box. Initially we have two enabled themes, the default theme and the default administration theme (which is only for the administration areas), and two disabled themes. By enabling more themes we can also allow our users to choose the look and feel they experience within the site.

Themes are administered through the **Appearance** link on the administration toolbar.

Theme management and pre-installed themes

The **Appearance** page lists all of the themes available to us in our Drupal installation:

Set and configure the default theme for your website. Alternative themes are available.

+ Install new theme

ENABLED THEMES

Bartik 7.0 (default theme)

A flexible, recolorable theme with many regions.

Settings

Seven 7.0

A simple one-column, tableless, fluid width administration theme.

Settings | Disable | Set default

To enable more themes for our users, we simply click the **Enable** link next to a disabled theme. We can also select **Enable and set default** if we wish to make one of the disabled themes the default theme:

DISABLED THEMES

Garland 7.0

A multi-column theme which can be configured to modify colors and switch between fixed and fluid width layouts.

Enable | Enable and set default

Stark 7.0

This theme demonstrates Drupal's default HTML markup and CSS styles. To learn how to build your own theme and override Drupal's default code, see the Theming Guide.

Enable | Enable and set default

From this screen we can also select which of the themes is used as the administration theme, and if the administration theme should be used when editing or creating content:

ADMINISTRATION THEME

Administration theme

Seven

Choose "Default theme" to always use the same theme as the rest of the site.

☑ Use the administration theme when editing or creating content

Save configuration

There are four pre-installed themes within our site; let's enable them all so that we can have a look at them and see what they look like. The pre-installed themes are:

- Bartik (the default theme)
- Garland
- Seven (the default administration theme)
- Stark

Let's take a look at these themes and how they differ.

Bartik

Bartik is the default Drupal 7 theme, and throughout the course of this book we have become very familiar with it. It's a clean and simple design, with three primary columns for content and blocks, a tabbed primary navigation, and user links at the top right-hand corner:

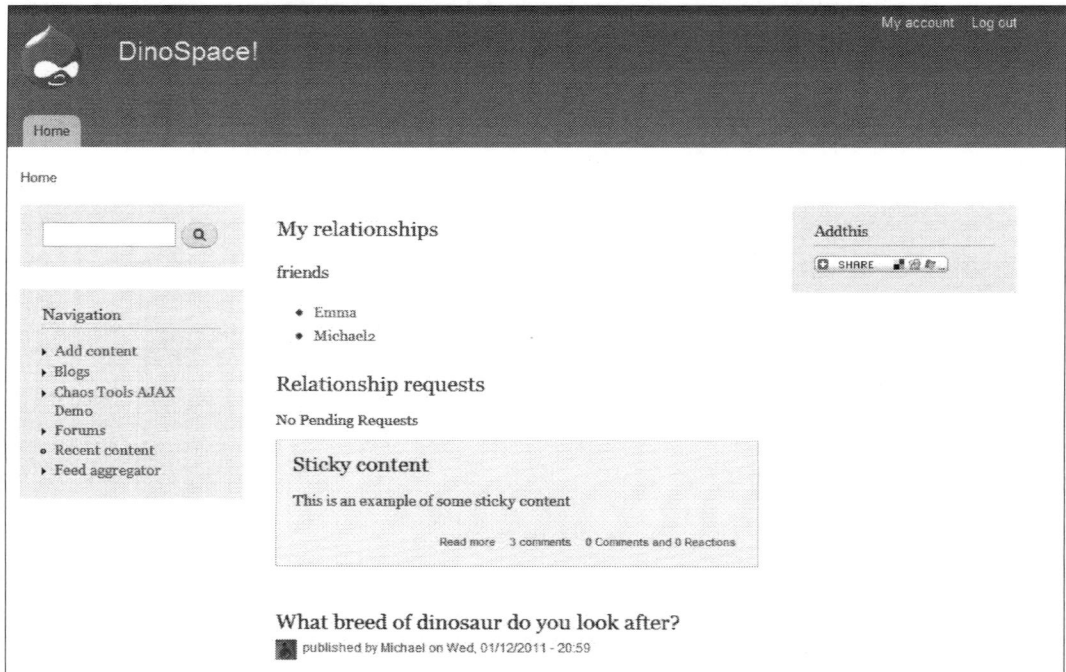

While this is a nice, clean, and user friendly theme design, the problem it has is that it is the default. Every Drupal 7 site comes with it out of the box; so if we (and other Drupal 7 sites) don't change it, it is difficult to differentiate the site from other Drupal 7 installations, which in turn puts users off. Thankfully, most websites chose to use a more custom theme and often use a theme which they have drastically customized to make their website more unique.

Garland

Garland will be familiar to readers of the previous version of this book, Drupal 6 Social Networking, as it is the default Drupal 6 theme. Again, it is a nice, simple, and clean design theme:

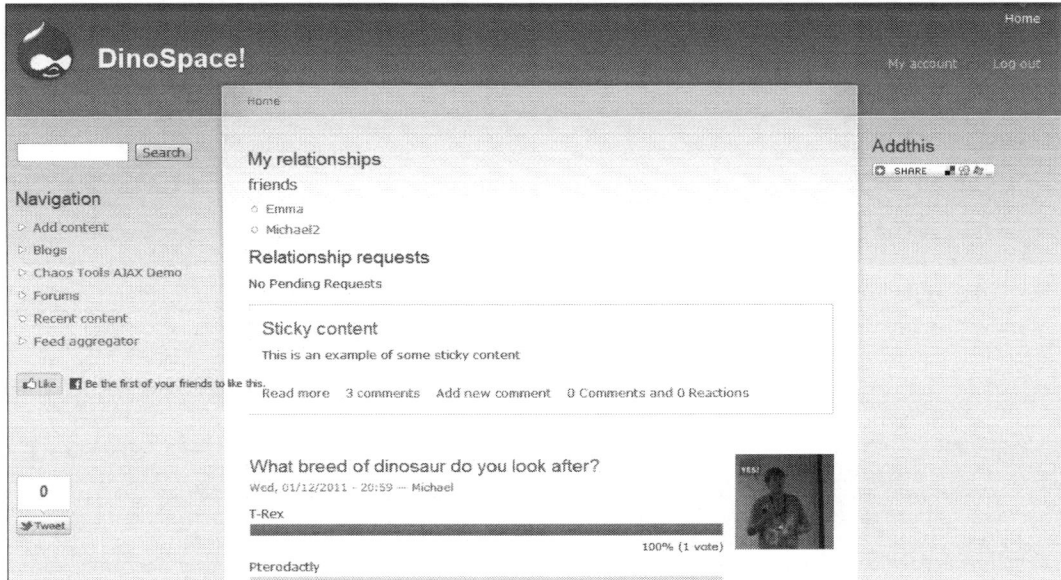

Certain key aspects, such as the primary links are hidden right at the top right-hand side of the page with much less prominence, though with this design there is clearly more emphasis on the site's content within the design, as opposed to Bartik which almost has content and columns displayed as "equals".

Seven

Seven is another theme we have gotten to know throughout this book. This is simply because this is the default Administration theme. We can, if we really want to, select this as the default frontend theme, but it doesn't contain support for many aspects of the Drupal theme because it is designed exclusively for administration areas.

Stark

The final theme which comes with our Drupal 7 installation is Stark. This is a completely "naked" theme which is designed to demonstrate the default HTML and CSS within Drupal:

This shows us the HTML markup which Drupal generates out of the box; it contains no template files, only a cascading style sheet. We can override this markup by creating suitable template files in a new theme of our own.

Contributed themes

There are huge numbers of themes available which have been created by professional designers, hobbyists, and Drupal enthusiasts. These can be downloaded from the Drupal website: `http://drupal.org/project/Themes`. This website lists available themes as well as the Drupal version for which they were designed. Screenshots of most of the themes are available so that we can see what the theme would look like, before downloading and installing. There are also themes available to download elsewhere, created by Drupal enthusiasts, and it is possible to commission a custom theme to be designed by a professional design company.

> **Make sure the version numbers match!**
>
> While downloading themes from the Drupal website, or elsewhere, ensure that they are compatible with the version of Drupal you have installed!

Installing contributed themes

To install a contributed theme which we have downloaded, we simply need to extract the contents of the downloaded file into the `/sites/all/themes folder` within our Drupal installation; this will display it in our administration area and allow us to enable it, and if we wish, set it as the default theme.

Customizing the default theme

Although it isn't really a good idea to use the default theme for our site, due to it being a common design, we can customize it. This is a useful approach if we are not able to, or don't have the time to, launch the site with a bespoke custom design. The customization options available to us include:

- The color scheme
- Which elements are used in the theme (for instance, the logo)
- The logo
- The favicon, or the "shortcut" icon

These settings can also be set globally for all of our installed themes, or individually on a per theme basis.

Themes are customized by clicking the **settings** link next to the theme in the **Appearance** section of the administration area.

Color scheme

The first set of options allows us to select a color set for the theme to use. Only a small number of themes support the color picker and color schemes. The available color schemes are:

- **Blue Lagoon**: the default color set; blue
- **Firehouse**: red
- **Ice**: light grey
- **Plum**: purple
- **Slate**: dark grey

Selecting a color scheme populates a list of the colors which are associated with it. We can alter the color scheme by using the color picker to change any of the colors:

Home » Administration » Appearance » Settings
Global settings   Bartik   Seven

These options control the display settings for the *Bartik* theme. When your site is displayed using this theme, these settings will be used.

COLOR SCHEME

Color set	Plum
Main background	#fffdf7
Link color	#9d408d
Header top	#4c1c58
Header bottom	#593662
Text color	#301313

Custom color sets

There is another option in the color scheme drop-down list, called Custom. This allows us to create a completely custom color scheme without having to modify one of the existing pre-defined color schemes.

Color set preview

Under the configuration options for the color scheme we have a preview section, which shows us what our theme would look like with the new colors applied to it:

Preview

Bartik

Home | Te Quidne | Vel Torqueo Quae Erat

Etiam est risus

Maecenas id porttitor Ut enim ad minim veniam, quis nostrudfelis. Laboris nisi ut aliquip ex ea.

Lorem ipsum dolor

Sit amet, consectetur adipisicing elit, sed do eiusmod tempor incididunt ut labore et dolore magna aliqua. Ut enim ad minim veniam, quis nostrud exercitation ullamco laboris nisi ut aliquip ex ea commodo consequat. Maecenas id porttitor Ut enim ad minim veniam, quis nostr udfelis.

ERISUS DOLOR

ETIAM EST RISUS

Maecenas id porttitor Ut enim ad minim veniam, quis nostrudfelis. Laboris nisi ut aliquip ex ea.

Donec placerat

Nullam nibh dolor

Blandit sed

Fermentum id

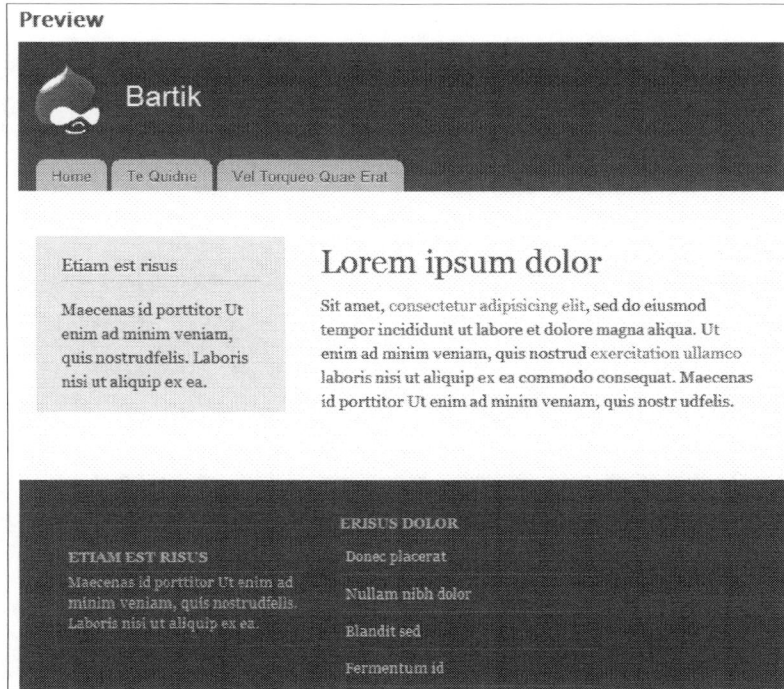

This allows us to get a feel for a particular color scheme before we decide to roll it out to all of our users.

Toggle display

The next set of configurable options for the theme are grouped together as **Toggle Display**. These allow us to select which features are to be included within the site's design. If we wanted to, we could disable the logo, remove the site name, remove the site slogan, and even remove the menu from the theme using these settings:

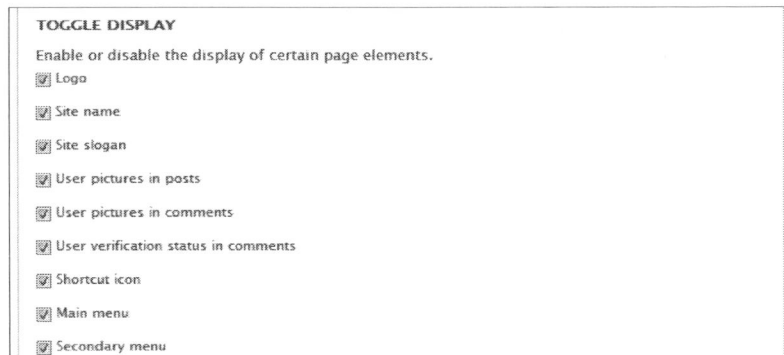

TOGGLE DISPLAY

Enable or disable the display of certain page elements.

☑ Logo

☑ Site name

☑ Site slogan

☑ User pictures in posts

☑ User pictures in comments

☑ User verification status in comments

☑ Shortcut icon

☑ Main menu

☑ Secondary menu

Unchecking the various options have the following effects:

- **Logo**: This will remove the logo from the theme
- **Site name**: This will remove the site name from the theme
- **Site slogan**: This will remove the slogan from the theme
- **User pictures in posts**: This will prevent display of a user's avatar when viewing their posts
- **User pictures in comments**: As **User pictures in posts**, but for comments
- **User verification status in comments**: If the user is using a verified account
- **Shortcut icon**: This will remove the favicon from being displayed
- **Main menu**: This will remove the primary navigation, usually the one displaying along the top of most common themes
- **Secondary menu**: This will remove the secondary menu, usually the one displaying down the left-hand side of most common themes

Logo image

Next, we can change the logo which is used on the theme. If we uncheck the **Use the default logo** box, we can supply our own logo using the form which appears, either by uploading a file or by pointing to an existing file:

This will replace the default Drupal "drop" logo displayed on our site.

Shortcut icons

A shortcut icon, more commonly referred to as a favicon, is a small logo typically displayed within our web browser next to the address bar or next to the title of the page within a tab in a browser. Similarly, for uploading a new logo we can upload a new favicon from the admin area too.

To create a favicon file, which we can use, there are a plethora of tools available online which will convert a full sized image or logo into a favicon for us. A popular one is the favicon generator from DynamicDrive: `http://tools.dynamicdrive.com/favicon/`.

The basics of creating a theme

Creating a theme from scratch is quite an in-depth process, and as well as requiring knowledge of Drupal's theming system, we also need to be able to create a design. Because of this, let us simply look at the basics of creating a theme, and how we could create a theme if we have an existing design to convert. There are many resources, listed later, which fully detail and document how to create themes for Drupal. This primer should give you enough knowledge to quickly convert a design you already have into a Drupal theme, provided you have knowledge of HTML and CSS. The full theme documentation should be followed to provide further assistance: `http://drupal.org/documentation/theme`.

Structure of a theme

Within Drupal a theme is comprised of the following files:

- `themename.info` (where `themename` is the name of the theme)
- A number of template files (ending in `.tpl.php`), containing HTML and PHP which override the default HTML Drupal generates (optional). Common template files to create include:
    - `comment.tpl.php` for the style of a comment
    - `maintenance-page.tpl.php` for the design of the maintenance mode page
    - `node.tpl.php` for nodes
    - `page.tpl.php` for pages
- `template.php` for conditional logic (optional)
- A logo and screenshot (optional, the screenshot is used in the themes list)
- Any stylesheets or additional resources we wish to use

These files are grouped together in a folder, and should be placed in the `sites/all/themes` folder. When a working theme is within this folder, it can be seen, installed, and used by our Drupal installation from the **Appearance** section.

Overriding specific parts of Drupal with a theme

We can use the theming system to override the design and layout of specific pages or specific types of pages, using template suggestions. For example, creating a file called `node--breed.tpl.php` would override the design of a page which was of node type breed for a particular breed of dinosaur, and `node--5.tpl.php` would override the design of the node with ID 5. A detailed list of template suggestions can be found on the Drupal website: `http://drupal.org/node/1089656`.

Creating the .info file

The `.info` file for the theme requires at least three properties to be defined:

- **Name**: The name of the theme
- **Core**: The version of the Drupal core that the theme is compatible with
- **Engine**: The template engine used
- A description is also recommended
- Any custom stylesheets can be implemented using stylesheet properties

These properties are set simply by listing the property name on a line followed by the equals character, and their value, as follows:

```
name = dinospacetheme
description = Drupal 7 Theme for DinoSpace
version = 1
core = 7.x
engine = phptemplate
stylesheets[all][] = dinospacetheme.css
```

Full details on the structure of the .info file can be found on the Drupal website: `http://drupal.org/node/171205`.

Rapidly building a theme

The quickest and easiest way for us to build a theme for our site is to take an existing theme, copy the templates, and replace them with new files which implement our own design. The pre-existing templates in these themes show the PHP code which is needed to display various bits of content.

Building a theme properly

Taking an existing theme and plugging in our own HTML code will certainly get a theme up and running quickly for us, but it won't give us a detailed understanding of creating themes. This is a topic which can and does fill several books. The following are recommended resources if you wish to create a custom theme, using best practices:

Drupal theming documentation: `http://drupal.org/theme-guide/6-7`

- *Introduction to Drupal 7 Theme Development*, a presentation from Drupalcon Chicago 2011, `http://drupaleasy.com/blogs/ryanprice/2011/03/introduction-drupal-7-theming-drupalcon-chicago-2011`

- *Drupal 7 Themes, Ric Shreves, Packt Publishing*, `http://www.packtpub.com/drupal-7-create-themes-with-clean-layout-and-powerful-css-styling/book`

Summary

In this chapter, we have taken a look through the Appearance section of the Drupal administration area, and used this to enable additional themes, enable and disable parts of the theme (for example, site slogan), update the logo and shortcut icon, and change the colors the theme uses.

We have also taken a brief look at the steps that would be involved in creating a custom theme for our site, so if we create a design to use, or commission someone to design the site for us, we could convert it into a theme for our site. This includes the core files required for a theme, where the theme files reside, and the structure of `.info` files.

With our theme customized, and some pointers for how we can create a custom theme, we can move onto *Chapter 9, Communicating With Our Users*.

9
Communicating with Our Users

With our social network almost complete, there is only one feature left for us to add, which is the ability to communicate with our users. While we can contact users individually (using the contact module, or by looking up their e-mail address), we can't get in touch with large groups, or our entire user base, at once. For instance, how will we inform our users of new changes to our site, which they may not know about?

In this chapter, you will learn about the following:

- Mailing lists, and how to integrate them to our signup process
- Allowing anonymous users to sign up to a mailing list using content blocks
- How to remind inactive users about your site
- Using content blocks to get our message across

Getting started

The following modules are mentioned within this chapter. It isn't recommended to download and install them all for use on a live site; however, you may want to download them to see which of the options discussed you wish to use:

- **Simplenews**: A simple newsletter module (`http://drupal.org/project/simplenews`)
- **Mimemail**: Allowing us to send HTML e-mails (`http://drupal.org/project/mimemail`)
- **PHPList**: To interact with the PHPList newsletter software (`http://drupal.org/project/phplist`)
- **Inactive_user**: To contact inactive site users (`http://drupal.org/project/inactive_user`)

A look back

Earlier in this book we looked at how our website communicates with our users on certain events, for instance when they sign up to our site. Within the **Configuration | People | Account settings** section, we have a group of settings called **E-mails**. These are the various templates which are used when our website needs to e-mail a user with information related to their account, including when a new account is created (with different templates depending on who created or approved the user account), when a new account is activated, when a user requests a new password, and when an account is blocked or canceled. The content of these e-mails can be very important depending on the nature of the website. In our DinoSpace site we may use a very informal, welcoming, and fun tone for our automated e-mails. A business focused website however would want to use a much more formal tone.

Modules send e-mails too!

Don't forget, many modules also have their own templates for the e-mails they send to our users. These can generally be easily modified too from within their sections of the Drupal administration area.

Direct contact with a user

Since we also previously installed the contact form module, we can also use that to communicate directly with individuals on our site. When we installed the module, the main reason was to allow other users to communicate with each other. However, there is no reason that we, as administrators, can't use that if we too wish to communicate with a user. This is particularly useful for things such as:

- Polite requests regarding their content or conduct on the site; particularly in light of user complaints
- Inviting them to become more active in the site; for instance, asking if they would be interested in becoming a moderator, or a content curator for our site

Alternatively, we could contact the user directly through e-mail, by looking up their e-mail address which is assigned to their user account. This is accessible from the administration area.

Mailing lists

Mailing lists are generally used to send marketing or promotional e-mails to a large group of individuals. Mailing lists software helps us manage our lists of users, performs find and replaces to insert users names and e-mail addresses (and other information) when sending the e-mail, and logs statistics.

E-mailing large groups of users introduces a number of problems for us as website owners. They are as follows:

- Many shared hosts limit the number of outbound e-mails that a user can send on a daily or even hourly basis.

- We have to be careful to make sure our e-mails don't get marked as SPAM; too many spam complaints and we will face retribution from our server provider; for example, being blacklisted so that all our e-mails are flagged as SPAM. There are numerous e-mail blacklisting services; if you get blacklisted you need to contact the various list maintainers to request removal.

- Even with our own dedicated resources, sending an e-mail to a large group of users can take time and use up our servers processing power. While installed mailing list software typically sends e-mails in batches, this could result in it taking some time to process the full list.

To alleviate this problem we can look at external mailing list systems which have hardware and software set up to cope with mass e-mail processing and delivery.

External mailing lists

There is a wide range of external mailing list systems available, and three such systems popular with the web community are as follows:

- Campaign Monitor (http://www.campaignmonitor.com/)
- Mail Chimp (http://www.mailchimp.com/)
- Constant Contact (http://www.constantcontact.com)

All three provide methods to integrate with websites and are well established and recommended. From personal preference, I'm going to use Campaign Monitor for this section of the chapter; however, Constant Contact has support for Drupal 7 in the form of a module available at http://drupal.org/project/constant_contact.

Automatic signup on user creation

The current Drupal module for Campaign Monitor is quite dated and isn't compatible with Drupal 7; however, with our new knowledge of the basics of Drupal module development let's create a basic module for this. This is a technical process; if you are not comfortable with creating modules or programming in PHP it is advisable to make use of Constant Contact and its module for Drupal instead, available at `http://drupal.org/project/constant_contact`.

When new users sign up to our Drupal site, the `hook_user_insert()` hook is called. All we have to do is write a new module, which implements this hook, and within the hook sends our new user to our Campaign Monitor list. More information is available on this specific hook on the Drupal website: `http://api.drupal.org/api/drupal/modules--user--user.api.php/function/hook_user_insert/7`.

Since the module we want to create is very basic, we only need two files, the appropriate `.info` file and the appropriate `.module` file. We should start by creating a new folder in our modules folder to contain this new module. I've called mine `mpcampaignmonitor`.

Our `mpcampaignmonitor.info` file simply contains the name, description, version, package, and the Drupal core it is compatible with. The code for this file is as follows:

```
name = Campaign Monitor
description = Integrate user sign up with campaign monitor
core = 7.x
package = "D7SN"
version = "1.0"
```

Our `mpcampaignmonitor.module` file has a `help` method which describes the module in the help screen, and an implementation of the `hook_user_insert()` function:

```php
<?php
// $Id$
/**
 * Display help and module information
 * @param path which path of the site we're displaying help
 * @param arg array that holds the current path as would be returned
 *    from arg() function
 * @return help text for the path
 */
function mpcampaignmonitor_help($path, $arg) {
  $output = '';
  switch ($path) {
    case "admin/help#mpcampaignmonitor":
      $output = '<p>'. t("Integrates with Campaign Monitor on user
      sign up") .'</p>';
```

```
      break;
   }
   return $output;
}
```

The implementation of the user_insert hook simply needs to make a call to the campaign monitor API, passing the name (if known, the following code sends the username in place of the name), e-mail address, our API key, and the ID of the list we want to subscribe the user to. The API Key and List ID can be found in the Campaign Monitor control panel.

As this is a very quick method to integrate external newsletters, the API key and list ID are simply stored as variables within the function. If we were distributing this code as a module to be downloaded, instead of writing it for use on our own site, we would ideally make those settings, which could be configured in the Drupal administration area.

Once the URL has been constructed containing the relevant details, it is processed with a simple fopen call as follows:

```
/**
 * Hook called on user create
 * @param array the array of form values submitted by the user.
 * @param object The user object on which the operation is being
 *   performed.
 * @param string The active category of user information being
 *   edited.
 * @return void
 */
function mpcampaignmonitor_user_insert(&$edit, $account, $category) {

   $apiKey = "OUR-API-KEY";
   $list = "OUR-LIST-ID";
   $url =
     "http://api.createsend.com/api/api.asmx/Subscriber.Add?ApiKey=";
   $url .= $apiKey;
   $url .= "&ListID=";
   $url .= $list;
   $url .= "&Email=";
   $url .= $account->mail;
   $url .= "&Name=";
   $url .= urlencode( $account->name );
   $newsletter_ping = fopen( $url, "r");

}
```

With this code created and in place, we now have a new module listed in the modules area for us to enable. Once enabled, users who sign up to our site will automatically be added to our mailing list.

Signup for anonymous users

To allow our anonymous users to sign up to our mailing list (or a separate mailing list for anonymous users to be notified of site news), we can simply get the signup code from our newsletter system and add it to a content block which only anonymous users see. We will be going through this process later in the chapter in more detail to provide an informative sign-up box to encourage users to join our site.

Alternative e-mailing options

There are a number of other e-mailing options available which we might want to consider for our site. Some of these are modules, others are third-party services, and there are some systems we can use to improve how Drupal sends e-mails.

PHPList

PHPList is a popular mailing list system written in PHP; if we chose to use this system we can use the PHPList integration module to do the following:

- Synchronize users from Drupal to our PHPList system
- Send targeting mailings based on the values of a user's profile
- Allow users to manage their PHPList subscriptions from within their account
- Bulk import into PHPList, if we already have a Drupal installation running, with many users

The PHPList software, which the module interacts with, can be downloaded from `http://www.phplist.com`.

> PHPList involves some server configuration; so if PHPList is the solution for you, make sure you read the documentation thoroughly.

Simplenews

Simplenews is one of the many modules available for Drupal which allow us to send e-mails to our users. One limitation of the Simplenews module is that it can't send to all our users; it requires users to subscribe to the mailing list first. We can manage the newsletter categories from the **Structure | Newsletters** section of the administration area:

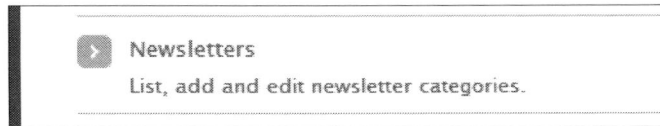

From here we can see the various newsletter categories, create new ones, and make changes to existing ones. We will walk through the process of creating a newsletter; however before we do, let's take a step back and think through the type of newsletters we would want to offer.

Our site will be a resource for a range of users with a range of interests and needs from our site. If we create a newsletter which is too specific or too generic, our users won't get any value from them. Instead, we can create a range of different newsletters for our users, for example:

- **DinoSpace News**: Keep up-to-date with the changes to our social network
- **Vacationing with your Dinosaur**: Holiday deals, destination reviews, and useful tips
- Carnivorous Dinosaurs update
- Herbivorous dinosaurs update
- Flying dinosaurs update

The full list of available newsletters will depend on the content and audience types of our site:

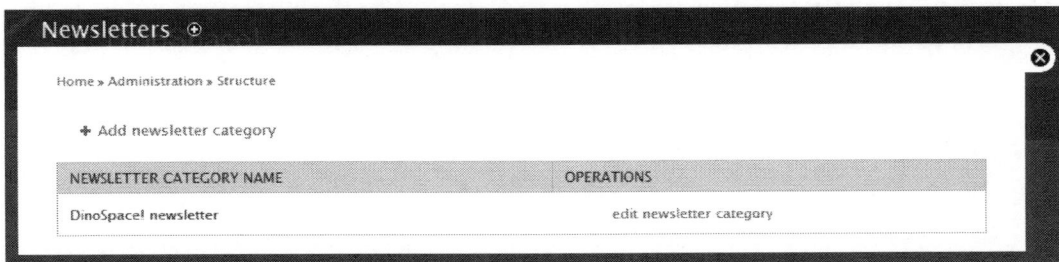

With newsletters in place, our users are able to manage their newsletter subscriptions from their profile, where it lists newsletters they have subscribed to, and provides a **Manage subscriptions** link:

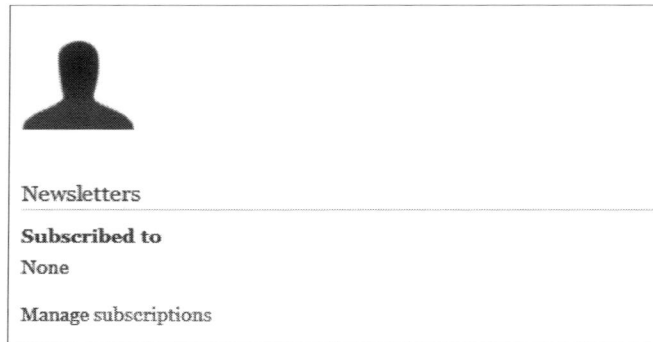

Newsletters

Subscribed to

None

Manage subscriptions

The manage subscriptions screen simply lists the newsletters and allows the user to tick or untick each newsletter depending on their preference:

NEWSLETTER SUBSCRIPTIONS

Select the newsletter(s) to which you want to subscribe or unsubscribe.

DinoSpace! newsletter

DinoSpace! newsletter categories.

Sending a newsletter with simplenews

With `simplenews`, newsletters are created as all content is created in Drupal; as a node. We simply create a new content element, with a type of **Simplenews newsletter**, if we installed the `mimemail` module, we can even send HTML formatted e-mails as our newsletter. You may also require the **MailSystem** module, depending on your server configuration.

When creating the newsletter, there is an option to select the newsletter category the newsletter should be sent to:

- Add this newsletter issue to a newsletter by selecting a newsletter from the select list. Send a newsletter or a test newsletter by selecting the appropriate radio button and submitting the node.
- Set default send options at Administer > Site configuration > Simplenews > Newsletter.
- Set newsletter specific options at Administer > Content management > Newsletters > Newsletters.

Title *

Body (Edit summary)

Text format Filtered HTML ▾   More information about text formats ⓘ

- Web page addresses and e-mail addresses turn into links automatically.
- Allowed HTML tags: <a> <em> <strong> <cite> <blockquote> <code> <ul> <ol> <li> <dl> <dt> <dd>
- Lines and paragraphs break automatically.

Newsletter category *

◉ DinoSpace! newsletter

The `simplenews` module comes with a range of settings, including:

- Default newsletter settings:
  - Format (plain text or HTML)
  - The default send action: either send a test e-mail to the test address or send out the newsletter
  - The test e-mail address, and if we want to override this by specifying the test e-mail address in the newsletter create screen
  - Details to display as the sender of the newsletter
- If anonymous users can subscribe, and if there should be a subscribe block on the site for them
- If newsletter subscriptions should be removed when a user is deactivated
- Subject and message for e-mails sent to subscribers when they subscribe
- Web address to take users to, once they have subscribed or unsubscribed from a newsletter
- How the e-mails should be sent
- If e-mails should be sent all in one go (a bad idea), or small batches at a time using the Drupal cron feature
- How many e-mails should be sent in each cron run
- If e-mails should be logged

These settings can all be found and managed in the **Configuration | Simplenews** section of the Drupal administration area.

Amazon Simple Email Service

Amazon have recently announced their new Simple Email Service (`http://aws.amazon.com/ses/`); this is a web-based service for sending e-mails. The benefits of using services like this is that their systems are designed for bulk e-mail sending. Unlike other e-mail services, this one allows e-mails to be sent for marketing purposes (that is, newsletters).

One `Drupal.org` community user recently integrated Amazon SES with their Drupal installation and encountered a problem with the way Drupal prepares the e-mails. If this is an approach you want to consider, they submitted a patch to work around this problem, which should be of use and is available at `http://drupal.org/node/1062616`.

Using content blocks to get our message across

We mentioned earlier about creating a content block to contain a newsletter signup form for our Campaign Monitor list. We can also use blocks to create content to communicate messages to our user base, or to directly target anonymous users to try and encourage them to sign up. Let's look at creating a content block just for our anonymous users.

Firstly, we need to enter the basics, such as the description, title, and body for the block. We create the block by navigating to **Structure | Blocks** and clicking the **Add block** link:

Block description *

join message for guests

A brief description of your block. Used on the Blocks administration page.

Block title

Join DinoSpace!

The title of the block as shown to the user.

Block body *

Hi there! Did you know that as a registered member of DinoSpace! you get access to all of these great features:
<ul>
<li>list features here</li>
</ul>
Not ready to join just yet? then why not sign up to our mailing list.
<!-- insert mailing list code here -->

Text format Filtered HTML

More information about text formats

- Web page addresses and e-mail addresses turn into links automatically.
- Allowed HTML tags: <a> <em> <strong> <cite> <blockquote> <code> <ul> <ol> <li> <dl> <dt> <dd>
- Lines and paragraphs break automatically.

Under **Visibility settings**, we need to select the **Roles** tab, and select the block to be visible only to anonymous users:

Visibility settings

Pages Not restricted	**Show block for specific roles** ☑ anonymous user
Content types Not restricted	☐ authenticated user
Roles anonymous user	☐ administrator ☐ temp
Users Not customizable	Show this block only for the selected role(s). If you select no roles, the block will be visible to all users.

Now all we need to do is go into the blocks administration area and select where we want the block to be displayed. Once we have done that, if we log out, we can see the block is displayed on our site:

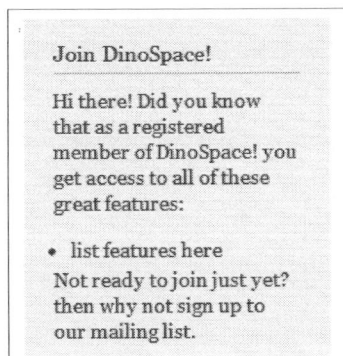

Join DinoSpace!

Hi there! Did you know that as a registered member of DinoSpace! you get access to all of these great features:

• list features here
Not ready to join just yet? then why not sign up to our mailing list.

Using theme customisations to indirectly communicate with our users

The look and feel (as defined by the theme we use) can also be used to communicate with our users. The following are some examples of what we could do:

• Display links to any mobile applications which we may have, if we detect the user is browsing the site on their mobile device

• Add a simple bar of information to the top of the site, perhaps relating to a specific feature

- Add (graceful and unobtrusive) information pop-ups using CSS (cascading style sheets) or using JavaScript libraries such as Fancybox (`http://fancybox.net/`)

- Adding a collapsible message, where the user can click an icon to expand an administrative message, which we can periodically update

These options require knowledge of HTML, CSS, and Drupal themes.

Inactive users: Please come back

So far, we have talked about getting in touch with either an individual user, all of our user base, or users of a specific mailing list they signed up to. Another scenario is that we might want to remind our inactive users about our site. The `inactive_user` module allows us to send reminders to users who have not been active within a certain period of time. This is made possible because Drupal records the time a user was last active. With this module we can hopefully entice some of our more inactive users back to the site. Unfortunately, this module is not yet ready for Drupal 7, though a development version is available. The module website should be periodically checked for updates or alternatives as they are developed, at `http://drupal.org/project/inactive_user`.

Summary

In this chapter, we looked at how we, as administrators, can communicate with our users using a variety of methods, including:

- Features we have previously covered in other chapters
- Newsletters and mailing lists
- Third-party mailing lists
- Content blocks
- Alterations to the Drupal theme

10
Deploying and Maintaining Your Social Network

With DinoSpace complete and functional, we are now ready to put the site online so that we can begin to attract users, and grow our website. As well as putting the site online, we need to keep security and maintenance provisions in mind, to ensure our site stays secure and well maintained should anything go wrong.

In this chapter, you will learn the following:

- How to deploy DinoSpace to the Internet, including looking at domain names, hosting providers, and the manual deployment process
- How to keep our site secure
- How to maintain our site
- How to back up our site, and restore it should the worst happen

Let's get started by deploying DinoSpace to the web!

Installing the modules

As usual, let's install any modules we will need during the chapter now, to save us time later. The modules we need are as follows:

- CAPTCHA: `http://www.drupal.org/project/captcha`

  Image Captcha is a part of the CAPTCHA package
- reCAPTCHA: `http://drupal.org/project/recaptcha`
- Mollom: `http://drupal.org/project/mollom`

These need to be downloaded, extracted to our modules directory, and then enabled so that we can configure and use them later.

Security

Our website, once fully in use, will contain lots of personal information of our users, including: their public profiles, their e-mail address, and content they have contributed which may not be publicly viewable. We also have all of the content on our site, which we want to keep safe. Essentially, security is important because we want to protect our website and the data of our users.

> **Data Protection legislation**
>
> It may be worth investigating Data Protection legislation in the country you reside in, and in the country your website is hosted in. As well as mandating how data must be kept secure, some countries, such as the UK, also have a register of Data Controllers who are responsible for data protection in a particular organization.

Because Drupal is an open source project, with fully readable code, we have both additional protections and risks regarding security compared to other non open source projects. Since the code is readable, anyone can look through the code and potentially find security vulnerabilities. However, because of the nature of the Drupal community, it is also very easy to report bugs and security issues, and get them fixed and patched quickly — the community act as security auditors. Once an issue has been patched, we would then need to download the new release, and upgrade our installation, based on the upgrade documentation.

Security advisories

There is a section of the Drupal website dedicated to security announcements, which makes it easy to keep up with the latest security patches released for the version of Drupal we are using. These security announcements are posted on this website: `http://drupal.org/security`.

It is also advisable to subscribe to the security announcements mailing list on this page, so that we can receive security announcements via e-mail; this saves us from continually checking this page for updates, alternatively, there is also an RSS feed for the content on this page which we could subscribe to.

Server security

The security of the server itself is one aspect that needs consideration. This can be broken down into two primary areas:

- Server software
- Firewall and network traffic

With shared hosting environments, there are some other considerations which we will discuss.

Software

Almost all software contain security vulnerabilities; once a vulnerability has been discovered, it is important to ensure that the software is upgraded or patched to prevent malicious users from exploiting these vulnerabilities. With managed hosting, we don't need to concern ourselves with server installed software, as our hosting provider should keep that up-to-date. However, if we want to concern ourselves with the software on our server (and check our provider is up-to-date), or if we are operating on unmanaged virtual or dedicated servers, we need to keep updated on security developments with:

- PHP
- MySQL
- Apache
- The FTP server software
- The SSH server-side software
- Operating system versions and kernel updates

This could be done by subscribing to any mailing lists found on the sites for those projects.

Securing the site with a firewall

Software and hardware firewalls can help protect our website from attack; these generally work by blocking access to certain parts of the server from certain computers (for example, allow anyone to access the website stored on the server, except users we explicitly banned, but disallow anyone to access aspects such as FTP or SSH unless explicitly permitted). Most web hosts can advise on their firewall setup, and documentation is available for firewalls that can be used on virtual and dedicated servers.

Shared hosting precautions

With shared hosting there are other considerations, in that other hosting customers have access to the same machine, it is worth checking if the following security provisions are in place when using shared hosting:

- **Open_basedir restrictions**: These ensure that code (for example, PHP code) only interacts with code in a customer's home directory, and certain shared areas, preventing another customer's code from interfering with ours
- **Jailed Shell**: This prevents a user from leaving their home directory when connecting to the server via SSH
- **Jailed FTP**: This prevents a user from leaving their home directory when connecting to the server via FTP, thus securing our site

Let's look at ways in which we can actively secure our Drupal installation by locking out spammers using the CAPTCHA and Mollom modules.

CAPTCHA

The **Completely Automated Public Turing test to tell Computers and Humans Apart (CAPTCHA)** module installs a test which proves you are human and prevents automated spam bots from signing up to our site.

The CAPTCHA module

Once the CAPTCHA module is enabled we can configure it from Configuration | People | CAPTCHA in the Administration area. From here we can configure which aspects of our Drupal installation require a CAPTCHA challenge, and which type of challenge should be used:

The forms which we enable CAPTCHA on will more than likely depend on the permissions associated with the form. If a form is only available to logged in users, then it makes sense to only associate a CAPTCHA challenge with the sign up form. If we are allowing anonymous users to comment on pages, then we may wish to add a CAPTCHA challenge to these forms too.

The CAPTCHA module provides two types of challenges out of the box:

- **Image**: The user has to enter the text which is generated within an image
- **Math**: The user has to enter the answer to a simple math problem

If we click the Examples button at the top, we can see examples of these challenges:

The reCAPTCHA module

The CAPTCHA module can be further enhanced by using the reCAPTCHA module; this provides a more advanced CAPTCHA system which also helps digitize books. There's more information on the reCAPTCHA project at their website: `http://www.google.com/recaptcha`.

Once we enable the reCAPTCHA module, we have a new tab under the Configuration | People | CAPTCHA screen:

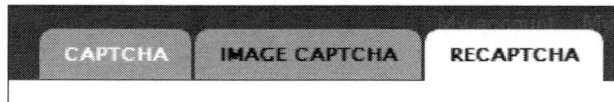

Because the reCAPTCHA service is provided by a third party and uses their servers, it is accessed via an API, and to use this API we need to request details known as keys to connect to it:

Home » Administration » Configuration » People » CAPTCHA

Public Key *

XXXXXXXXX

The public key given to you when you registered at reCAPTCHA.net.

Private Key *

XXXXXXXXXX

The private key given to you when you registered at reCAPTCHA.net.

☐ Secure Connection

　　Connect to the reCAPTCHA server using a secure connection.

☐ AJAX API

　　Use the AJAX API to display reCAPTCHA.

▸ THEME SETTINGS

Save configuration

Beneath each of the key boxes are links to register and request API keys; these links send a copy of our web address to the registration form, to pre-populate the form for us. Once we have signed up and entered our public and private keys, we can use reCAPTCHA.

We now have an additional option when selecting which CAPTCHA challenge to use, allowing us to specify the reCAPTCHA option. The examples page has also updated, including an example of the reCAPTCHA module:

CHALLENGE *"RECAPTCHA"* BY MODULE *"RECAPTCHA"*

Type the two words:

10 more examples of this challenge.

Using CAPTCHA can be irritating to users when they sign up, so it is important to use this feature with care. Measure the amount of SPAM accounts that are registering on the site, and use your judgement to decide when to enable it.

SPAM prevention

In the event that a spammer does sign up to our site, either a human spammer, or if the CAPTCHA system is bypassed, we can run user submitted content through a SPAM system to detect if their submissions are genuine or not.

Mollom

Mollom provides two main services: it analyses text to determine if the contents is SPAM, and it also offers CAPTCHA. If we wish, we can even use its CAPTCHA features in place of the CAPTCHA features setup with the reCAPTCHA and CAPTCHA modules.

Let's set up Mollom to work alongside our current CAPTCHA setup, but with an additional backup of its own CAPTCHA system if it detects a SPAM posting. This works by sending certain form submissions, such as a new page, comment or forum post, to the Mollom web service for analysis. If Mollom determines this to be SPAM, the user is then asked to complete a CAPTCHA test.

As with reCAPTCHA, Mollom is a third-party service and requires us to sign up to get API details so that we can use their service, these should be entered in Administration | Configuration | Content Authoring | Mollom | Settings, there is a sign up link to allow us to obtain the API keys.

> ⊗ The Mollom API keys are not configured yet.
>
> **▾ ACCESS KEYS**
>
> To use Mollom, you need a public and private key. To obtain your keys, register and login on mollom.com, and create a subscription for your site. Once you created a subscription, copy your private and public access keys from the site manager into the form fields below, and you are ready to go.
>
> **Public key**
>
> Used to uniquely identify you.
>
> **Private key**
>
> Used to prevent someone else from hijacking your requests. Similar to a password, it should never be shared with anyone.

Once we have the API keys installed, we need to instruct Mollom as to which forms to protect, via the Forms tab.

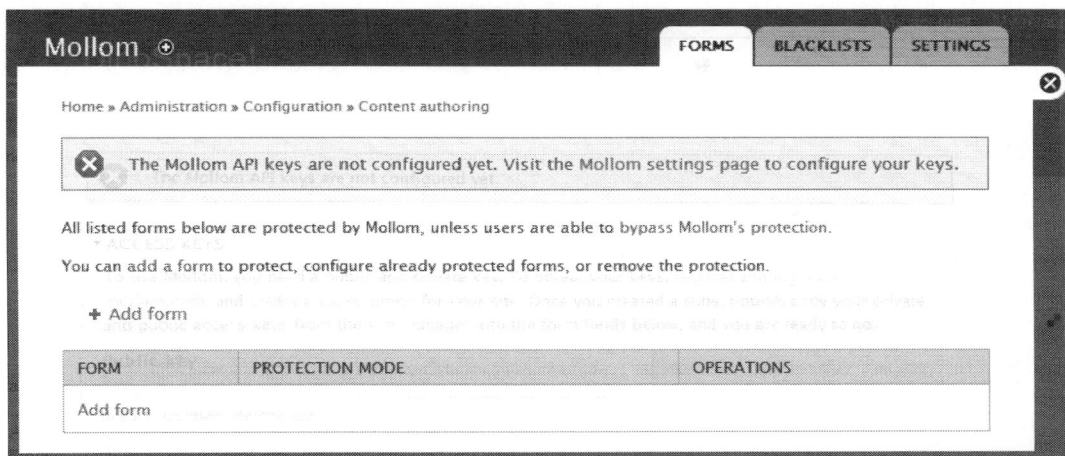

When adding a form, we first select the form to protect, then we have options to do the following:

- Protect the form by using Mollom to analyze the contents of the form submission
- Protect the form by using a Mollom supplied CAPTCHA
- Analyze the text for spam or profanity
- Select the fields of the form to analyze with Mollom
- Set if posts should be discarded or sent for manual moderation if they are identified as spam

Passwords

As the website owner, our passwords can provide access to the administration area of the website; our hosting account password also gives complete access to our website (even elements which may not be powered by Drupal), databases, e-mail, and statistics, so it is important that we use secure passwords.

Passwords which are not secure can be obtained by users guessing, automated dictionary attacks where a computer goes through a list of words trying them as the password, or by social engineering.

Strong passwords are generally difficult to guess by any of the previously mentioned methods, and here are some suggestions for making a strong password:

- Use both letters and numbers
- Make use of special characters such as @, /, \, #, *, &, and so on
- Make all of your passwords unique, otherwise if someone guesses your Drupal password, they may be able to gain access to your personal e-mail, other websites you are a member of and so on, if the passwords are all the same
- Include spelling mistakes to make the word harder to guess
- Don't include personal information such as dates of birth, names of family, and so on
- Consider using numbers in place of some letters

Drupal has a built-in JavaScript checker, which will advise whether it thinks a user's password is secure or not.

Deploying

There are quite a number of stages to go through to put DinoSpace online, so that it can be accessed on the Internet. Typically, this will involve the following:

1. Choosing and registering a domain name
2. Signing up with a hosting provider
3. Setting the nameservers for the domain
4. Creating a database on the hosting account
5. Exporting our local database
6. Importing our local database to the hosting account
7. Changing some of our database records
8. Changing our database configuration options
9. Uploading the files for our site
10. Testing

Choosing a domain name

Hopefully, by this stage, you will have already decided on the domain name you wish to use. With a site such as DinoSpace we could either combine the two names as one word, or we could hyphenate the name; this gives us more options should the TLD (top level domain, for example, `.com`) for our name be taken.

Sites such as `DomainTools.com` have whois lookup tools on them, which allow you to see if a particular domain name has been taken. Most domain name registrars also have these. They are an ideal starting point to check domain name availability.

Some website owners took advantage of international TLDs to form part of their web address, for example, `dinospa.ce` (`.ce` isn't a valid TLD, however), so this is another option if there is a relevant TLD, though for country specific TLD's sometimes there are restrictions on who can register a domain through them.

Registering a domain name

Once we have found a domain name which suitably represents our site, and is available, we can register it through a domain name registrar.

For around $10USD you should be able to register a `.com` domain name for a year, or a `.co.uk` domain for two years.

Popular domain name registrars

There are a number of popular domain name registrars, including the following:

- NameCheap (`www.namecheap.com`)
- GoDaddy (`www.godaddy.com`)
- 123-reg (`www.123-reg.co.uk`)

Signing up with a hosting provider

Signing up with a hosting provider generally involves choosing a hosting provider, selecting a suitable hosting package from their offering, supplying personal information, and supplying billing information to pay for the hosting.

Once signed up, most hosts send over a welcome e-mail including login details within an hour or so, once they have activated the account.

Choosing a web hosting provider

Hosting is a very big market on the Internet, and there are a large number of hosting providers available. There are also a number of different types of hosting provider available, including:

- **Shared hosting:** In shared hosting, lots of customers have space and resources on a single server, for example, A Small Orange.

- **Virtual Private Servers**: In virtual private servers, a small number of customers have access to dedicated resources on a single server, in the form of a dedicated virtualized instance of the server, giving the customer complete control, for example, SliceHost.

- **Cloud Hosting**: This is similar to VPS hosting, in that it is a virtualized server, except that the resources are generally spread over many machines, and the resources are not dedicated, allowing the hosting to use as much or as few resources as required, by making use of more physical machines, for example, Amazon EC2.

- **Dedicated Servers**: In dedicated servers, an entire machine is dedicated to one customer / website, with complete control to the customer, for example, Rackspace.

- **Co-location**: This is the same as dedicated servers, but the customer purchases their own equipment, and rents space in a data centre to house the servers and connect them to the Internet, for example, The Planet.

As our Social Network will be starting off small, it is advisable to start with either a shared hosting package, a small VPS, or cloud hosting. These should allow us to start with a small amount of server resources, for a low cost, and increase the resources as our site becomes more popular. Normally with shared hosting, accounts can be upgraded to include more space or bandwidth, though not additional processing power, with VPS and cloud providers, the specification of the server and the processing power allocated can often be upgraded and downgraded as necessary.

We will discuss VPS and cloud hosting in more detail in *Chapter 11, Planning for Growth.*

When looking at potential web hosting providers, the following factors should be taken into account:

- The amount of web space offered: We need to at least cover the space for our files, and a reasonable amount left over for user uploads.

- For VPS / Dedicated servers, the amount of dedicated memory we have access to is also important, as when all of the RAM is used up, servers make use of SWAP space on the disk, which is much slower.

- The amount of bandwidth required (data transferred from the web server to customers and other visitors per month): The amount we need will depend on traffic to our site, but it's important to see what happens when you exceed your bandwidth. We also need to check if this bandwidth is for upload and download, some providers include unlimited upload bandwidth, so updating our site won't use any of our bandwidth limit.

- Any service level agreements in place, such as a guaranteed uptime, or turn-around time for hardware replacement.

- Minimum contract term: How long are you are tied in for.

- Acceptable usage policy, to ensure they don't prohibit any of the functions of our social networking website: Some hosts limit outgoing e-mail traffic to prevent spam, which could affect some of our notification e-mails.

- To have software installed on the server, we obviously require PHP, MySQL, sendmail, and Apache with the `mod_rewrite` module.

- If we have full SSH root access (essential for VPS / dedicated servers so they can be fully managed).

- What level of support they offer (some hosts even lend a hand if a script isn't playing nicely on their servers).

- Cost and any benefits for paying monthly or annually.

Web-based control panels, such as cPanel or Plesk are included with most standard web hosting accounts. This makes many administrative tasks easier, including the following:

- Setting up and managing e-mail accounts
- Setting up and managing databases
- Viewing statistics, access, and error logs
- Performing backups, restoring from backups, and so on

One of the most common control panels is cPanel, and is included with most shared hosting and **Virtual Private Server (VPS)** providers. Some aspects of this chapter contain instructions specific for cPanel (manual deployment, and backing up and restoring), as well as alternative instructions for power users using the command line (assuming SSH access is enabled on the hosting account, this can normally be requested for shared hosting accounts: as for VPS/Dedicated servers, check that you are given full root access via SSH).

Packt Publishing has a book available specifically for cPanel, should you be interested in learning more about it: *cPanel User Guide and Tutorial* by *Aric Pedersen* (www.packtpub.com/cPanel/book).

Considerations for hosts for social networking websites

A few additional considerations worth keeping in mind, specifically for social networking websites, are as follows:

- Are websites backed up regularly automatically? If they are not, you could always write your own backup cron job script (SSH access would be helpful for this).
- What security measures are in place?
- Do the hosting accounts scale nicely?
- Can you pre-purchase additional bandwidth in advance of exceeding a limit?
- How many concurrent users can the hosting account cope with?

Popular web hosting providers

Some popular web hosting providers include the following:

- Slicehost (`www.slicehost.com`) is a Virtual Private Server provider, designed for developers with functionality to easily upgrade and downgrade server capacity.
- A Small Orange (`www.asmallorange.com`), who also provide shared hosting accounts, virtual servers, and dedicated servers.
- MediaTemple (`www.mediatemple.net`) is a provider of scalable virtual servers, with a control panel to make things as simple as with standard shared hosting accounts.
- VPS Net (`www.vps.net`).
- 1&1 Internet Inc. (`www.1and1.com`) provide shared hosting accounts, virtual servers, and dedicated servers for larger websites and web applications. However, be careful as their lower end shared hosting accounts don't support databases, such as MySQL.

Research hosting providers

Web Hosting Talk (`www.webhostingtalk.com`) is a popular discussion forum focusing on discussing the web hosting industry, containing many reviews and comparisons. It is worthwhile taking some time to research the different providers before signing up with one. It is also worth asking your potential host directly if they have hosted Drupal accounts, if they are familiar with the requirements for Drupal, and if they have any accounts optimized for Drupal.

Setting the nameservers for the domain

Once we have our domain name registered, and a hosting account set up, we need to change the nameservers of our domain to those of our hosting provider. This ensures that any traffic to our domain name is directed to our hosting account.

When signing up to a hosting provider, their welcome e-mail will generally include a reference of their nameservers; these are the addresses to servers which translate DNS requests for that particular domain name into IP addresses of the servers the site is hosted on. They are typically of the form `ns1.hostingproviderabc.com` and `ns2.hostingproviderabc.com`. Some domain registrars require the IP address of the servers as well as the hostname.

Full information on how to set the nameservers can be obtained from your domain name registrar, changes made to nameservers can take up to 24 hours to take effect.

Creating a database on the hosting account

Let's look at the two most common ways to create databases on a hosting account, firstly using the popular control panel cPanel, and secondly using phpMyAdmin when logged in as a user with suitable permissions (permissions to create users and databases, such as the root user).

With cPanel hosting control panel

Let's walkthrough creating a database on the hosting account using cPanel.

> This section assumes a hosting account with cPanel installed.

The first stage is to log in to our control panel (this is usually `www.yourdomain.com/cpanel`), and within the Databases section click the MySQL® Database Wizard icon. This will allow us to create a database and a user with permissions to access this database. The screenshot is as follows:

Next, we enter name for the new database; this is normally then combined with the hosting accounts username, so the database name `network` would become `dinospac_network`. Once we have entered a name, we need to click **Next Step**, to move on to the next stage of the database wizard:

Step 1: Create A Database

New Database: `network`

Next Step

Then we need to create a user within MySQL, which will connect to the database server to access the database we have just created. It is important to use a secure password for this, the Generate Password button to have cPanel automatically generate a secure password for us.

Once we have entered the username and password, we need to click the **Next Step** button:

MySQL® Database Wizard

Added the database

Step 2: Create Database Users:

Username: `dinospace`   *Seven characters max

Password: `···········`

Password Strength:
Very Strong (100/100)

Generate Password

Password (Again): `···········`

Next Step

Now that we have a database and a database user, we need to grant permissions for that user to be able to manage the database. Let's check the ALL PRIVILEGES checkbox and click the Next Step button again:

We now have a database on the server and a database user that can access the database. These are the details we will need for our configuration file.

With appropriate privileges on PHPMyAdmin

Assuming we have suitable permissions allowing us to create a database and a database user, we can use phpMyAdmin to create a new database and a user with permissions to use it. We will create a new user for MySQL, and set it to have its own database. We need to click the Privileges tab first, shown in the following screenshot:

On the privileges screen, we need to click the **Add a new User** link, shown in the following screenshot:

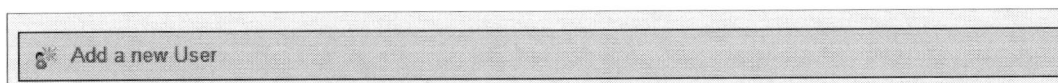

From here, we give the user a username, select the host from which the user can connect (normally localhost), and set a password (or we can use the Generate button to generate a secure password randomly for us).

We should select the **Create database with same name and grant all privileges** option under Database for user. This will create a database called `dinospacenetwork`, and give the `dinospacenetwork` user privileges to use it.

Once we submit the form, we have our new database and our database user. The reason we want a new database user, as well as a new database, is that should we have a vulnerability in our code, which would allow a user to access our database, it would only allow them access to this one database. Similarly, if there was a vulnerability in another application, they couldn't get to our database (unless of course, we used the root database details).

The following screenshot shows the create new user form:

Exporting our local database

With our database set up on the server, we now need to export the database we have on our local development installation. This can be done by selecting the database and then clicking the Export tab in phpMyAdmin.

From here, we can select which tables we wish to download, and have the option of either exporting the database as SQL, or as a download containing SQL, as shown in the following screenshot:

```
┌─View dump (schema) of database────────────────────────────────────────────────────────┐
│ ┌─Export────────────────────────────┐ ┌─Options──────────────────────────────────────┐ │
│ │      Select All / Unselect All     │ │ Add custom comment into header (\n splits lines)│ │
│ │ ┌────────────────────────────────┐ │ │ ┌──────────────────────┐                      │ │
│ │ │ actions                      ▲ │ │ │ └──────────────────────┘                      │ │
│ │ │ activity                     ▣ │ │ │ ☑ Comments                                   │ │
│ │ │ activity_access                │ │ │ ☐ Enclose export in a transaction            │ │
│ │ │ activity_comments              │ │ │ ☐ Disable foreign key checks                 │ │
│ │ │ activity_comments_stats        │ │ │ SQL compatibility mode                       │ │
│ │ │ activity_messages            ▼ │ │ │ ┌─────────────┬─┐                           │ │
│ │ └────────────────────────────────┘ │ │ │ NONE        │▼│                           │ │
│ │ ○ CodeGen                          │ │ └─────────────┴─┘                           │ │
│ │                                    │ │ ⑦                                            │ │
│ │ ○ CSV                              │ │ ┌─ ☑ Structure ─────────────────────────────┐ │ │
│ │ ○ CSV for MS Excel                 │ │ │ ☐ Add DROP TABLE / VIEW / PROCEDURE / FUNCTION / EVENT │ │
│ │ ○ Microsoft Excel 2000             │ │ │ ☑ Add IF NOT EXISTS                       │ │ │
│ │                                    │ │ │ ☑ Add AUTO_INCREMENT value                │ │ │
│ │ ○ Microsoft Word 2000              │ │ │ ☑ Enclose table and field names with backquotes │ │
│ │ ○ LaTeX                            │ │ │ ☐ Add CREATE PROCEDURE / FUNCTION / EVENT │ │ │
│ │ ○ Open Document Spreadsheet        │ │ │ ┌─Add into comments──────────────────────┐│ │ │
│ │ ○ Open Document Text               │ │ │ │ ☐ Creation/Update/Check dates          ││ │ │
│ │ ○ PDF                              │ │ │ └────────────────────────────────────────┘│ │ │
│ │                                    │ │ └───────────────────────────────────────────┘ │ │
│ │ ◉ SQL                              │ │ ┌─ ☑ Data ──────────────────────────────────┐ │ │
│ │ ○ Texy! text                       │ │ │ ☑ Complete inserts                        │ │ │
│ │ ○ XML                              │ │ │ ⑦                                         │ │ │
│ │                                    │ │ │ ☑ Extended inserts                        │ │ │
│ │ ○ YAML                             │ │ │ ⑦                                         │ │ │
│ │                                    │ │ │ Maximal length of created query           │ │ │
│ │                                    │ │ │ ┌──────────────────────┐                  │ │ │
│ │                                    │ │ │ │ 50000                │                  │ │ │
│ │                                    │ │ │ └──────────────────────┘                  │ │ │
│ │                                    │ │ │ ☐ Use delayed inserts                     │ │ │
│ │                                    │ │ │ ☐ Use ignore inserts                      │ │ │
│ │                                    │ │ │ ☑ Use hexadecimal for BLOB                │ │ │
│ │                                    │ │ │ Export type                               │ │ │
│ │                                    │ │ │ ┌─────────┬─┐                             │ │ │
│ │                                    │ │ │ │ INSERT  │▼│                             │ │ │
│ │                                    │ │ │ └─────────┴─┘                             │ │ │
│ │                                    │ │ └───────────────────────────────────────────┘ │ │
│ └────────────────────────────────────┘ └──────────────────────────────────────────────┘ │
│ ┌─ ☑ Save as file ───────────────────────────────────────────────────────────────────┐ │
│ │ File name template¹: ┌──DB──────────┐  ( ☑ remember template )                       │ │
│ │ Compression: ◉ None ○ "zipped" ○ "gzipped"                                           │ │
│ └──────────────────────────────────────────────────────────────────────────────────────┘ │
└─────────────────────────────────────────────────────────────────────────────────────────┘
```

Importing our local database to the hosting account

With a copy of our local development database exported, we can import it into our hosting account using the Import tab on the server's phpMyAdmin, where we simply upload the SQL file (if we exported as text, we would use the SQL tab to paste the SQL into and import the database).

> In most cases, there is a 2 MB limit on file uploads. This can cause problems for importing a large active site, however, we are only importing our skeleton database so this shouldn't be a problem. For importing and exporting large databases, you should use SSH, as discussed later in this chapter.

We now have our database set up and working on the production server!

Changing the database settings

In order for our live Drupal installation to connect to the database on the server, we will need to update the configuration file to contain the connection details for that database.

The database connection details are located in the settings.php file (in the sites/default folder). We need to download this file, and open it with a text editor (or a PHP editor, such as Crimson editor).

Within the file we need to edit the `$databases` array which should be between lines 181 and 195. Within this section of code, we simply update the database (for the name of the database we are connecting to), username, password, and host variables to reflect those of our hosting account:

```
$databases = array (
  'default' =>
  array (
    'default' =>
    array (
      'database' => 'drupal_live',
      'username' => 'drupal_live',
      'password' => 'oursecurepassword',
      'host' => 'localhost',
      'port' => '',
      'driver' => 'mysql',
      'prefix' => '',
    ),
  ),
);
```

Uploading the site

With the configuration file updated, and the live database set up, we can now upload all of our files to the server. To upload the website files from our development environment to our production environment, we need to use an FTP client. One such example of an FTP client is FileZilla, a free FTP client available for download.

Within FileZilla, we simply enter the web address of the site, and our FTP username and password and then click Quickconnect:

Secure FTP

If you have SSH access, instead of leaving the port field blank, you could supply port number 22. This would force the connection to be secure, using SSH.

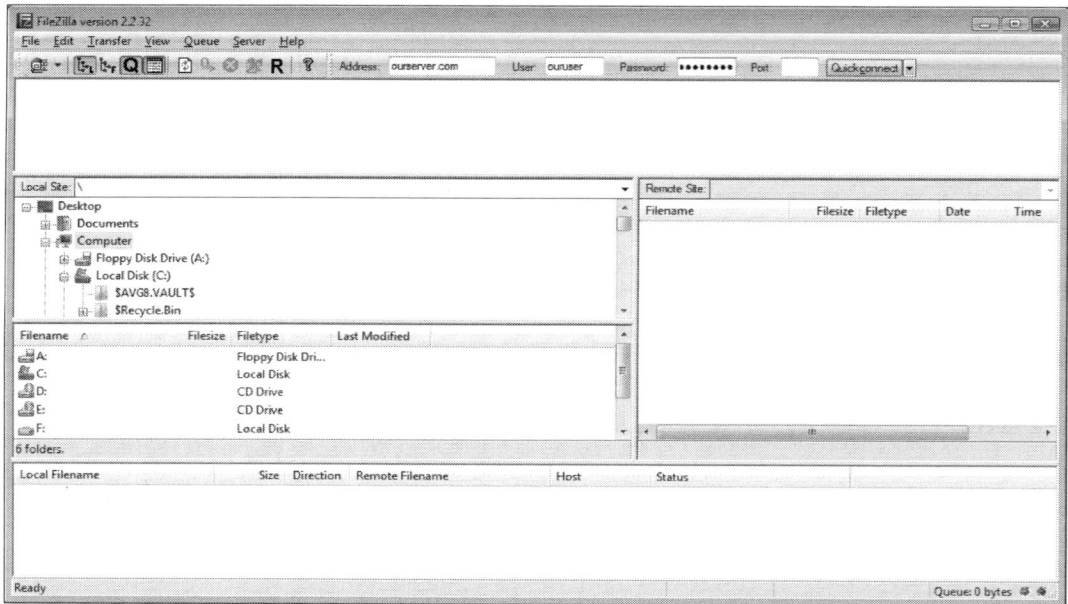

Once the FTP client is connected, we simply drag the files from the relevant folder on our development environment in the Local site pane on the left to the relevant folder within Remote site pane on the right. Commonly, the folder on the server would be either public_html or htdocs, and files within these folders are generally made accessible to the public through a web browser.

Permissions on certain folders, such as the uploads folder, will need to be changed to allow write access. More information regarding these permissions can be found on the Drupal website: http://drupal.org/node/244924.

Testing

We now have a domain name, a suitable hosting environment, our Drupal installation is within our hosting environment, and a live database is set up, the next stage for us is to visit the live site in our browser to check everything is working as intended.

Maintenance

From time to time we may wish to perform some maintenance on our site; let's look at three common ways of maintaining our installation:

- Automated maintenance: Cron
- Making changes and updating our site
- Analysing Drupal reports and performing maintenance accordingly

Cron

Cron is the automated execution of tasks by our server. Many Drupal modules perform regular maintenance tasks (for example, pruning log files), by using cron these tasks can be automatically performed at specific intervals.

Setting up cron jobs is quite technical, and depends on your hosting provider too, as not all hosting providers allow cron jobs to run. You should contact your web host for more information on setting up a cron job.

The Drupal handbook online contains more information about setting up cron. `http://drupal.org/cron`.

Looking up the secure cron URL

If you are comfortable with setting up a cron job, you will need to generate a secure cron URL from Drupal. This is a web address which when called by our cron scheduler, will perform various automated tasks for Drupal. With Drupal 7 this URL is secured, preventing other users from manually triggering our cron tasks.

The URL can be obtained from Administration | Reports | Status:

Cron maintenance tasks   Last run 1 hour 7 min ago

You can run cron manually.

To run cron from outside the site, go to http://localhost/drupal7/cron.php?
cron_key=04W5_b2mlZ_OcJOkjLdXg_v1hbopdMAePnmnqQel29w

Performing maintenance

When we decide to make some major changes to our site, it is a good idea to put the site into maintenance mode. This prevents other users from accessing the site at a time when they are more likely to experience errors resulting from changes being made as they are browsing the site.

There is a maintenance option within Drupal specifically for this purpose, it turns the website offline to our users, and displays a message of our choice. This option is found under Administration | Configuration | Development | Maintenance mode.

From here we just need to tick that we want to **Put site into maintenance mode**, and enter a Maintenance mode message to be displayed to users who try and access the site.

If we now go back to the homepage of the site, there is a message there to remind us, as an administrator, that the website is in offline mode and our users won't be able to access the site:

If we log out, we can see that the site is inaccessible, and we are presented with the message we set earlier.

> **Logging into an offline site**
>
> To log back into the site we need to go direct to the user page, which will prompt us to log in. For example,. `www.dinosapce.net/user/` (`?q=user` if Nice URL's not enabled)

Upgrading Drupal

When new versions of Drupal are released, we may wish to upgrade to a newer version, especially if it is a new security release. Upgrading is quite a straightforward process; however, one thing we do need to be careful of is our modules. If we upgraded to a new major release of Drupal (for example, Drupal 8) we would probably find most of our modules would not work. When new releases are available, with security updates, a message is displayed in the administration panel. Although the upgrade process may vary from upgrade to upgrade, the process generally involves the following:

- Downloading the new version of Drupal
- Backing up your website
- Backing up your database
- Uploading the files from the new version to the site
- Visiting our site and accessing the `update.php` file to make any necessary database changes

Of course, full detailed documentation is provided within each upgrade.

Reports

Drupal provides us with a number of reports in the administration area which can help advise us of areas where maintenance may be required. These reports include the following:

- Recent log entries of various events which have been recorded, including users logging in, e-mail problems, and actions relating to content
- Top 'access denied' errors listing attempts by users to access content they are not permitted to see
- Top 'page not found' errors listing the top access attempts to pages which don't exist on our site

- Available updates, lists updates which are available for our modules and themes
- Status report which checks for problems with our site, for example, if cron is set up

How can these help?

If we are finding a lot of access denied errors then we are likely to have a link in a menu or page, which most of our users can see, to pages they shouldn't be able to access. We should then look for this link and remove it. Similarly if we are having a lot of "page not found" errors for certain pages, then we may have a link to a page which does not exist and we should remove the link. Alternatively, it may be due to a page we removed, we could set up a redirect to a replacement page, or put up a page explaining why the page was removed.

The available updates report can help us keep our modules up-to-date, when upgrading modules and themes it is advisable to turn the website into maintenance mode, to prevent our users experiencing any errors.

Backing up and restoring your social network

Backing up and restoring our site is one of the most important maintenance tasks to do, as if something goes wrong with our site, server, or host, we would want to be able to restore the site quickly. Ideally, backing up should be automated, if you have purchased backup provisions with your hosting account, you may have automated backup options available in addition to the ones listed as follows:

With cPanel

Within the main cPanel interface, in the Files section there is a link to the Backups area.

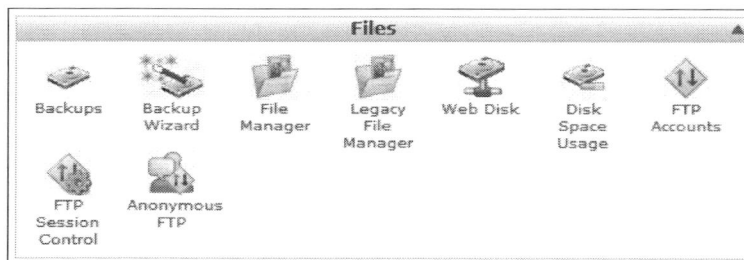

We can download a copy of our Home Directory (all of the files and most of our settings), and also a copy of the database from this section. Simply clicking the relevant backup buttons will prompt us to download the backup files from the server:

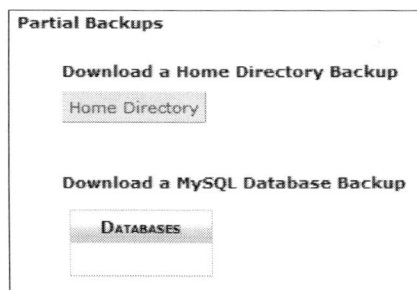

Partial Backups

Download a Home Directory Backup

Home Directory

Download a MySQL Database Backup

DATABASES

It is essential that we keep these files stored somewhere safe and secure.

Restoring the site and database

To restore from a backup we need to ensure we are logged into cPanel, and then click the Backups button to go to the backups section, as we did when backing up the site.

On the right-hand side of this screen are the options to **Restore a Home Directory Backup** and to **Restore a MySQL Database**:

Restore a Home Directory Backup
Choose File   No file chosen   Upload

Restore a MySQL Database
Choose File   No file chosen   Upload

To restore from the backups, all we need to do is browse for the file we wish to restore from, and then click Upload.

> When restoring any existing database or home directory, content will be removed, so only do this if you really need to. If you need to gain access to a specific file that you need to back up, decompress the home directory backup, look for the file, and upload it to your site using an FTP client.

Using the command line

An alternative method to back up and restore our site is by using the command line.

Command-line access and Putty

Most shared hosting accounts won't provide command-line (SSH) access by default, but many will enable it on request for your account. Simply file a support ticket with your host to request this, and if they allow it, they will provision it for you.

To connect to the server using SSH, you can either use the terminal interface on a Mac or Linux, or on Windows use a program such as Putty, a free SSH client available from: http://www.chiark.greenend.org.uk/~sgtatham/putty/.

Backing up the site and database

Once connected through SSH to the server, we need to navigate to the location of our site. In most cases, this will be /home/ourusername:

```
cd /home/dinospac/
```

Then we can compress the public_html folder to a single file, using:

```
tar cvzf backup.tar.gz public_html
```

With the folder compressed, we need to move it to within the public_html folder, so we can download it by visiting oursite.com/backup.tar.gz:

```
mv backup.tar.gz public_html/backup.tar.gz
```

The following command exports our database to a web-accessible location on our server, where we can download it using a web browser:

```
mysqldump -u username -p databasename > /home/dinospac/public_html/
backup.sql
```

After executing this command, we will be prompted for our password, and then we can download the file from our browser.

Once downloaded, it is important that we remove the database.sql and backup.tar.gz files immediately, so that they are not downloaded by anyone else.

Restoring the site and the database

Assuming we upload the `tar.gz` file into our server, we can decompress it with the following command:

```
tar -xvf backup.tar.gz
```

Assuming we upload the SQL file onto our server, we can import it with the following command (the database should be emptied, or be a new clean database, first):

```
mysql -u username -p databasename < /home/dinospac/backup.sql
```

Do they work?

Backing up the site, and knowing how to restore it in an emergency is only half of the battle; we also need to ensure that our backups work! We can test our backups by extracting them and setting them up on a localhost machine, and this should be done regularly to test the integrity of backups.

Summary

In this chapter, we looked at how to deploy our social networking site onto the Internet, how to keep spammers out using Mollom and reCAPTCHA, and how to keep it maintained using the maintenance mode, reports, and cron to keep everything running smoothly. We also looked into keeping backups of our site in case anything went wrong, and how to restore from a backup if we need to. Hopefully, we won't need to use the restore feature, but it is important to know how to use it in case we do.

11
Easing Growing Pains

As we get more and more users, and our social network becomes more popular, we will be faced with two new challenges: growth and scalability. Hopefully, this will be a problem we are faced with as a result of the marketing and promotion topics discussed in *Chapter 12, Promoting Our Site*.

As site usage increases, more and more resources on our web server are consumed. Depending on the hosting provisions we use and the resources at our disposal, this can lead to a slower experience for our users, a server failure, or some users being unable to access the site. We can help mitigate against this by looking at how we can get the most out of our server hardware, by improving our site, and how we can scale by adding more resources (not just by adding more servers).

In this chapter, you will learn the following:

- How to speed up load time of content for anonymous users by caching it
- How to use third-party caching engines to increase performance
- How NoSQL solutions can help
- How we can free up server resources by outsourcing tasks
- What content delivery networks are and how they can help
- How we can examine our own custom code to keep it performing well
- Server performance tweaks to Apache, MySQL, and PHP
- More about scaling and redundancy options

Let's look at how we can improve the performance of our Drupal-powered social network, and plan for growth!

Basic performance tips

In the administration area under **Configuration | Development | Performance** we have a few performance options:

CACHING

☐ Cache pages for anonymous users

☐ Cache blocks

    Block caching is inactive because you have enabled modules defining content access restrictions.

Minimum cache lifetime

<none> ▼

Cached pages will not be re-created until at least this much time has elapsed.

Expiration of cached pages

<none> ▼

The maximum time an external cache can use an old version of a page.

BANDWIDTH OPTIMIZATION

External resources can be optimized automatically, which can reduce both the size and number of requests made to your website.

☐ Aggregate and compress CSS files.

☐ Aggregate JavaScript files.

We can cache pages for anonymous users and blocks within our site. This takes a copy of the content and stores it outside of our database—either in the server's memory or on the file system. This reduces the work the server has to do to load these pages. We can also instruct Drupal to aggregate and compress our CSS and our JavaScript files, so that when a user visits our site, those files are generated and downloaded quicker, with fewer HTTP requests, helping to slightly reduce the load that our server is under.

Introduction to caching and caching options

Caching systems can reduce the number of database and file system requests the website makes when our users access it, by storing commonly used data in the system's memory (this is known as caching).

When we needed to access the contents of a commonly used file or frequently accessed database record, the information is already cached and we simply check the cache when we need to access the data. For example, our static pages such as the about page, contact page, policies, and so on, are not going to change frequently so they can be cached and then quickly accessed when requested. Drupal 7 has been improved to be more compatible with such systems, including the following:

- APC: http://drupal.org/project/apc
- Memcache: http://drupal.org/project/memcache
- Varnish: http://www.varnish-cache.org/trac/wiki/VarnishAndDrupal

NoSQL options

There are a number of database systems available which are schemaless, useful for storing large amounts of data which doesn't need to relate to other data, such as logs, pages, documents, and so on. Examples of systems available include MongoDB and CouchDB. Generally, each individual record defines its own structure and fields, allowing such systems to be flexible to the data they are needed to store.

In some cases, where we are working with very large data sets, we can gain a performance benefit by using something like MongoDB to:

- Store Drupal fields
- Store cached items
- Store user sessions

There is a module available which provides integration with MongoDB at http://drupal.org/project/mongodb. More information on MongoDB itself can be found at http://www.mongodb.org/. Unfortunately, it isn't possible to simply install Drupal from the start with MongoDB, we can only use databases such as this to store the information mentioned previously. Installation details for MongoDB can be found on their quick start guide at http://www.mongodb.org/display/DOCS/Quickstart.

For more information about using Drupal and MongoDB, see the video of the presentation by Doug Green and Károly Négyesi at the Drupalcon Chicago: http://chicago2011.drupal.org/sessions/practical-mongodb-and-drupal.

Can't someone else do it?

Drupal and our web server do a number of tasks which can easily be offloaded onto other services, either free of charge or at minimal cost.

Statistics

By default, the statistics module is disabled within Drupal. This is a module which would allow us to collect usage statistics about our site. While these statistics are a good thing, if we used Drupal to collect and manage them, we would be adding to the work we need it to do in the course of powering our social network. Instead, we should leave the module disabled and look to use third-party services, which do an excellent job of logging statistics and visualizing them for us. In particular, there is Google Analytics, a free comprehensive statistics package, where all the logging and processing is done by Google—saving our servers the need to process that data. You can sign up for a free account at `http://analytics.google.com`. Google Analytics provides a very detailed breakdown of our website's visitors and content popularity, whereas Drupal's default statistics focus on content popularity. We can use this data to analyze the location of our users, the technical capabilities of their computer, and subsequently continually tailor our content for the people who actually use our site.

Sending e-mails

At various times, our site needs to send out e-mails to our users; most of these are transaction-based e-mails and are sent in response to a particular action, for example, "Michael added you as a friend", or "Your password reset e-mail". This is another aspect we can outsource to another provider, and for a few benefits as follows:

- We don't have our server running outgoing e-mail services

- We can see delivery reports for our e-mails, and use techniques to help reduce our e-mails being marked as spam

- We can process bounces easily; for instance, deactivating users where their welcome e-mail bounces

One such service which takes this off our hands is Postmark at `http://postmarkapp.com/`, which provides us with the first 1,000 e-mails free of charge, and then charges $1.50 for every thousand e-mails we send. A module is available to allow Drupal to plug directly into Postmark at `http://drupal.org/project/postmark`.

E-mail services

More server focused than related to Drupal itself, if we are using a server which we control (that is, a VPS or dedicated server), instead of having the server deal with our private e-mail accounts, which consume storage and processing resources on the server, we can offload that too. One potential option is Google Apps, a cloud-based e-mail service for organisations and companies using the same technologies as their standard Gmail service. With this, we don't need to install any e-mail services on our web server, and simply set the MX record of our domain name to redirect e-mail traffic to the Google servers. For more information, and to sign up, see `http://www.google.com/apps/intl/en/group/index.html`.

Hosted Apache Solr search

The default search feature relies on Drupal periodically indexing our website, which in turn consumes our server's resources. One alternative is to use Acquia's (the commercial company supporting Drupal) hosted Solr search service. It doesn't take all of the work away from our Drupal installation, as it still needs to communicate with our site to access the site's data, but it worries about building and maintaining the search index for us. For more information see the Acquia search service web page at `http://acquia.com/products-services/acquia-search`.

Using content delivery networks

A content delivery network is a network of servers with a number of different geographic locations. When a user visits a website which uses a CDN, static files such as user downloads, images, style sheets, and JavaScript libraries are downloaded from the visitor's closest server on the Content Delivery Network. This reduces the number of connections to our primary web server, and increases the speed at which the site loads for the user (while in most cases it won't speed up the PHP processing or the HTML transfer, the images, and other supporting files, are usually larger and take longer to download).

CDN module

The CDN module (`http://drupal.org/project/cdn`) allows us to easily set up our Drupal installation to serve various images, files, and other assets from accounts we have set up with content delivery networks:

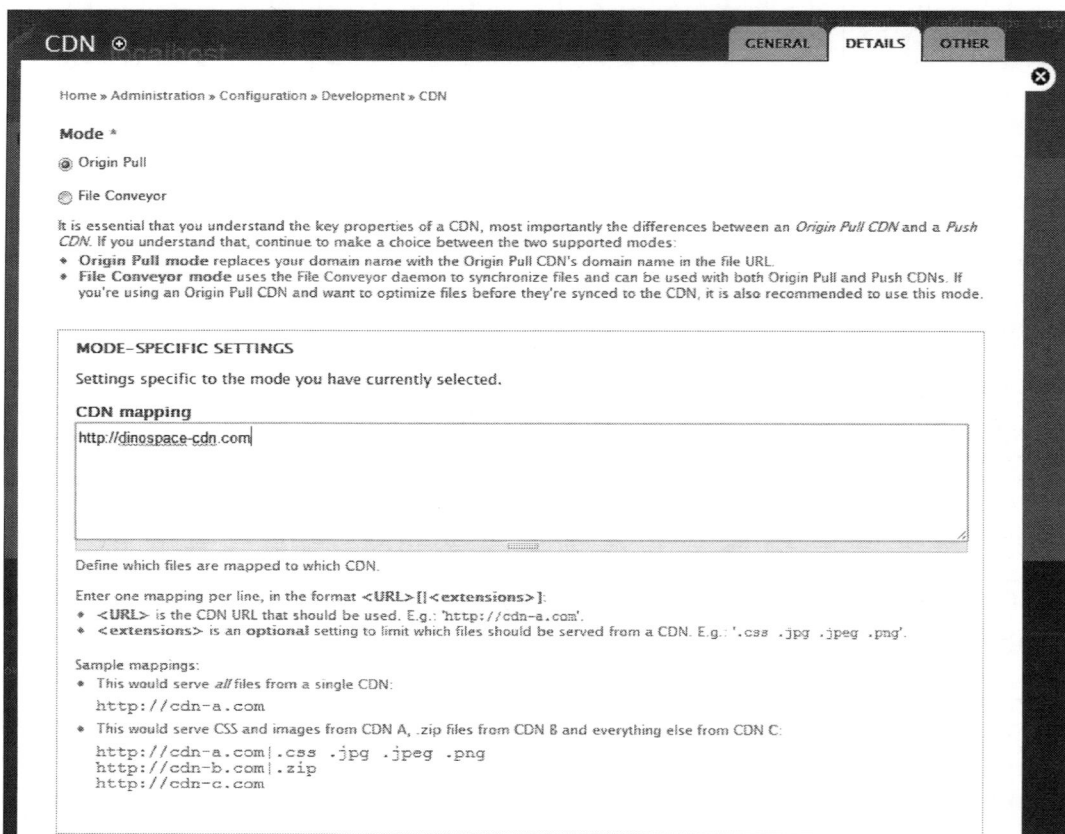

Code improvements and custom modules

One of the most important factors when it comes to the speed, performance, and scalability of our site, is our code. By improving the performance of our code, it consumes fewer resources, allowing us to get more out of our current hardware.

This book has assumed that we have used existing modules to power our Drupal Social Network, however, if we start to expand our Social Network with our own custom developed modules, we might want to look at improvements we can make to our code. We can also use these tricks; if we find certain modules are having a detrimental effect on our site, to work out what is causing the problem, and allow us to fix it (we could even submit the fix as a patch to the module author on `Drupal.org`). There are many user groups and discussion forums (a simple Google search will turn up ones related to particular issues) where we can join to ask and answer questions. By answering questions on topics we have experienced with; other users will be more inclined to help us with our issues.

So, what can we do to improve our code performance?

- We can profile our code to look for problems
- We can look for slow MySQL queries which we can optimize
- We can compress our output

Code profiling

We can profile our code to find bottlenecks in our code, so that we know which aspects need improvement or refactoring. Profiling tools, such as Xdebug (`http://xdebug.org/index.php`), are integrated into PHP to run as our scripts run, logging performance information to a file, which we can analyze using another suitable tool (with Xdebug, we can use tools such as KCacheGrind and WinCacheGrind).

Slow queries

If a query takes too long to run causing Drupal to wait, it may either reach a timeout preventing it from displaying anything to our user, or our users may get impatient and leave our site.

> This section assumes we have access to our MySQL configuration files; that is, that we are on a VPS or Dedicated server.

MySQL can be configured to log slow queries, allowing us to see which queries are taking too long to run, so that we can investigate and improve the queries or improve the database scheme itself, that is, by adding more suitable indexes. To enable the slow query log, we simply add the following line to our MySQL configuration file (my.ini file):

```
log-slow-queries = dinospace_slow_queries.log
```

Once enabled, the query log by default logs queries which take longer than 10 seconds to complete, we can change this by adding the following line to our configuration file:

```
set-variable = long_query_time = 2
```

Compression

By compressing our website's output, we can reduce network latency between the server and the user, and reduce bandwidth usage, making the site load faster. While the code won't be generated any quicker, it should be received by the user faster.

This can be done either with some Apache configuration, or by tweaking our PHP installation. The Apache option involves installing and enabling the mod_deflate Apache extension. More information on this can be found online, see: http://httpd.apache.org/docs/2.0/mod/mod_deflate.html and http://www.howtoforge.com/apache2_mod_deflate.

The PHP option involves using zlib (http://php.net/manual/en/book.zlib.php); this isn't installed with PHP by default on Linux installations, but can be installed fairly easily — contact your web host for further information.

Once installed, there are a number of different ways it can be enabled to compress the output, we can either enable it directly in our PHP.INI file, or if we have suitable access, we can dynamically set / override the INI files value in our PHP script, with the following line of code at the top of our index.php file:

```
ini_set('zlib.output_compression', '1');
```

Alternatively, if we are not able to set INI file values, we can use object buffering to not send anything to the browser initially, buffering the output instead. Once all the output has been buffered the compression handler is called to compress the output and send it to the browser. To do this, we simply put the following line of code at the top of the Drupal index.php file:

```
ob_start( 'ob_gzhandler' );
```

Server performance and configuration

The topics we have discussed so far focus on code changes, or introducing other services to reduce the work our web server needs to do. Our site runs on services which are highly configurable in their own right, including Apache, MySQL and PHP—all of which can be configured and tuned for performance using their various configuration files.

Apache

Our Apache configuration file (name and location depend on the setup of the server) contain settings relating to how many connections can be accepted, timeout period, and so on.

The maximum number of clients which can connect to the server at any one time is set by the `MaxClient Directive` in the configuration file; this can be increased to allow more connections to the server, provided we have sufficient resources to allow this of course. More information is available at `http://httpd.apache.org/docs/2.0/mod/mpm_common.html#maxclients`.

The length of time a process can take before Apache times out the request is set in the `Timeout Directive`, and we can reduce this to prevent processes which are likely to time out from consuming as much processing time. More information is available at `http://httpd.apache.org/docs/2.2/mod/core.html#timeout`.

Apache has some useful performance tuning information on its website to help get higher performance out of the server. More information can be found at `http://httpd.apache.org/docs/2.0/misc/perf-tuning.html`

MySQL

We can optimize MySQL for high availability and performance. Packt have published a book on this topic,"*High Availability MySQL Cookbook*", *Alex Davies*, `https://www.packtpub.com/high-availability-mysql-cookbook/book`.

Alternative web servers

An alternative to increase the performance of our web server is to use a different web server, such as lighttpd or nginx, which are lightweight web servers, designed for speed and performance:

* `http://nginx.org/`
* `http://www.lighttpd.net/`

Scaling our resources

With our installation optimized, and our server's resources being utilized as best as they can, we now need to look into how we can scale our systems to easily provision more resources as and when we need them. Options available include the following:

- VPS Cloud Hosting, which generally involves either of the following:
    ° Adding more resources to a virtualized server
    ° Paying for only the resources we use

- Adding additional servers for certain functions

VPS cloud hosting

Cloud hosting is generally a form of VPS (Virtual Private Server) hosting, where one or more physical machines have one or more virtual servers running on top of them. In most cases, a high specification server has a number of virtualized servers running on top of it, each with dedicated and guaranteed resources available, acting as far as the customer is concerned, as their own dedicated server. When we start our website, we won't need too many resources, so we could happily share the resources with other users on the same server; as the site grows, we could upgrade our account to use more resources. Some cloud solutions also allow a VPS instance to run on several physical machines, either for redundancy (should one go down, others kick in), or to provide more resources. By virtualizing the server, we don't need to spend money on new hardware when we need to upgrade, or wait while a technician upgrades or replaces hardware.

A number of cloud hosting providers offer ways to upgrade the resources required dynamically, so should the site experience a spike in traffic, more resources would be provisioned. Two examples of such providers are Amazon with their EC2 service (Amazon Elastic Compute Cloud) and VPS.NET.

With Amazon EC2, we would only be charged for the resources our website uses, be it storage space, bandwidth, or CPU time, which has the advantage of growing and shrinking to meet our needs. VPS.NET have auto-provisioning functionality, so that should load, storage space, or memory usage exceed a certain threshold, it can automatically add more resources. The main difference here is that you are charged based on a set dedicated amount of resources.

By starting with a scalable VPS provider, we can have our website up and running with generous resources at a low cost, and can add and remove resources as and when required easily, and if we wish, automatically.

Additional servers

Either in addition to VPS / Cloud hosting, or with dedicated servers, we could add additional servers to the infrastructure, with each server performing certain operations; for instance, a dedicated MySQL database server, a dedicated Apache server, a dedicated server for sending outgoing e-mails, a Memcached server, and so on. The advantage is that each server can be specially optimized for the services running on it, as well as providing more resources for each aspect. The downside is that it introduces network latency, as database query results and so on, will have to be transferred over a network to the web server, and then sent to the user. If MySQL is hosted on a separate server, then it should be located on the same network with a low latency link (hardware and data center permitting).

Adding redundancy to our setup

As DinoSpace becomes more popular, the consequences of downtime become more severe. Each second of downtime is time that new users are turned away from the site, leading them to potentially look elsewhere. It is also the time where existing users may be put off from the site, and may look into alternative sites which may be more reliable. This point is emphasised by the media coverage and public reaction each time a popular social website, such as Twitter or Facebook, goes offline.

Redundant systems should help reduce or eliminate downtime, by providing backups of everything, including the following:

- Replicated database servers: If our primary database server goes offline, a backup server kicks in. The data on this backup is up-to-date because it would constantly replicate from the primary server.

- Redundant network connections to the data centre: Should one particular connection become congested, or suffer failure, another provider's connection can be used.

- Redundant web servers: Should one suffer an outage.

Most redundancy options are dependent on the services available from the data center the servers are hosted within. Provided we have access to shared IP addresses, provided by the server provider / data centre, we can set up a fallback server using Heartbeat. The primary server sends a heartbeat to the secondary server; if the secondary server doesn't receive a heartbeat in a certain time limit, then it activates and traffic is routed to the secondary machine instead. More information is available on the project's website at `http://www.linux-ha.org/wiki/Main_Page`.

Slicehost has an excellent tutorial on setting up Heartbeat (the only slicehost specific aspect is requesting a failed over IP address) at `http://articles.slicehost.com/2008/10/28/ip-failover-slice-setup-and-installing-heartbeat`.

Keep an eye out...

Pressflow (`http://pressflow.org/`) is a distribution of Drupal designed with performance, scalability, and high availability in mind. At the moment, they only have a version available for Drupal 6, although Drupal 7 contains a number of improvements they have recommended. A version of Pressflow is in development for Drupal 7, so it is worth keeping an eye out for that for further performance enhancements.

Summary

In this chapter, we looked at how we can get more from our servers, our software, and from our Drupal installation, by:

- Speeding up load time of content for anonymous users by caching it
- Using third-party caching engines to increase performance
- Looking at NoSQL solutions for large data sets and certain aspects of Drupal
- Outsourcing tasks, including the following:
    - E-mail sending
- Statistics
    - E-mail services

- Leveraging Content delivery networks
- Profiling code for our own custom modules
- Tweaking to Apache, MySQL, and PHP
- Exploring scaling and redundancy options

Now that we have looked at how to cope with growth, scalability, stability, and performance issues, we can begin promoting our site and getting in as many users as we can, which we will look at in *Chapter 12, Promoting Our Site*.

12
Promotion, SEO, User Retention, and Monetization Strategies

With DinoSpace up and running, and now that we are more comfortable in handling our site's future growth, we need to get members to our site, as without members our social network will fail (unless we were setting up DinoSpace for a select group of people who we know). Let's look at useful promotion, marketing, search engine optimization, and user retention concepts, to help us increase our user base, and keep our users.

In this chapter, you will learn the following:

- How to promote sites online using:
    - Pay-Per-Click campaigns
    - Advertising space
    - Newsletters
    - Social marketing
- How to keep the search engines happy
- On-site and off-site search engine optimization
- Some customer retention tips
- Some tips to help make money from the site

It is important to note, that this isn't a technical chapter, and the contents covered can (and do) fill several books. The purpose of this chapter is to give you some valuable insight, hints, and tips which can help you increase the performance of your website in the search engines, and to promote the site through other ways, to help ensure it is a success.

Promotion and marketing

Marketing can range from some simple online marketing, advertising, or PPC campaigns. Let's take a look at some of the marketing methods available to us.

Online advertising

There are a number of different online advertising techniques available for us to take advantage of, including the following:

- Pay-Per-Click advertisements
- Purchasing advertising space
- Newsletter advertising

Pay-Per-Click

Pay-Per-Click advertising only costs us each time a visitor clicks on an advert and goes through to our site. When looking at or negotiating cost-per-click rates with advertisers, it is important to work out how many of these visitors are likely to join DinoSpace (our conversion rate), so we can decide how much we wish to invest in a PPC campaign.

If we had a monetization strategy in place for our site, for example, paid advertisements on the site, we could work out how much each user earns us, which would help us to establish how much we could invest in PPC, combined with our conversion rate, to ensure we don't lose money. Of course with this type of site, in the early stages, it is essential to build up the user base, even if it doesn't earn us any money initially.

Most PPC services allow us to set daily and monthly budgets, so that when a daily maximum is reached our advert is no longer displayed until the next day, when a new daily limit is in effect.

Let us now take a look at how most PPC services work:

1. We sign up to a PPC network.
2. We provide information about our site, and some personal information.
3. We provide billing information, either a credit card number, or we make payments in advance.

4. We select the keywords we wish to target (for example, "dinosaur breeding tips"; these are words which visitors may type into a search engine, or the page may have content related to these keywords for adverts displayed on pages, triggering our adverts), as well as any information on the visitors we want to target (for example, UK users).

5. Finally, we set a budget for how much we would be willing to pay for each click, the maximum we would be willing to spend in a day, and so on.

Once the campaign is up and running we can generally log in to a control panel and see how much of our budget has been spent, and how much we are paying on average per click. The monthly budgets mean if we don't pre-pay, and instead provide credit card information, we are never billed more than we have agreed to.

One thing that advertisers are often concerned about is the possibility of fraudulent clicks. For example, a competitor could perform a search to find our advert, and then repeatedly click our advert. This would cost our campaign budget, and not give us a return, because the clicking was not by a potential new sign-up. To prevent this from affecting advertisers, and ruining the reputation of advertising networks, most of them have systems in place: tracking duplicate clicks and crediting the accounts of advertisers when this occurs. It is important to ensure that the PPC network we chose has provisions for detecting fraudulent clicks, so our money isn't wasted!

Search engine PPC networks

Many search engines also provide their own PPC advertising network, three of which are listed in this section. The algorithms employed by many of these search engines determine how much a click is likely to cost based on the site itself and its position in the natural search engine rankings.

A site that is completely unrelated to dinosaurs (and more specifically unrelated to, supplies, breeding tips, health care tips, and so on, for keepers of dinosaurs), would probably need to pay more than a relevant site for the same (dinosaur-related) keywords with search engines, as the relevancy of the site (generally determined by its existing search engine rankings) affects the cost.

Three of the most popular search engine advertisement networks are:

- **Google:** (http://www.google.com/ads/)
- **Yahoo!:** (http://sem.smallbusiness.yahoo.com/searchenginemarketing/index.php)
- **Microsoft:** (http://advertising.microsoft.com/search-advertising)

Most search engines also allow their advertising networks to be used on third-party sites, so apart from appearing as a sponsored link on search engine results pages, the site will also display on websites, which decide to display adverts from that particular advertisement network, and also contain relevant content to the advertisement.

One important thing to remember about competing sites is that most PPC networks allow us to enter sites where we don't want our advert to appear, so if a competitor displays adverts, and ours appears on theirs, we can detect this through their control panel, and add them to the list to prevent our advert displaying, hopefully increasing our return on investment.

Pay-Per-Action—A look to the future

Pay-Per-Action is a new scheme being investigated by a number of PPC networks, where you only pay when a visitor performs a certain action on your site. This could involve registering for an account, entering their e-mail address in a newsletter box, or making a purchase. This is still very much at the research and development stage for most networks; however, it is worth keeping an eye on the progress in this area.

For DinoSpace, the bonus for us would be that we only paid each time a user registered on our site and created a profile. Of course, we would pay more per action than we would per click, but in theory we should only pay when we get results, giving us guaranteed return on investment.

The downside to PPA schemes, is that for sites which display such advertisements, they may not necessarily make as much money (for example, sites currently displaying Google Adwords) because there may not be any actions performed, despite a large number of clicks.

Advertising space

A number of websites offer advertisement space, generally on a monthly basis, which can often be a great way to generate new traffic and bring new customers to a site. There are a few simple points to take into account when considering renting advertising space from a site:

- Does the site you are looking to advertise on compete directly with your own site? If so, they probably wouldn't accept your advert, nor would it be an ideal place to advertise. The visitors have already clicked through to their site, and would probably not be inclined to go elsewhere. Thinking back to our DinoSpace social network, this means we wouldn't want to advertise on fictitious sites such as:
    - DinoNet
    - DinoPlanet

- Is the site relevant to ours? If the site is relevant (but non-competing), then we are more likely to get clicks through to our site, as visitors will be interested in the area we work in.

- Is the site we are advertising on reputable? If the site has a bad reputation, that reputation will come to us by association. Visitors will see we are associated with the site, and that will affect their view of our site. It is important to spend some time checking a site's reputation; it may even be worth contacting the owner of the site to find out some background or history about the site and the owner.

- What are the statistics for the site like? If the site does not get many visitors, then it isn't worth us advertising on it. It is important to find out statistics from the website owner, including visitor numbers and preferably some information on the demographics of users. If the site has a small number of visitors, then it would be important to ensure that payment is for a certain number of impressions or clicks, as opposed to a set period of time. Services such as Google Analytics provide this information; however, there are many providers available who can process the raw log files on the hosting server, and generate statistics from that.

Warning: Keep the search engines happy!

Search engines hold a lot of power when it comes to promoting websites, as they run a number of advertisement networks, and list websites organically in their search results pages. We need to ensure we stay on their good side, and keep them happy, otherwise we will feel their wrath and have our rankings in their results pages penalized.

Getting penalized by search engines

Page listings in **Search Engine Results Pages** (**SERPs**) are determined by search engines by a number of different metrics, including age of domain name, content on the site, and also the number of incoming links to a site. With Google, this link factor, along with some other metrics, makes up a page rank. Depending on a site's page rank, the links the site has to other sites (outbound links) can gain page rank from this. Links from one site to another are classed as a vote, and it assumes that the site owner was happy to display that link, and that they approve of the site, and wish to attribute a vote to it, improving its page rank.

In some cases, paid advertisements are seen as a way to buy increased page rank, which search engines see as a way of "spamming" their search index. Many search engines, including Google, have anonymous online reporting tools, where users can report paid links on websites, which are then investigated and the involved sites are penalized with regard to their rankings in the SERPs.

Keeping them happy

The sale and purchase of links and adverts isn't wrong on the Internet, it is just the sale or purchase of links to adjust page rank, and so, most search engines take into account some additional information within a link that indicates that the site owner does not wish for the link to receive their "vote" when calculating page rank. This attribute should be used for any paid advertisements or links, to ensure neither the site selling nor the site buying the adverts are penalized for this. The solution is to add `rel="nofollow"` to the link, so we would end up with a link such as this:

```
<a href=http://www.packtpub.com rel="nofollow">Packt Publishing</a>
```

This does not mean that we need to add this attribute to all of our outbound links, only links that are paid for.

Here are some useful tips to ensure you stay in the good books of the most popular search engines:

- Don't buy or sell links, only buy advertising space from reputable sites (and ensure the advert has the `rel="nofollow"` attribute
- Ensure that all adverts on your own site contain the `rel="nofollow"` attribute
- Be wary of e-mails offering to place advertisements on your site

Hopefully, by following these tips and taking a common sense approach, you won't jeopardize your search engine rankings.

Newsletter advertising

There are a large number of online newsletters available, many of them targeting specific niche markets. It would be useful to advertise our stores within e-mail newsletters that are relevant to our store; for instance, an e-mail newsletter that is sent to all prop managers at theatre companies.

This method involves quite a lot of research, finding suitable newsletters, and discussing with the owners of the newsletters to negotiate advertising pricing.

> Don't forget to consider the points we discussed earlier, with regards to advertising space, when looking at advertising on newsletters. The tips apply to both forms of advertising quite well.

Newsletters

There are a number of newsletter systems available, which we can use to send newsletters to our customers or interested parties. Visitors to our site could leave their e-mail address to indicate they are interested in our site, but are perhaps not ready or convinced enough to join our site, and instead would like us to e-mail them every now and then with new information on what is happening with our social network.

One particularly popular newsletter system is Campaign Monitor; this not only makes it easy to manage many lists of subscribers, but also provides advanced tools to track the success and performance of newsletter campaigns, with metrics such as:

- How many users opened the e-mail?
- How many times did users open the e-mail?
- Which links were clicked on, by whom, and how many times?
- Which e-mail clients were used?
- Who, or how many users, unsubscribed from the newsletter, forwarded it to a friend, or reported it as spam?

These metrics are not accurate, as the techniques used to detect how many times an e-mail has been opened rely on images within the newsletter, thus requiring the user to set their e-mail client to display images. However, they are useful as a basic indication of minimum statistics.

It is also possible to integrate the newsletters with stats programs such as Google Analytics. One final feature worth mentioning, is that Campaign Monitor, MailChimp, and many other newsletter systems, also allow us to preview the contents of the newsletter in various different e-mail clients to ensure the newsletter will look as intended. For all of our subscribers, along with this, it can also run the e-mails through spam filters to detect if it is likely to be flagged as spam.

Social marketing

While it may seem contradictory, it makes sense to also make use of other, non-competing, social networks to promote DinoSpace. Most existing social networks have provisions for user and business information as well as profile data including website addresses. Examples of this include creating a Facebook fan page for our site, adding the site's URL to our Facebook and MySpace profiles, and to our Twitter accounts. These extra links could help with additional promotion; even if they only bring one or two new members, it is still worthwhile.

It is important however to not use competing social networking sites to promote our site on, as such promotion is likely to be removed, and does not help our reputation. Sites such as Facebook are large and generic, so provided we are promoting a site such as DinoSpace, which is specific and targets a niche market, we would be encouraging users to also join our site, and not encouraging them to abandon the site for ours.

Viral marketing campaigns

Viral marketing is a relatively new marketing concept, which revolves around utilizing social networks. One particular example of viral marketing is utilizing video sharing websites such as YouTube and promoting videos which advertise our site, for instance, spoof or gimmicky videos which engage the viewer, and encourage them to either join our site or help us promote our site. We could use this to make a short training video on "the care of dino eggs" which we could then post to various education and learning websites such as eHow.

This technique is probably more suited to large social networking sites with large marketing budgets, that are trying to promote a brand. Information on using YouTube in particular was recently posted on a technology blog called TechCrunch, which can be found at `http://www.techcrunch.com/2007/11/22/the-secret-strategies-behind-many-viral-videos/`.

Twitter

We could use Twitter, a social network that aims to tell your friends and followers what you are doing, to keep up-to-date with our users. One potential method is to create an announcement Twitter account to post news, updates, and feature releases, in addition to keeping an eye out for comments or feedback from customers on the social network, and responding to them, perhaps taking into account their ideas or suggestions for new features for us to implement.

RSS feeds

Many websites offer content to their users through **Really Simple Syndication (RSS)**, which allows them to read the content, such as blog articles, latest products, recommendations, and reviews, and so on, off-site in their favorite RSS reader.

For DinoSpace, we could use this to display the latest public content which has been posted to our site, or a list of new updates to the site, or if we wanted to be really clever, we could give each user a custom RSS feed link which contains the latest additions to their status feed, though this could hinder any monetization options which involve on-site advertisements. One potential counter to this, is displaying advertisements within RSS feeds, something which is slowly becoming more common, and is certainly worth investigating.

Services such as Google's FeedBurner allow us to monitor our users' usage of RSS feeds, and gather statistics from them.

Search Engine Optimization

One way to increase traffic to our website is through **Search Engine Optimization (SEO)**. This involves ensuring the content and the structure of our site are well optimized for search engines, making it easier for them to access our sites, and digest the important content. The other aspect is with regards to inbound links to our site.

Therefore, search engine optimization can be broken down into two primary areas:

- On-site search engine optimization, focusing on changes to the actual website itself
- Off-site search engine optimization, focusing on building up a reputation for the website through reputable, high quality, inbound links

Let us take a brief look at these two methods.

On-site SEO

On-site SEO requires us to ensure that the website itself is suitably structured, and the content is appropriate and up-to-date, encouraging search engines to index the site, and helping them realize which content is most relevant within the site.

Headings

Properly structured pages make use of appropriate headings to break down the content of the document into sections. The content within these headings is also considered highly by search engines. It is important that we don't fill them with too much content; three to seven words should be sufficient, keeping with the feel of a heading. The different levels of headings indicate their importance within the page (heading level one is most important, level two less, and so on). There is much discussion on the web design community about what a first level heading should contain—either the name of the site or the name of the page. Personally, I find the name of the page more appropriate and more relevant in terms of optimization too. There should only be one instance of the h1 tag on a page, however there can be any number of lower level headings.

Internal links

Having links to other pages within the site is a very simple and useful way to improve search engine performance. The trick is to make use of relevant sentences, using the relevant keywords as hyperlinks, and also ensuring that the titles of the link are suitably optimized. Take the example of a novelty hat category page. A poorly optimized link would be:

```
To see Dino friendly restaurants our members have reviewed <a
href="dfr/">click here</a>
```

The link has no context to search engines, and contains no meaningful information. A more meaningful, and therefore, search engine friendly link would be:

```
Why not view our members' reviews of <a href="reviews/dinosaur-friendly-
restaurants/" title="Reviews of Dinosaur friendly Restaurants made by
our members">Dinosaur friendly restaurants</a>
```

All these small changes do make a difference!

Up-to-date, relevant content

One of the most important things about a website is its content. Visitors like content to be fresh and up-to-date. By the same token, search engines also like this, as it shows the site is related to the user's search, and that it is relevant because it is regularly updated.

Page meta data

An older method for search engine optimization was to take advantage of the meta tags within an HTML document. Because this was widely abused, it isn't as effective as it once was; however, it is still a useful technique. Some sites have their description text in search engine results pages showing as the text from their description meta tags.

The two important meta tags are `keywords` and `description`. The `keywords` tag allows us to associate a number of keywords with our content, and the `description` tag allows us to associate a friendly, easy-to-read description to the page. Because search engines penalize sites that hide some content from their users (with the purpose of it being shown only to the search engines, to make the search engines think the site was more relevant for certain phrases or keywords), this technique was abused as a legitimate way to have text that was unrelated to the page (or repetitions of related content) to try and boost rankings, and as such the search engines don't put as much emphasis on these now.

The meta tags are contained within the `<head>` section of an HTML document. An example of the `keywords` and `description` tags in use is as follows:

```
<meta name="description"
      content="DinoSpace is a vibrant, buzzing community for keepers
of Dinosaurs, sharing health-care, breeding and leisure tips" />
< meta name="keywords"
        content="dinosaur, keepers, help, community, health, reviews,
friendly, leisure, supplies" />
```

While the search engines don't take these into account too much, it is still important not to overuse them, as that indicates to the search engines that the site is trying to abuse the meta tags and their purpose.

Site speed

One very new edition to the list of factors to a site's ranking in search engines is the speed of the site, as announced by Google in April 2010. Sites that take a while to load are penalized. More information can be found on the Google blog available at: `http://googlewebmastercentral.blogspot.com/2010/04/using-site-speed-in-web-search-ranking.html`.

There are a number of tools available to help monitor and improve the speed of your website. Some potential tools include:

- YSlow from Yahoo!: `http://developer.yahoo.com/yslow/`
- Page Speed browser plugin: `http://code.google.com/speed/page-speed/`
- Articles on speeding up your site: `http://code.google.com/speed/articles/`

Search engine goodies! Sitemaps and tools

Many search engines provide a number of tools to help webmasters improve the performance of their sites in the search engines, and to help webmasters with the best practices. Google has a number of webmaster tools, a collection of tools geared towards helping webmasters manage the errors within their site, and is available for use, freely. Webmasters can also create a sitemap in XML format, to tell Google of all of the pages within our site, their importance within the scheme of the site as a whole, and how frequently they are updated, to help them decide when to return to re-index the updated content.

The webmaster tools in general, outline errors such as duplicate content, duplicate meta data within pages in the same site, as well as broken or forbidden links. More information can be found on the following pages:

- `https://www.google.com/webmasters/tools/home?hl=en`
- `http://www.google.com/support/webmasters/bin/answer.py?hl=en&answer=40318`

Off-site SEO

Off-site SEO relies on promoting the website on various other websites through inbound links, which is why it is referred to as off-site SEO. This is a particularly large area, and some companies spend very large amounts of money on this, though of course this is all relative to the amount of return they get on their SEO investment. Off-site SEO is particularly useful for gaining rankings for specific keywords within the search engines.

Inbound links, as we discussed earlier, are an important metric in determining the ranking of websites within the SERPs. One of the easiest ways to generate inbound links is with existing social networks, or social websites (forums in particular), by adding a link to the website within our personal signatures on discussion forums. This needs to be done carefully and considerately. If we were to sign up just to promote our link, we would be seen as a spammer, and most sites would deactivate our accounts. Posting comments on relevant blog entries or articles with a link back to our site is also useful, provided the comments are appropriate, relevant, and our own site does not compete with the article or blog in question.

Some examples of services that SEO agencies offer as part of an off-site campaign include the following:

- Writing articles for relevant blogs or article networks with links back to our site
- Guest blog posts on other blogs

- Online distributed press releases
- Link baiting (articles, content, or applications designed to generate many comments, blog trackbacks, forwarding, and linking to; often this is done by posting on controversial topics within a specific niche, or by viral marketing)
- Link building (building high quality, relevant inbound links)

What to look for in an SEO company

Search engine optimization is very much an art as opposed to a science. If you are considering using a search engine optimization firm to help, here are some useful tips if you do wish to use a company to manage SEO strategy:

- Nobody can guarantee results, so watch out for companies that claim they do.
- SEO is a long term investment; however, watch out for minimum terms imposed by the companies. By the same token you should appreciate that results take time, so small (3 – 6 months) minimum terms are acceptable.
- SEO and PPC are not the same; some companies claim to offer SEO, when all they do is set up Google Adwords.
- Find out about their link building campaigns to ensure they build relevant links that won't have a negative effect in the long term.
- Audit trails: Do they provide a log of work they do, links they acquire, webmasters they contact, on-site changes? Most won't give much information, as it is what is paid for, but make sure you get some indication of work performed.
- Reports: Ensure you are updated regularly with search engine performance, and the effect their work is having on the rankings.

User retention

Another important aspect of marketing, is marketing with existing users, keeping them coming back to the site to make the site more useful and relevant for other users.

E-mails for the user's action

Regular e-mails can remind users about the site, if they have forgotten about it, or not had time to visit for a while. We don't want to send them lots of e-mails to nag them into returning, but, we can e-mail them with relevant updates. For example, when someone tries to connect with them on the site, or when they receive a message through the site, we e-mail the user to notify them of this.

This also doubles as a reminder to our users, and if the user connecting with them is of interest to them, it may help members who have lapsed in their interaction with the site to return.

User feedback

By asking the user for feedback, and ideas for improvement, they can feel more engaged and involved in the site. This also gives us feedback to use, ideas to discuss, and new features to implement.

Hello there!

As we discussed earlier, newsletters are a great way to remind a user that our site is still around, without their being a specific reason. Perhaps just to tell them what they have been missing out on, or to ask for feedback on why they haven't participated in a while, or to tell them about new developments and features on the site. We could also add a poll to our site, to help engage interaction, and use a start and end date to keep it up-to-date. This could be included in our e-mails, as well as being prominent on our site.

Monetization options

One other important consideration is how to monetize our site. While DinoSpace hasn't been designed to make a profit, it may be useful to try and recuperate expenses such as hosting fees. Some simple options to get you started:

- **Cafepress.com / Spreadshirt**: Create merchandise with your site's logo on, and earn a percentage from sales. This could be prominently promoted on the site.

- **Google Adsense**: Advertisement blocks from Google on the site earn money on a per-click basis; alternatively, integrating a Google search feature provides a less obtrusive form of advertising.

- **Affiliate Marketing**: Become an affiliate of sites such as Amazon, where relevant products can be promoted on the site and a commission earned.

Final tips: Web stats

We can monitor the statistics and performance of our site, using a number of stats tools which are available. One such product is a very powerful statistics and analytics package called Google Analytics, available from Google, completely free of charge. This is useful for us to see which pages our visitors are using, and which pages are being ignored, allowing us to either promote them more heavily, or to focus on the more popular areas of the site.

There are also ways to integrate Google Analytics with e-commerce installations, to try and help us to determine average income per visitor; this is particularly useful when making use of PPC marketing, as it links in with Google's own PPC network, AdWords.

We can sign up for Google Analytics on `http://analytics.google.com/`, where we are supplied some HTML code to insert into our site's footer template, so that it can begin tracking our statistics.

We can also use tools like this to monitor bounce rates, to see how and why our users leave our site and from which pages they decide to leave; we can also see where the visitors come from, so we know which advertising sites or sites we have links on are helping us. Statistics on error pages can be useful to help us find links which are broken, or incoming links which are outdated, so we can either correct the broken link, or put a redirect in from an outdated inbound link to the new location of a moved page.

Modules to consider

There are a number of other modules which can help with SEO, although not all of these are available for Drupal 7 at the time of writing. It is worth investigating these too:

- SEO Checklist
- Nodewords
- Global Redirect
- Path Redirect
- XML Siteman
- Google Analytics

Summary

In this chapter, we looked into effectively marketing and promoting websites and social networking websites with online marketing techniques, search engine optimization, and user retention strategies. We also looked briefly into how we may wish to monetize our site.

Now that your social networking site is up and running, and ready for new users through these promotion strategies, it is over to you to make your new social network a success.

A
Setting up a Local Development Environment

In order to test our Drupal installation before putting it online, we need to set up a local development environment, which needs to include:

- A web server; for example, Apache
    - ° The Apache rewrite module

- PHP
    - ° The GD image manipulation library

- A database server; for example, MySQL

Let's look at installing WampServer to get a local development environment running on a Windows computer, the commands to install Apache, PHP, and MySQL on Linux (a LAMP setup), and where to download and how to install MAMP for a Mac.

WampServer for Windows

There are a number of bundled installers available for Windows which provide support for Apache, MySQL, PHP, and their administration. One such program is WampServer, which can be downloaded from the project website: http:// www.wampserver.com/en/. There are versions for both 32 bit and 64 bit operating systems, so be sure to download the one for your operating system.

Installing WAMPServer

First things first, let's download WAMPServer from their website. Once downloaded, we then need to run the installer. The first stage of the installation is the standard overview screen, confirming that we are installing WampServer 2 on our computer, so let's click **Next**:

The next step is to read through the licence agreement which governs the software, select that **I accept the agreement**, and then click **Next** to proceed:

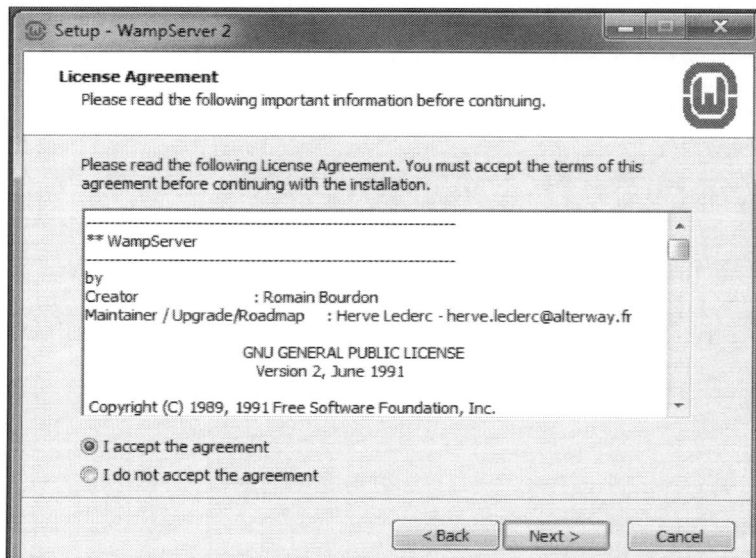

Next we need to select where we want to install WampServer, and click **Next** again:

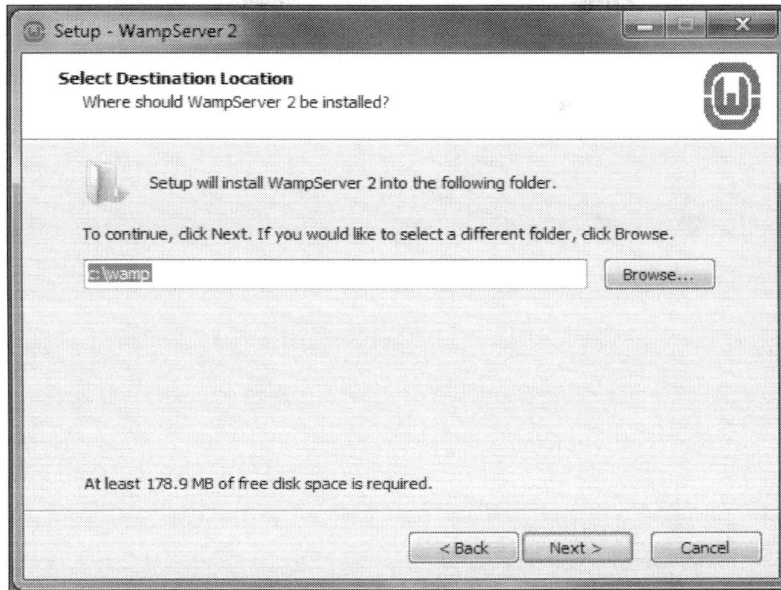

Before installing on our computer, WampServer then presents us with a review of the options we have selected to confirm; once we are happy with the details we click **Install** to start installing WampServer on our computer:

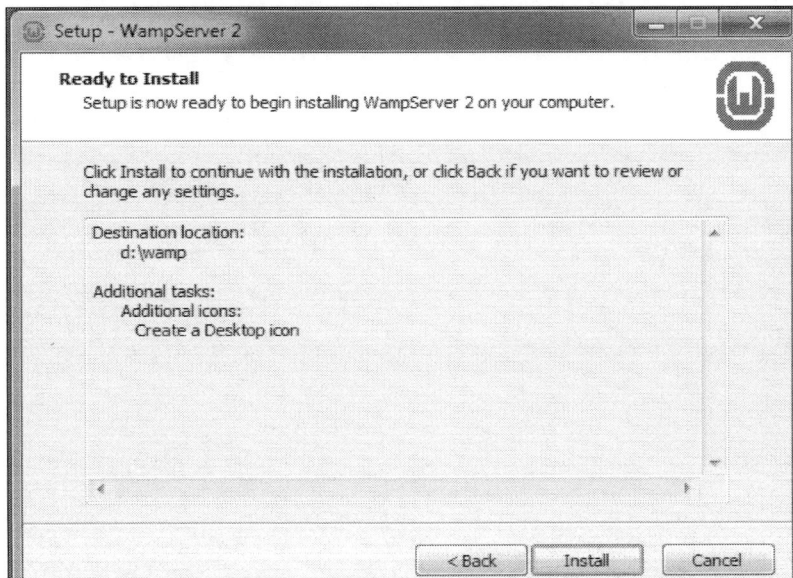

WampServer then starts installing; this process typically takes less than five minutes:

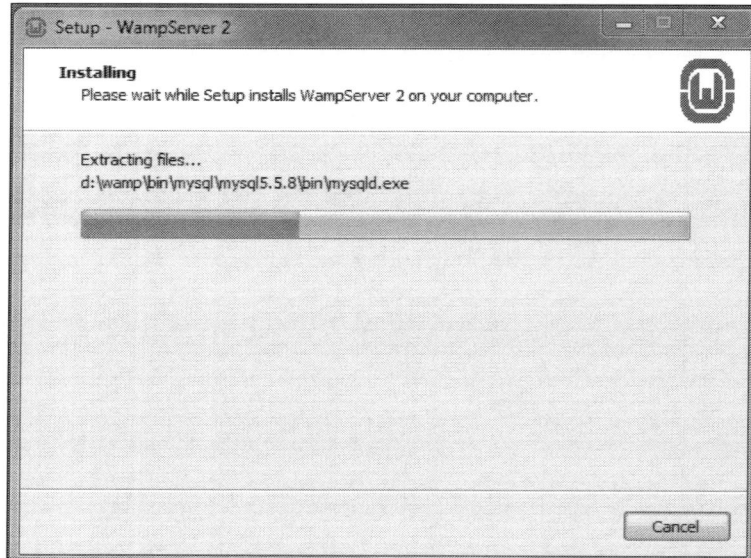

Once the installation has completed we are asked to confirm our primary web browser, by default it has selected Internet Explorer; if we are happy with that we should click **Open**. Otherwise we should browse for an alternative browser first. Next the installation asks for details for PHP mail; on most installations we won't be able to send mail from PHP scripts because we have no mail server installed, so just click **Next**:

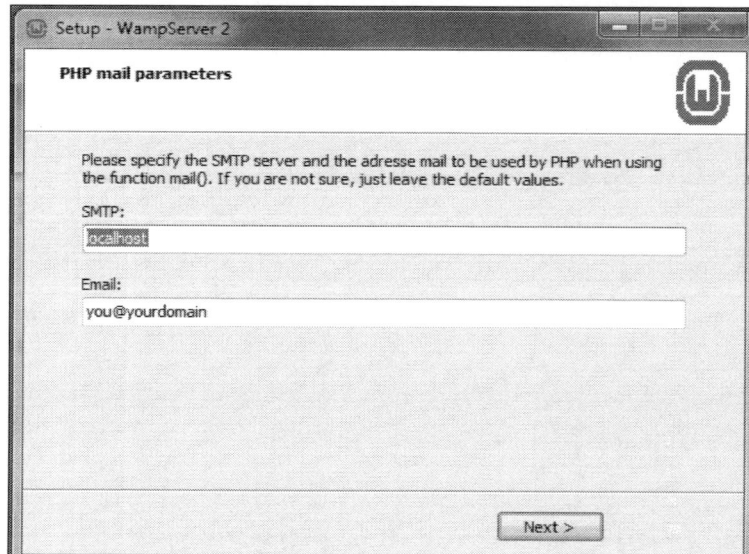

We now have WampServer installed; if we click **Finish**, WampServer will start:

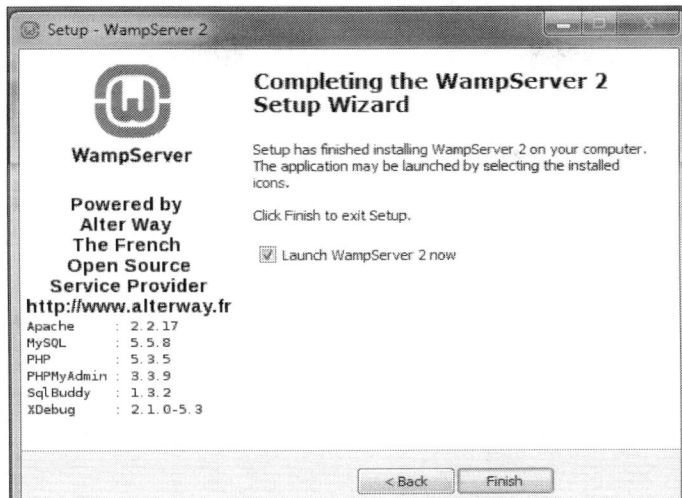

Apache not starting?

If WampServer won't start (the icon in the system tray will be red or orange), this is likely because something else is utilizing the computer port Apache runs on (port 80). Programs such as Skype do this, so you may need to close other applications before trying to start WampServer.

When WAMPServer starts for the first time, we will be prompted by the Windows Security Alert to allow apache to communicate over our network.

Now we have WampServer installed on our local computer; let's take a brief look at it, and then enable the PHP GD module and the rewrite the module for Apache.

WAMPServer overview

When WampServer is running it is displayed in our computer's system tray alongside the clock. Clicking the icon displays a menu where we can configure our server, and start or stop various services:

Putting the server online would allow web pages on our computer to be accessible to other computers on our network, and potentially via the Internet. We can quickly start, stop, and restart the services, configure each of them, quickly open the folder containing our websites files, and quickly open our website or database manager in a web browser.

Configuring WampServer

Within the WampServer menu the **Apache**, **PHP**, and **MySQL** options allow us to configure the various services. We can install modules and add-ons to the different components, or we can edit the configuration files for them.

There are two main features we will need enabled:

- GD for PHP
- Rewrite_module for Apache

Configuration Files

The files `my.ini,` `php.ini,` and `httpd.conf` are the configuration files for the three services; although we shouldn't need to edit these for our website, it is important to know where they are, in case we do need to change them later, as they control a lot of how the software works. These three files control a lot of how the software works and there is more information is available on their respective websites for the functions of each of the files. We can use the `php.ini` file to allow larger files to be uploaded by editing the `upload_max_filesize` and `max_post_size` sections to support larger files.

GD2

PHP's GD2 module is a graphics library that allows PHP to easily manipulate and manage images, including resizing images, recreating images, adding watermarks to images, and so on. Drupal has a number of image features which require an image module to be installed with PHP. By default, GD2 is installed with WampServer, but it is important that we check this and know where the setting is.

PHP's modules are enabled and disabled by clicking the WampServer logo in the system tray selecting **PHP** and then **PHP Extensions**.

From here we can enable or disable the GD2 extension:

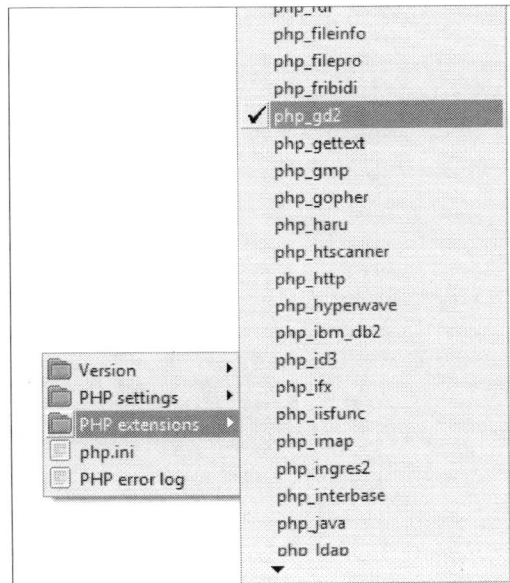

Rewrite module

Apache has a module called rewrite which allows it to rewrite URLs, in particular to make them more friendly by rewriting URLs such as /home/about to index. php?q=home/about.

A number of Drupal's modules make use of this feature if it is available, so let's enable it! It can be enabled from **Apache modules** within the **Apache** menu:

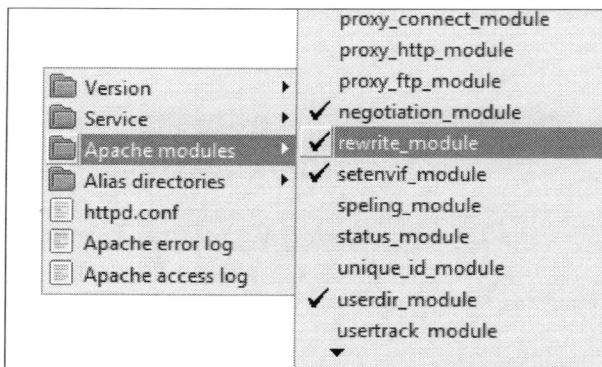

Linux

The exact installation instructions for Linux vary depending on the distribution used; however, the following instructions should work for Ubuntu and other Debian based distributions like Debian itself. You might want to consider using a program such as VirtualBox (http://www.virtualbox.org/) to run a Linux web server on top of your Windows or Mac (or even Linux if you wish for your development environment to be virtualized) computer, to effectively test the Drupal site on a Linux environment before putting it online.

Install Apache

In order to install Apache, run the following command:

```
sudo apt-get install apache2
```

Enable the rewrite module and restart Apache

In order to enable the rewrite Apache module, run the following command:

```
sudo a2enmod rewrite
sudo /etc/init.d/apache2 reload
```

Chapter No.

Install PHP

To install PHP, run the following command:

```
sudo apt-get install php5
```

Enable MySQL and GD

In order to enable the MySQL and GD extensions for PHP, run the following commands:

```
sudo apt-get install php5-mysql php5-gd
sudo /usr/sbin/apache2ctl graceful
```

Install MySQL

In order to install MySQL, run the following command:

```
sudo apt-get install mysql-server mysql-client libmysqlclient15-dev
```

Install phpMyAdmin

In order to install phpMyAdmin run the following command:

```
sudo apt-get install phpmyadmin
```

Mac

First we need to download the application from the project website: http://www.mamp.info/en/mamp/index.html. To install it we simply drag the file into the applications folder. Full documentation for the project is available on their website: http://www.mamp.info/en/documentation/index.html.

Summary

We now have a local development environment set up complete with Apache, PHP, and MySQL, wherein we can test our Drupal social network installation.

B
Installed Modules

The following **third-party contributed modules** are downloaded and subsequently installed during the course of this book.

Chapter 1 to Chapter 3

No third-party contributed modules are installed within Chapters 1 – 3; only core modules are used.

Chapter 4

The following contributed modules are downloaded and installed as part of Chapter 4:

Module	Location
Gravatar	`http://drupal.org/project/gravatar`
Follow	`http://drupal.org/project/follow`
Field collection	`http://drupal.org/project/field_collection`
Entity	`http://drupal.org/project/entity`

Chapter 5

The following contributed modules are downloaded and installed as part of Chapter 5:

Module	Location
Flag	http://drupal.org/project/flag
Heartbeat	http://drupal.org/project/heartbeat
Rules	http://drupal.org/project/rules
Chaos tool suite	http://drupal.org/project/ctools
User relationships	http://drupal.org/project/user_relationships
Panels	http://drupal.org/project/panels
Views	http://drupal.org/project/views
Guestbook	http://drupal.org/project/guestbook
Organic groups	http://drupal.org/project/og

Chapter 6

The following contributed modules are downloaded and installed as part of Chapter 6:

Module	Location
Disqus	http://drupal.org/project/disqus
AddThis	http://drupal.org/project/addthis

Chapter 7 to Chapter 8

No third-party contributed modules are installed within Chapters 7 – 8.

Chapter 9

The following contributed modules are downloaded and installed as part of Chapter 9:

Module	Location
Simplenews	http://drupal.org/project/simplenews
Mimemail	http://drupal.org/project/mimemail
PHPList	http://drupal.org/project/phplist
Inactive_user	http://drupal.org/project/inactive_user

Chapter 10

The following contributed modules are downloaded and installed as part of Chapter 10:

Module	Location
CAPTCHA	`http://www.drupal.org/project/captcha`
reCAPTCHA	`http://drupal.org/project/recaptcha`
Mollom	`http://drupal.org/project/mollom`

Chapter 11 to Chapter 12

No third-party contributed modules are installed within Chapters 11 – 12.

Index

E

Elgg
about 17
URL 17
e-mailing options
PHPList 218
Simplenews 219
Entity module
downloading 107
URL 128, 293
examples, Social Networking
British Telecom 9
Dell 9
NameCheap 9
Netgear 10
external mailing lists
about 215
automatic signup, for user creation 216, 217
sgnup, for anonymous users 218
external mailing list systems
about 215
Campaign Monitor 215
Constant Contact 215
Mail Chimp 215

F

Facebook
about 12
features 12
Facebook Applications 18
Facebook Connect 18
Facebook style statuses (microblog) module
URL 161
favicon file
creating 209
Field collection module
downloading 107
URL 293
field_create_field function 178
field_create_instance function 178
file module 98-101
Find us on Facebook, integrating in Drupal 174
Flag module
URL 128, 294

Follow module
downloading 107
URL 293
using 118

G

Garland 203
GD2 module 289
Global Redirect 281
Google Analytics
about 258, 281
URL 281
Google Apps 259
Google OpenSocial 18
Gravatar module
about 106
downloading 107
Gravatars
configuration options 121
enabling 121
group content type
about 149
configuring 150
creating 149
groups, formatting 151
user context, adding to group 151
groups 148
groups, for DinoSpace!
about 148
closed, membership options 148
invite only, membership options 148
membership options 148
moderated membership, membership
options 148
new users group 148
open membership, membership options
148
T-Rex owners groups 148
UK Dinosaur owners group 148
guestbook module
about 160
URL 128, 294

H

Heartbeat module
URL 128, 294

user centric home page
about 123, 124
triggers 123
user_insert hook
implementing 217
user interaction, in DinoSpace!
enabling 127
groups 148
modules, installing 128
relationships 128
user activity stream 139
user profiles, commenting on 160
users, contacting 147
user management
about 107
bulk user operations 112
user account, cancelling 111
user account, deleting 111
user, creating 109
user, editing 110
user list 108
users, filtering 108
users, searching 108
users, sorting 108
user, suspending / blocking 110
users, viewing 108
user profiles
commenting on 160
creating 115
user relations activity
about 139, 147
heartbeat template, creating for friend relationship 140, 141
in action 146
rule, creating for each relationship type
142-146
template, creating for each relationship type
140, 141
User relationships module
URL 128, 294
user retention
about 279
e-mails, with relevant updates 279
user feedback 280
user roles 76
users
contacting 147

V

Varnish
URL 257
Views module
URL 128, 294
viral marketing 274
VPS.NET 264
VPS (Virtual Private Server) hosting 264

W

WAMP 21
WampServer
configuring 288
for Windows 283
GD2 module 289
installing 284-287
overview 288
rewrite module 290
webmaster tools 278
websites output
compressing, Apache configuration used
262
compressing, PHP installation used 262
WinCacheGrind 261

X

XAMPP 21
Xdebug 261
XML Siteman 281

Y

Yahoo!
URL 269
YSlow from Yahoo!
URL 277

Z

zlib 262

[PACKT] open source ✳
PUBLISHING   community experience distilled

Thank you for buying
Drupal 7 Social Networking

About Packt Publishing

Packt, pronounced 'packed', published its first book "*Mastering phpMyAdmin for Effective MySQL Management*" in April 2004 and subsequently continued to specialize in publishing highly focused books on specific technologies and solutions.

Our books and publications share the experiences of your fellow IT professionals in adapting and customizing today's systems, applications, and frameworks. Our solution based books give you the knowledge and power to customize the software and technologies you're using to get the job done. Packt books are more specific and less general than the IT books you have seen in the past. Our unique business model allows us to bring you more focused information, giving you more of what you need to know, and less of what you don't.

Packt is a modern, yet unique publishing company, which focuses on producing quality, cutting-edge books for communities of developers, administrators, and newbies alike. For more information, please visit our website: www.packtpub.com.

About Packt Open Source

In 2010, Packt launched two new brands, Packt Open Source and Packt Enterprise, in order to continue its focus on specialization. This book is part of the Packt Open Source brand, home to books published on software built around Open Source licences, and offering information to anybody from advanced developers to budding web designers. The Open Source brand also runs Packt's Open Source Royalty Scheme, by which Packt gives a royalty to each Open Source project about whose software a book is sold.

Writing for Packt

We welcome all inquiries from people who are interested in authoring. Book proposals should be sent to author@packtpub.com. If your book idea is still at an early stage and you would like to discuss it first before writing a formal book proposal, contact us; one of our commissioning editors will get in touch with you.

We're not just looking for published authors; if you have strong technical skills but no writing experience, our experienced editors can help you develop a writing career, or simply get some additional reward for your expertise.

[PACKT] open source ✲
community experience distilled

PUBLISHING

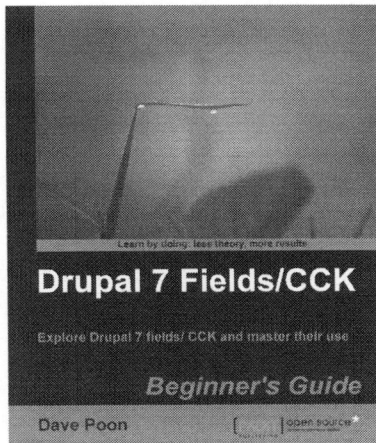

Drupal 7 Fields/CCK
Beginner's Guide

ISBN: 978-1-849514-78-1   Paperback: 288 pages

Explore Drupal 7 fields/CCK and master their use

1. Step-by-step guide to building your own Drupal 7 website using the Drupal 7 fields system

2. Specifically written for Drupal 7 development and site building

3. In-depth coverage of theming fields in Drupal 7

4. Discover the new fields system from the database perspective

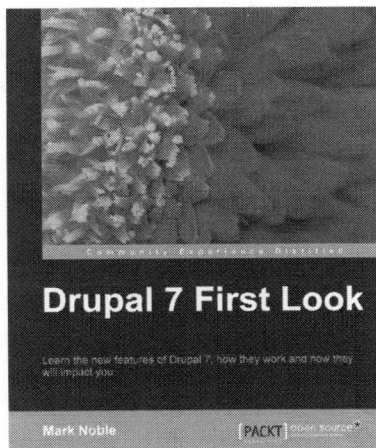

Drupal 7 First Look

ISBN: 978-1-849511-22-3   Paperback: 288 pages

Learn the new features of Drupal 7, how they work and how they will impact you

1. Get to grips with all of the new features in Drupal 7

2. Upgrade your Drupal 6 site, themes, and modules to Drupal 7

3. Explore the new Drupal 7 administration interface and map your Drupal 6 administration interface to the new Drupal 7 structure

4. Complete coverage of the DBTNG database layer with usage examples and all API changes for both Themes and Modules

Please check **www.PacktPub.com** for information on our titles

4028494R00182

Printed in Great Britain
by Amazon.co.uk, Ltd.,
Marston Gate.